CW01456060

VIKING SOCIETY FOR NORTHERN RESEARCH

TEXT SERIES

GENERAL EDITORS

Alison Finlay and Carl Phelpstead

VOLUME XVIII

GUTA LAG

THE LAW OF THE GOTLANDERS

GUTA LAG

THE LAW OF THE GOTLANDERS

Translated and edited by Christine Peel

VIKING SOCIETY FOR NORTHERN RESEARCH
UNIVERSITY COLLEGE LONDON
2009

ISBN: 978-0-903521-79-6

The printing of this book is made possible by a gift to the University
of Cambridge in memory of Dorothea Coke, Skjaeret, 1951.

The cover motif is based on the image from a seal, found in Bro parish in
Gotland. The image is dated 1280 and the seal is considered to date from
circa 1225–50, which makes it the oldest recorded of all the Scandinavian
provincial arms. The image is encircled in an inscription: GUTENSES:
SIGNO: XPISTVS: SIGNATUR: IN: AGNO. The first half of this has been
variously translated 'I represent the Gotlanders', 'I am the symbol of
Gotland' and 'The Gotlanders are represented by this seal'. The second
half has been translated: 'Christ is represented by the lamb' and 'Christ's
symbol is the lamb'. Later versions, in particular for the town of Visby,
show several variations, including a reversal of the image and a gloria on
the ram, both of which are considered to be more usual. See *KL*, s.v.
Landskapssegel; Siltberg 2005, 284–98.

Printed by Short Run Press Limited, Exeter

CONTENTS

PREFACE

After the publication of *Guta saga* in the Viking Society Text Series, I was encouraged by Professor Richard Perkins to continue my research work with a PhD thesis. This addressed the body of the manuscript of which *Guta saga* formed an addendum, the fourteenth-century law codex called *Guta lag* 'the law of the Gotlanders'. The study also involved comparison with a later manuscript, a copy of a lost fifteenth-century original. It was always the ultimate aim to have this thesis published by the Viking Society, and when it was accepted in 2006, I started to consider how best to present it.

It was decided at an early stage to publish only the translation, and to omit the Gutnish texts and the glossary. This decision was made with regret, but to include these would have made the publication beyond the scope of the Text Series. Most of the remaining content of the thesis has been included, with necessary re-formatting and improvement. The manner in which the two major documents were to be presented was also not decided upon immediately, and the final result is to some extent a compromise. The text of the fourteenth-century B 64 Holm has been taken as the basis and minor deviations in AM 54 4to have been presented in footnotes, with major differences shown in separate Additions. This is similar to the manner in which Schlyter presented the material in his volume.

We were fortunate in obtaining a generous grant from the Dorothea Coke Memorial Fund, which has enabled us, amongst other things, to reproduce pages of the manuscripts to a high quality.

I owe a debt of gratitude to Dr Perkins for his original suggestion and supervision of my studies, to Dr Carl Phelpstead for his helpful and perceptive editorial assistance on the content of the work and to Dr Alison Finlay for her patient and thorough editing of my manuscript and her uncomplaining acceptance of my last-minute thoughts.

My husband again showed exceptional patience during my studies and the production of this volume. His proofreading, particularly of lists of amendments, has been invaluable, but the remaining errors are my own.

Finally, I would like to thank the staff in the libraries in London, Stockholm and Copenhagen who helped me to satisfy the requirements for chapter and verse, which it has become so much a part of my nature to insist upon.

Christine Peel

INTRODUCTION

THE KINGDOM OF SWEDEN first began to take shape in the Viking Age when a number of independent provinces around and to the north of Lake Mälare acknowledged the same king and principal heathen temple at Uppsala. There was no central administration, however, and each province had its own assembly, law and legal system. To the south and west of these provinces lay Västergötland and Östergötland and, still further south, provinces belonging to Denmark, each again with its own laws. The island of Gotland also had its own law and administrative system and was more or less independent. The two most important of the provincial laws, and those that form the basis for the other preserved law texts, were those for Östergötland and Uppland (the province in which Uppsala lay).

Although all the preserved redactions of the provincial laws are post-Conversion, most exhibit traces of older traditions. The extent to which they do so depends not only on the age of the manuscripts in question but also on the extent to which they retain independence from the two main provincial laws. *Guta lag*, the law of the Gotlanders (subsequently referred to as *GL*), differs radically in a number of respects from any of the mainland provincial laws. The differences are not only in the content but also in the presumed administrative structure in force at the time. These differences are discussed in detail in sections III and IV of this Introduction.

Mainland provincial laws were all superseded by a national law, *Magnus Erikssons landslag* (*MELL*), between 1347 and 1352, and at some time before 1357 this was supplemented by a town law, *Magnus Erikssons stadslag* (*MEStL*). The former was revised to some extent under King Kristoffer of Bayern (1440–48). These two law codes remained in force until 1734 when a unified Swedish law was established. In contrast to the mainland provinces, Gotland, for reasons laid out below, effectively retained its own provincial law until 1645, when it finally came under permanent Swedish rule.

I *Gotland's medieval historical background*

The following brief history of Gotland in the Middle Ages is presented in order to clarify the context in which *Guta lag* was written. The first known literary reference to Gotland's belonging to the Swedish state is in the ninth-century description in Old English of Wulfstan's voyage through the Baltic (*Orosius*, 16, line 28), although Wessén (*SL* IV, 306) and others contradict Wulfstan's claim (see *GS*, xxxiii–xxxv). In particular, Rydberg (*STFM* I, 40) argues that Gotland was independent of Sweden in the tenth century.

Later runic inscriptions, notably the Torsätra stone in Uppland (U 614) from the second half of the eleventh century, indicate that there was conflict between Gotland and mainland Sweden during that period, and tribute was collected from the islanders. By the twelfth century Gotland was certainly subject to Sweden in some respects. A document in Latin from the time of Pope Callixtus II, which lists bishoprics in a number of countries, including those of Scandinavia, is held in the Biblioteca Medicea Laurenziana in Florence. This document is dated to *c*.1120 and forms part of the Ashburnham collection; it is catalogued as *Codex (Laurenzianus) Ashburnham 1554.* The library acquired the collection in question in 1878 on the death of Lord Bertram, fourth Earl of Ashburnham. The text of the document, commonly called *Florensdokument* in Swedish, was first published by Delisle (1886, 70–75). As well as enumerating the Swedish bishoprics, it lists *Guthlandia* as one of the *insulae* of Sweden. Although the usual sense of *insula* is 'island', the list includes other, non-insular districts. Since, however, the document contains a number of obvious errors, its reliability on the matter of Gotland's relationship to Sweden must also be questionable (Delisle 1886, 75; Fabre and Duchesne 1910, Introduction, 41–43; Tunberg 1913, 28; *DS* Appendix 1, 3, no. 4; *GV*, 449–51).

A lost document from the reign of Emperor Lothar III (1125–37) apparently gave Gotlanders statutes of rights and freedom, but the oldest preserved such document is the Declaration of Artlenburg (*Artlenburgprivilegiet* or *Artlenburgfördraget* in Swedish), drawn up in 1161 (or possibly 1163) by Henry the Lion, Duke of Saxony and Bavaria. This document, in Latin, contains various reciprocal provisions relating to trade, inheritance, personal protection, and fines for violations against the person, but none of these is mentioned in *GL*. The oldest extant copy is dated 1225, the year in which Mariakyrkan in Visby was consecrated. It was originally kept in that church but is now preserved in the town archives of Lübeck. The document is edited in *Sveriges traktater med främmande magter* (*STFM*) I, 78–79, no. 42 (Yrwing 1940, 109–37; 1978, 109–16; *SL* IV, lxxxi; *KL* s. v. *Handelsfred*; *GV*, 455–59).

Although Gotland does not figure in the corpus of West Norse literature to any great extent, it is mentioned a number of times in connection with St Olaf. Snorri in Chapter 77 of *Óláfs saga helga* links it with Öland under the bishopric of Östergötland (*ÍF* XXVII, 109). Accounts of visits by St Olaf to Gotland are to some extent contradictory, but it seems certain that he visited the island on at least two occasions and possibly three (*ÍF* XXVII, Chapters 7 and 192; *GS*, xxxvi–xxxviii). The purpose of Olaf's first visit in 1007 or 1008, when he was twelve, was to exact tribute, but later visits seem to have been incidental to his voyage to and/or from Russia in 1029 and 1030. One of these later visits may have resulted in the introduction of Christianity to Gotland, or at least in the baptism of individual Gotlanders, but it is questionable whether a general conversion of the whole of the population resulted. Gotland took St Olaf as its patron saint, but this may have been influenced more by colourful legend than by an historical event. Church building in Gotland seems to have been initially the result of private initiative (see Chapter 3, lines 22–23). It cannot have started later than about the middle of the twelfth century, since by that time Gotland was evidently incorporated into the See of Linköping. The Cistercian monastery of Beata Maria de Gutnalia was founded at Roma in 1164, a daughter house to that of Nydala in Småland, which implies that Christianity was firmly established in Gotland by that date and that there were already close links with Sweden (Pernler 1977, 57, 61–62, 65).

In 1195, at the instigation of Bishop Meinhard of Livonia, Gotlanders apparently took part in a crusade in Livonia, which embraced what is now southern Estonia and northern Latvia (Yrwing 1940, 59; 1978, 123; Christiansen 1997, 81, 114). It appears that shortly after this, or at the beginning of the thirteenth century, commitment to an annual levy (*laiþingr*) for the Baltic crusades was established in Gotland, although Rydberg (*STFM* I, 71) dates this arrangement to *c*.1150 (Yrwing 1940, 58–59; 1978, 21–22). The Gotlanders agreed to supply seven manned warships for these crusades, or, alternatively, pay forty marks in coin for each ship not provided. One ship was to be funded by each sixth district (*siettungr*) and the seventh ship, it is assumed, by the inhabitants of Visby. These included both Gotlanders and Germans. The latter had been part of the resident population of merchants, probably from the twelfth century, before the Hanseatic League was formed (see pp. xi–xii below). The option of a payment in money rather than men was presumably offered in deference to the importance of trade between Gotland

and her Baltic neighbours (see Yrwing 1978, 21). Details of these arrangements appear in *Guta saga*, the short legendary history of Gotland that forms an appendix to the manuscript B 64, although there is no record of when they were put in place (see *GS*, 12–14 and notes).

There are further records of Gotlanders actually refusing to take part in crusades, such as those in 1199 to Livonia and in 1226 to the Baltic island of Ösel, presumably because they were unwilling to jeopardise their trading relationships with these countries (Björkander 1898, 27–28; Yrwing 1963, 94; Pernler 1977, 62, 108; Yrwing 1978, 124; 1991, 164).

Although Gotland was attached to the See of Linköping in Öster-götland, it was Archbishop Andreas Suneson of Lund, a Danish province at that time, who appears to have taken most interest in the island. He visited Gotland in 1207, a circumstance that has led to the supposition that it was he who initiated the writing of the first manuscript of *GL*. A letter from Pope Innocent III dated 1213 (*DS* I, 178, no. 152) concerns the abbot of Gotland and rural deans of the northern and southern districts (*Northlanda* and *Sutherlanda*), linking them to the diocese of Lund. Pernler (1977, 153–54) argues that Lund is in this document most probably an error for Linköping, and as the Archbishop of Lund was primate of Sweden at the time, superior to the Archbishop of Uppsala, a mistaken reference to the archdiocese here, instead of the diocese, might be understandable. Eight years later, in 1221, Archbishop Suneson, together with Bishops Karl and Bengt of Linköping, wrote a letter (*DS* I, 690, no. 832) setting out the arrangements relating to visitations by the bishop to Gotland. The contents of this letter may be compared with information given by *Guta saga* on the same topic (see *GS*, 10–12 and notes).

During the thirteenth century, there was considerable correspondence from the papacy concerning the level and distribution of tithes payable in Gotland. In 1217 Pope Honorius III confirmed tithe laws previously arranged for Gotland between Archbishop Suneson and Bishop Karl of Linköping (*DS* I, 190, no. 168). No document containing the original agreement survives, but the laws apparently differed from those in other Swedish provinces, where the bishop normally received a third of the remaining tithe, after a third had been paid to the parish priest. The parish church and the poor then each received the same proportion as the bishop (i.e. two ninths of the whole). It seems that allocation of a portion of the tithe to the bishop was a later innovation, perhaps replacing *ad hoc* payments for individual services rendered (e.g. church consecrations). *GL*'s is the only tithe law in Europe with no modification in favour of the bishop. That arrangements for Gotland occasioned some dissatisfaction in Linköping is suggested by a letter from Pope Gregory IX in 1230 confirming them (*DS* I, 257–58, no. 256), against protests from Bishop Bengt. In 1253 Pope Innocent IV had to issue the same edict to Bishop Lars (*DS* I, 366, no. 411). At the same time he issued statements of protection relating to the people and clergy of Gotland (*DS* I, 365–66, no. 410). He also confirmed the right of the priests to elect their own rural deans and the people to select their pastors (*DS* I, 366–67, nos 412 and 413). Whether Gotland succeeded in resisting later encroachments into the various elements of the tithe is doubtful and in all probability some of the tithe collected for parish churches was diverted to building the cathedral at Linköping. Since, however, there are no parish accounts covering the fourteenth and fifteenth centuries, this must remain a matter for conjecture (*SL* IV, 247–48 note 14; Pernler 1977, 133–44).

So far as the secular, as opposed to the ecclesiastical history of Gotland is concerned, it is evident that trade, in particular into and out of Visby, was of strategic importance in the late twelfth and early thirteenth centuries. A dramatic rise in Baltic transit trade in the eleventh to thirteenth centuries is possibly related to the decline in the importance of Birka, activity by Gotlandic merchant farmers (*farmannabönder*) filling the resulting vacuum (Yrwing 1978, 104–05, 138–40). The goods most traded were skins, but wax, iron and weapons were also significant. That Gotlanders had been trading in the Baltic and beyond during the Viking period is supported by finds of silver in almost every parish on the island and by finds in the Baltic countries of artefacts of Gotlandic design. The existence of a Gotlandic trading station in Novgorod and documentary evidence of trade with England in the form of customs declarations and literary references also show that trade flourished over a wide area before Visby emerged as a Hanseatic town (*HansUB* I, 270, 283, 281, 322; Bugge 1899, 151–71; Bohman 1951, 35). In 1229 Pope Gregory IX wrote to the Bishop of Linköping, the Cistercian abbot of Gotland and the rural dean of Visby to ask them to prevent trade first with the Russians (*DS* I, 253–54, no. 250, 27th January 1229), who were harassing Finnish converts, and then with unconverted Finns (*DS* I, 255–56, no. 253, 16th February 1229). The first request in all probability referred to Gotlandic merchants; the latter did so explicitly and was an attempt to enforce a previous interdict by Honorius III in 1221 (*DS* I, 220–21, no. 206, 13th January 1221). This is again evidence that the Gotlanders valued their Baltic trade and were reluctant to relinquish it, even in the cause of defending Christianity (see Pernler 1977, 196–97).

The building of Mariakyrkan in Visby started in the early thirteenth century and this ambitious project must reflect the success of the town itself, largely as a result of its association with the Hanseatic League. According to a letter dated 1225 from Bishop Bengt (*DS* I, 241, no. 231), which is the first written record of a German population in Visby, the church was to be consecrated as a parish church for both resident Germans and visiting merchants involved in Hanseatic trade. Björkander (1898, 88–89 notes 2, 3, 4) considers that the church was built primarily for the new German visitors, but that it was not their only church. Yrwing (1940, 223–38; 1978, 114–15) argues that the reference is to both a permanent and a transient German population and that Germans had started to inhabit Visby from the twelfth century and had possibly had an earlier church on the same site.

From about the middle of the thirteenth century, tension began to rise between the merchant farmers of the countryside and the largely German inhabitants of Visby. This was initiated by the actions of Lübeck and Hamburg in 1252, when they declared themselves representatives of the merchants of the Holy Roman Empire and excluded the Gotlandic merchants. Although the latter were granted safe conduct through Saxony in 1255, and their rights as expressed in the Declaration of Artlenburg (see p. viii) were reiterated, by 1280 the German inhabitants of Visby had made their own arrangements with Lübeck and later Riga to the exclusion of non–German merchants. Trade with England had also been reduced considerably by 1255, with only one Gotlandic merchant mentioned in records of fur trading (*HansUB* I, 475; Yrwing 1978, 28, 138). In 1282 the situation worsened and Frisians and Gotlanders were forbidden to trade in the North Sea. There was even an attempt to prevent the English trading in the Baltic.

By 1288, conflict between Visby and the rest of Gotland was inevitable and there was a bitter civil war. This resulted in a victory for the inhabitants of Visby, who then raised a wall around the town. Magnus Ladulås took advantage of the situation to punish the townspeople and force them to confess that they had broken their duty to the king in building the wall without permission. For this they paid a fine of 2,000 marks of silver with further sums at regular intervals, and agreed to allow the other Gotlanders to send messengers to the king. The viability of foreign trade by the merchant farmers of the countryside had, however, been destroyed. At the same time Magnus confirmed his sovereignty over Gotland, as well as new tax laws, which he had introduced in 1285, i.e. an annual levy tax to be paid whether the fleet was called out or not. The inhabitants of Visby retained their independence from the rest of Gotland, but at the expense of a humiliating surrender to the king of Sweden (Yrwing 1978, 27–33). One advantage that they did gain was their own law in German, *Visby stadslag* (the town law of Visby, *VStL*), which appears to have been set down in the early part of the fourteenth century. As a result, ordinary Gotlanders were slowly reduced to a population of domestic freehold and leasehold farmers, a situation that considerably worsened when King Valdemar Atterdag of Denmark invaded Gotland in July 1361.

In 1360 Valdemar had retaken Skåne and Blekinge from Magnus Eriksson and, early the following year, he had invaded Öland and captured the castle of Borgholm. On 27th July a well-equipped Danish force defeated an army of farmers, inflicting heavy losses. The citizens of Visby seem to have taken no part in the fighting and two days later Valdemar confirmed their ancient rights and privileges (*DD* III:6, 65–66, no. 69), simply replacing Sweden with Denmark in the agreements drawn up (Yrwing 1978, 46–49). The situation in the remainder of Gotland is less clear, and on 26th July 1364 Albrekt of Mecklenburg, who had seized power from Magnus, appeared to be in a position to pledge Gotland to Count Henry of Holstein for 4,000 marks of silver, or at least to be able to promise to do so (*STFM* II, 337–43, no. 368). This promise was never fulfilled, however, and in 1389 Albrekt lost power in Sweden to Queen Margareta. In the period from 1395 to 1398, Albrekt had regained control of Visby, while the remainder of the island was in Danish hands under Sven Sture. The latter cooperated with the Vitalian Brotherhood, a band of pirates in the pay of members of the Mecklenburg family. They were at that time destabilising the Baltic, and in 1396 Albrekt's son Duke Erik took command of the Vitalians in Gotland, and of Sven Sture himself. When Erik died of the plague in the following year, Sven Sture took over both the Vitalians and, effectively, Gotland (see Yrwing 1978, 51–52).

The damage to Baltic trade that this piracy caused, and advances made by Margareta in creating a Scandinavian superpower, led in 1398 to intervention by the Teutonic Order. They seized power in Gotland and took responsibility for both Visby and the rest of the island from Duke Johan of Mecklenburg on behalf of Albrekt, confirming that open trade was permitted in Visby and that taxes would not be imposed by the

Order, or by anyone to whom the island was pledged (*STFM* II, 585–87, no. 424, 5th April 1398). In the following year, Albrekt pledged the island to the Order in return for 30,000 gold nobles. Of these, 20,000 were to be waived in respect of the costs incurred by the Order in the rescue operation. This arrangement was clearly intended to prevent Queen Margareta from claiming Gotland from either party. In this it failed and finally, in 1407, Margareta agreed to pay the newly appointed Grand Master 9,000 nobles in respect of the castle of Visborg, which the Order had started to build in Visby. In November the following year, the Grand Master confirmed that he had received the sum named and was content to hand both Gotland and the castle to Erik of Pommern, joint monarch of the Union with Margareta, on the sole condition that Visby retain its ancient rights and privileges. All outstanding claims by the Teutonic Order for the cost of rescuing, maintaining and defending Gotland (i.e. the 20,000 nobles mentioned above) had been abandoned, as the task had become an economic liability, which they were perhaps only too relieved to surrender (see Schück 1945, 199–205; Yrwing 1978, 53–54).

The power struggle over Gotland continued through the fifteenth and the first quarter of the sixteenth centuries, but in 1526 it finally ceased to be a bone of contention in Scandinavia and became an unimportant Danish province for 119 years. More than two hundred years of conflict and uncertainty, during which Visby lost its place in the Hanseatic League as early as 1470, had completely obliterated Gotland's importance in Scandinavian and Baltic trade (Schück 1945, 205–20).

II *Preservation of* Guta lag

The text of *Guta lag*, the law of the Gotlanders, is preserved in eight manuscripts. Two of the medieval manuscripts, one vellum and one paper, are in Gutnish and it is these that are presented in the translation here. The others consist of a vellum manuscript in a mixture of Middle High German and Middle Low German, two Danish paper manuscripts, a paper manuscript containing a number of later provisions in Danish and two eighteenth-century paper manuscripts in Gutnish. All eight manuscript traditions are taken into consideration when attempting to construct a stemma.

There are four further manuscripts that contain only the historical appendix to the law, referred to as *Guta saga*. These are not considered in the present study, but are described in the introduction to *Guta saga*. *The History of the Gotlanders* (xii–xiv).

A. *Holm B 64*

This octavo vellum-bound manuscript, held in Kungliga Biblioteket (the Royal Library) in Stockholm, is the only medieval vellum manuscript of *GL* in the original Gutnish. The text of *Guta lag* covers forty-two leaves, followed by eight leaves containing the text of *Guta saga* (*GS*, x). Schlyter (*CIG*, i, iv) dates this manuscript, which he calls '*A*', to about the middle of the fourteenth century. Wessén (*LG*, xxvi) and others support this dating. The manuscript was discovered in Gotland *c*.1680 and taken to Stockholm, where it was passed to the archive of antiquities by Professor Andreas Spole (†1699) and subsequently used by Johan Hadorph for his edition (1687). Hadorph states elsewhere that the manuscript (B 64) was 'några åhr sedan igen funnin uthi en Kyrckia der på Landet ibland orenligheet, såsom en förkastat Ting' (several years ago found in a church in the province, amongst the rubbish, like a thing rejected). The chapter numbers in the table of contents, which is written in two columns, have been inserted by a later hand and the table of contents itself differs slightly from the content. The nature of the differences (e.g. the inclusion of references to slaves, missing from the text) suggests that the table reflects an earlier redaction of the text. The language of three chapters (62, 63 and 65) and of *Guta saga* is later than that of the other chapters. Chapter 64 (24f in this translation) has been omitted from its proper place (according to the table of contents) and inserted between Chapters 63 and 65 (*GU*, vii–x; *GLGS*, vii–xii; *SL* IV, lxv). The same scribe is responsible for the whole manuscript and it seems likely, as Wessén suggests, that most of these inconsistencies existed in his original. This manuscript is hereafter referred to as B 64 and its content, perhaps unfortunately, as the *A*-text, following Schlyter's designation.

B. *AM 54 4to*

This paper manuscript, bound in vellum, is in Den Arnamagnæanske Håndskriftsamling at the University library in Copenhagen and is designated '*B*' by Schlyter (*CIG*, xii). According to a statement on folio 55r, David Bilefeld copied it in 1587 from a manuscript (no longer extant) dated 1470. AM 54 4to consists of fifty-seven numbered leaves. On folios 55v to 57v is a table of contents. A further leaf at the front is inscribed *Anno Dei MDLXXXVII*, and a separate leaf attached to the manuscript has a note by Árni Magnússon repeating the information on folio 55r. David Hansson Bilefeld was born in Denmark and received a German education. He came to Gotland in 1569 as tutor to the sons of the Danish governor Jens Bilde and in 1571 was appointed headmaster in Visby. At the date of the production of AM 54 4to he was parish priest in Barlingbo and rural dean (*proastr*) of the northern riding (*þriþiungr*) of Gotland. Bilefeld was appointed suffragan Bishop of Gotland in 1592 and died in 1596 (Pipping 1901a, 72; Lemke 1868, 22–23). The text of Bilefeld's manuscript differs from the *A*-text in that sections relating to the children of priests and to the sale of and theft by slaves missing from B 64 appear in AM 54 4to. The provisions concerned seem to be older than those in sections where the texts agree, and were thus likely to have been deliberately omitted from B 64 or its original (see *GLGS*, xviii; *SL* IV, lxvi). This circumstance supports an assumption that AM 54 4to, and hence the manuscript of 1470, although of a later date than B 64, represents an earlier state of the law. The text of AM 54 4to is hereafter referred to, again perhaps unfortunately, as the *B*-text.

C. *Holm B 65*

This is an octavo vellum manuscript, lacking covers, from 1401, held in Kungliga Biblioteket, Stockholm, and containing a medieval German translation of *GL*. It contains the text of the law and a German translation of *Guta saga*. Following the vellum leaves are attached thirteen paper leaves, the first nine and last two of which contain two sets of Danish statutes, written in a mid-sixteenth-century hand. One set is dated Christmas Eve (*helig afton*) 1492 and the other 1537. The first is complete, but only the first two and a half chapters of the latter are included. According to information in the manuscript itself, the German translation was prepared under instructions from Johann Techewicz, who was captain (*houptman*) of the Teutonic Order in Gotland. The translation itself was executed by Sunye (known only by his given name), recorded in June 1402 as superintendent at St George's Hospital, Visby (*SD* I, 143, no. 195) and later apparently as rural dean of the northern riding of Gotland (see Pernler 1977, 167). Schlyter (*CIG*, xiv) considers that the text is a mixture of Middle High German and Middle Low German, such as was probably spoken by the German residents of Visby, but this has been challenged by Ekelund (1906, 9, 32, 34) and others. The translation contains the chapters concerning the sale of and theft by slaves, but not the other extra provisions in AM 54 4to, nor the three additional (latest) chapters in B 64. The last thirteen chapters are in a different sequence with respect to both B 64 and AM 54 4to. The translation in B 65 is designated *tyGL* by Wessén (*SL* IV, lxvi). The manuscript Holm B 65 is hereafter referred to as B 65 and its content as *tyGL*.

D. *AM 55 4to*

This mid-sixteenth-century paper manuscript, containing a Danish translation of *GL*, is held in Den Arnamagnæanske Håndskriftsamling at the University library, Copenhagen. It is bound in a paper cover, inscribed *Den gamle Gullands Low*. On the title page, as well as the words *Gullans Lovf*, is the name of the owner: Claudius Christophori F. Lyschander and '† 1623'. The first two leaves contain a table of contents, which does not wholly agree with the text itself and is written in a different hand. The text of the law is followed by some notes on coinage in the same hand and an outline, in a later hand, of an alphabetical index, which has not been completed. Wessén, who designates the text in the manuscript *daGL*, thinks that the translation might have been made in connection with a declaration by King Hans I in 1492, confirming the validity of 'then gamble Gudlandtz lough' (the old Gotlandic law), supplemented by certain other provisions contained in manuscript Holm C 81 4to described below (see *SL* IV, lxvii, lxxxvii). According to Schlyter (*CIG*, xvii), however, the manuscript was probably written out by the translator himself, which would place it approximately fifty years later in date. Three chapters present in the medieval Gutnish manuscripts are missing from this translation; it contains, however, seven chapters that do not appear in the other texts and three that differ in content from similar provisions elsewhere in the text. The last thirteen chapters are in a different sequence from the last fourteen of the three preceding manuscripts and the chapter on taxes is omitted. The provision concerning the sale of slaves is present, but not that concerning theft by slaves. AM 55 4to therefore evidently follows a tradition independent of the three manuscripts previously described, and is of value in respect of the provisions not found elsewhere, since it in all probability throws light on a lost Gotlandic original.

E. *Holm C 81 4to*

This paper manuscript from the late sixteenth century, bound but lacking covers, is held in Kungliga Biblioteket, Stockholm. It contains in complete form the two sets of Danish statutes, which are to be found in truncated form in B 65. On one of two blank leaves at the beginning a later hand refers to the first set of statutes as that laid down by King Hans I in 1492. The second set of statutes was, according to its rubric, drawn up in 1537 by King Christian III Frederiksson.

F. *GKS 3363 4to*

This vellum-bound paper manuscript is held in Den Gamle Kongelige Samling (GKS) of Det Kongelige Bibliotek (the Royal Library) in Copenhagen. A number of supplementary notes are inserted at the end of the manuscript. It has two title pages, one inscribed *Lex Gothlandica 1470 scripta* and the other *Exaratum Anno MDLXXXVII*. The catalogue details state: '*Lex Gothlandica, ad exemplar 1470 exerat, manu O. Sperlingii jun.* 1687'. This date is presumably the date assigned to the manuscript. It is an imperfect, although largely careful copy made by Otto Sperling (†1715), a professor in Copenhagen, and was intended to consist of the Gutnish text with a Latin translation on facing pages. Only the first two and a half chapters and the chapter headings have been translated, however. Since it gives the years 1470 and 1587 on the title page, the Gutnish would appear to be a copy of Bilefeld's manuscript, AM 54 4to, as stated by Schlyter (*CIG*, xix), and thus does not represent an independent tradition. This manuscript is not listed in Gigas's catalogue (1903–15) of Scandinavian manuscripts in Det kongelige Bibliotek.

G. *Kall 650 4to*

This unbound paper manuscript is held in Kalls Samling of Det Kongelige Bibliotek, Copenhagen. The collection was the property of Professor Abraham Kall (†1821) and was inherited by Det kongelige Bibliotek in 1821. The Gutnish of the manuscript (on the verso pages) is an exact copy, apart from a number of misreadings, of GKS 3363 4to and hence ultimately of Bilefeld's manuscript. Kall 650 4to was executed at almost the same time as GKS 3363 4to (i.e. late seventeenth or early eighteenth century). This manuscript is likewise not listed in Gigas's catalogue (1903–15).

H. *Holm B 68 4to*

This paper manuscript, also bound in paper, and held in Kungliga Biblioteket, Stockholm, is a Danish translation of *GL* from the beginning of the seventeenth century and is a copy of AM 55 4to. Schlyter (*CIG*, xix) considers the scribe to be Swedish on the grounds of his handwriting and orthography. There are a number of spaces left in the manuscript, presumably for later insertions that were never completed.

Stemma

From an analysis of the preserved manuscripts of *GL* described above a tentative stemma may be proposed:

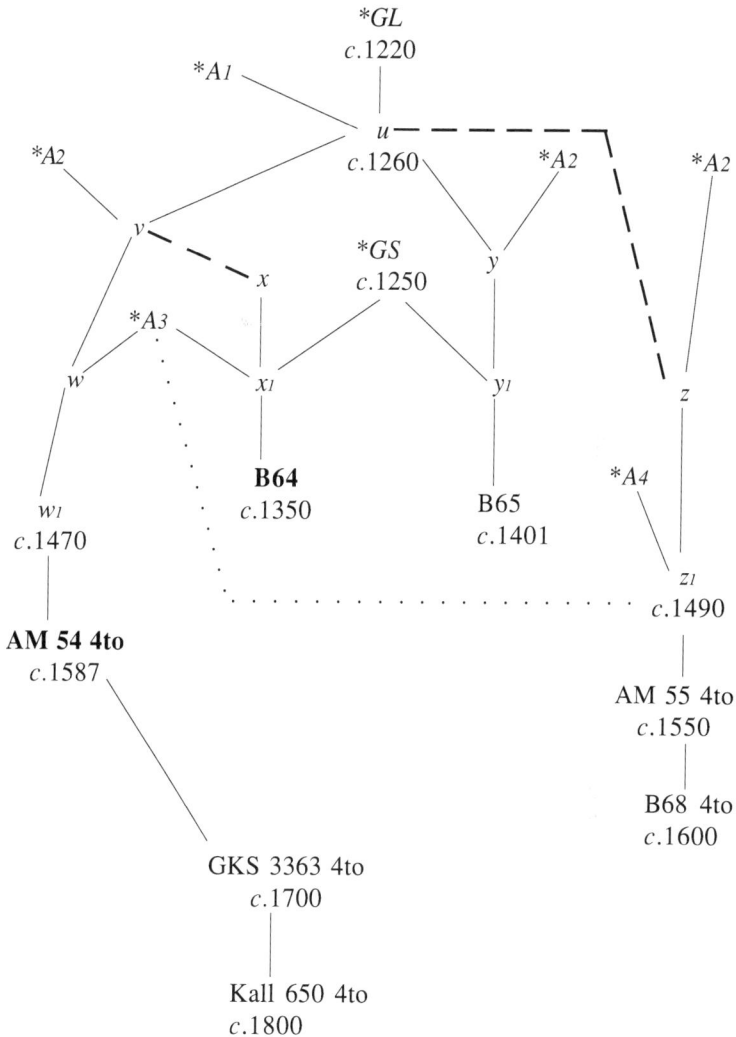

The argument in favour of a single, 'original', manuscript for *Guta lag*, probably written at the instigation of Archbishop Suneson of Lund, is presented in section V. Correspondence between the archbishop and others in the early thirteenth century suggests that no written law code existed for Gotland before that time. This being the case, it seems reasonable to assume that the outcome was a single manuscript, which was then copied, added to and translated as circumstances changed and the need arose. The consistency of the core statutes in all the extant manuscripts also supports this assumption.

Following Wessén's suggestions (*SL* IV, lxiv–lxviii), it seems likely that the surviving complete manuscripts that are not obviously copies (A–D above) represent four different traditions, here designated *w*, *x*, *y* and *z*. Of these, *w* and *x* are assumed both to be derived from a common source *v*. Two arguments for this are: (1) the presence of some errors common to B 64 and AM 54 4to, such as that noted in the footnote to Chapter 32, lines 12–13, and (2) the identical sequence of the fourteen later chapters, which is not the case in the other two traditions. Pipping points out (*GLGS*, xviii note 1) that Bilefeld could have had B 64 to hand when he made his copy and been influenced by it. He certainly had access to B 64 at some time, since he has made annotations in it, e.g. the number 27 in the margin on folio 22r, which is in his handwriting (see Pipping 1904, 16–18). Pipping observes, however, that Bilefeld appears to have had access to a third manuscript (which Pipping calls *X*) when making his copy of the one dated 1470 (see *GLGS*, xvii–xviii). Pipping reaches this conclusion in his edition of AM 54 4to, where he considers various marginal notes that Bilefeld made in his manuscript and points out their differences in orthography both from the main text (and hence presumably from the manuscript of 1470) and from B 64 (see Pipping 1901a, 73–81). In addition, the number '27' written by Bilefeld on folio 22r of B 64, alongside Chapter 20, does not refer to the equivalent chapter in AM 54 4to, which is 26, and so, argues Pipping, must refer to the equivalent chapter in *X*. Since Pipping's *X* has not survived, there is little that can be conjectured concerning its content or age, and it has been excluded from the stemma.

If it is assumed that the first manuscript of *GL* dated from *c*.1220, there must have been a later manuscript group, designated *u*, that contained the provision, designated *A_1* on the stemma, relating to inheritance by daughters of non-Gotlandic (i.e. Swedish) men and which is present in all the extant manuscripts (e.g. at the end of Chapter 24 in B 64 and in Chapter 36 in AM 54 4to). Manuscript group *u* can be dated to the second half of the thirteenth century at the earliest, since the inheritance law could not have been included prior to 1260, when Birger Jarl introduced it into Swedish law (Pipping 1926, 247–50).

The miscellaneous provisions (designated *A_2* on the stemma) contained in Chapters 48–61 of B 64, which Wessén also considers to be later than the main corpus, must have been added after the writing of *u*, and independently in each of the traditions *v*, *y* and *z* (as indicated) since these fourteen chapters are in different sequences in three of the four complete manuscripts, but in the same sequence in B 64 and AM 54 4to. The late fifteenth- and early sixteenth-century Danish statutes, which are present in B 65 and Holm C 81 4to, clearly represent a separate tradition, outside that of the main text. They are not included in the stemma.

The *w* tradition represents an early version of the law, deriving from *v*, which retained the specific provisions relating to slaves and the children of priests. At some point various additions to existing provisions concerning hair pulling, toasts at weddings, and inheritance by women (designated *A_3* on the stemma) were absorbed into the text. A copy of this version, dated 1470, was used by Bilefeld in writing AM 54 4to, the *B*-text, and this in turn was copied by several later scribes (e.g. as GKS 3363 4to and Kall 650 4to).

The *x* tradition derives similarly from *v* but omits the provisions concerning the children of priests and the sale of and theft by slaves, presumably when clerical celibacy was enforced, and slavery became less common because of economic, rather than moral, circumstances. Lis Jacobsen (*GGD*, 6) infers from this that *x* represents a later stage of the law than *w*, *y* or *z*. The first manuscript with these omissions, shown by a broken line from *v*, Pipping assumes was made *c*.1300, i.e. shortly before B 64 was written. Since the table of contents in the latter refers to the provision relating to the sale of slaves not contained in the text, it seems that B 64 was written at a time of transition in the law. At some point, represented by x_1, the heterogeneous additions (*A_3*) made to the *w* tradition were included, but not absorbed into the body of the text as they were in the *w* tradition, appearing instead in Chapters 62, 63 and 65. Whether this happened before or after the omissions in question were made is not possible to determine, since no change was made to the table of contents to incorporate them. *Guta saga* (*GS*), which was not part of the *w* tradition, was also appended at or around this stage. The *x* tradition is represented only by B 64, the *A*-text.

The *y* tradition, represented by B 65 (*tyGL*), contains some of the older provisions, namely those concerning the sale of and theft by slaves, but not the additions (*A_3*) found in the *w* and *x* traditions. On this basis, Jacobsen considers that the German translation represents the oldest preserved content. At some point, however, say y_1, the text of *Guta saga* was translated and incorporated into B 65.

Finally, the *z* tradition, which is represented by AM 55 4to and its copy B 68 4to (*daGL*), omits some of the provisions that might be regarded as original, shown by a broken line from *u*. Some, but not all, of the provisions assumed to have been later additions are included (shown by the dotted line leading from $*A_3$) as are others that have no equivalents elsewhere (designated $*A_4$ and forming Chapters 13, 52, 54, 55 and 57–59 of the named manuscripts).

As a supplement to the stemma, Appendix A contains a table showing the differences in content and sequence of chapters in the four principal manuscripts (A–D above) and thus the four manuscript traditions.

III *Nature and content*

A. *The nature of* Guta lag

There are three scholarly opinions concerning the character of the original text of *Guta lag*, and thus the existing manuscripts. Richard Steffen (1943, 40) contends that the 'original' text of *GL* was produced by a priest, and that it was partly theoretical in nature, reflecting an ideal rather than an achieved legal framework. In support of this view Bengt Söderberg (1956, 13) points out that a wergild of twenty-four marks of silver must have been equivalent to a large farm complete with its contents and movables. Since only wealthy landowning families could have considered paying such a fine, it might be assumed that for others the price must have been their life or liberty, a process that started when the killer fled to an area of asylum with his close family. Such an assumption, i.e. that the fines were unrealistic, changes the balance of the law as presented in the manuscripts. Instead of fines taking precedence over other forms of punishment, the old system of retaliation would seem still to hold good, in defiance of the new principle of reconciliation.

Karl Westman (1912b, 16–18) uses the terms *rättsbok* and *lagbok* in the context of Swedish provincial laws. He defines the former as a record of the law in force at a particular date, recorded from the words of law speakers as an *aide mémoire*. A suitable English translation of *rättsbok* might be 'justice book'. Westman cites the older law of Västergötland (*ÄVgL*) and the law of Östergötland (*ÖgL*) as examples of this type. He contrasts these with a number of other provincial laws, particularly those from Svealand, that is, the laws of Uppland, Södermanland and Hälsingland (*UL*, *SdmL* and *HL*), which he designates *lagböcker*. Westman defines these as systematic, normalised codes prepared by lawmakers from existing written records. These were presumably designed to incorporate the complete legal process. *Lagbok* would be usefully translated as 'statute book'.

Westman does not classify *GL*, or certain other provincial laws, for example those of Dalarna and Västmanland and the younger law of Västergötland (*DL*, *VmL*, *YVgL*). Hafström (1970, 25, 27) holds that all the law texts from Götaland were justice books and by implication includes *GL* in this category, but Wessén (*LG*, xix) places *GL* in the second of Westman's categories rather than the first, and refers to the concluding words of the law:

> Þa en nequarar atbyrþir kunnu þar verþa sum ai hittas hier, þa skulu þar slitas miþ domera tali ok þair þet sueria et þet sein ret guta lag ok siþan skrifas hier i.

> If some occurrence should take place, which is not to be found here, then it must be decided by the majority of judges, and they are to swear that these are proper laws of the Gotlanders, and then they are to be written down here.

On the basis of this provision he holds that *GL* appears to be a formally accepted and applied text. He contrasts this with the older law of Västergötland and the law of Östergötland, which he agrees with Westman to be private records of the law at a particular date, written by men involved with legal matters as *aides mémoires*, i.e. justice books. On the other hand, Holmbäck (*SL* I, xv–xvi; *MELLNT*, xiv–xvi) considers that *GL* as preserved represents a private record of the law that applied in the province at a specific time (i.e. a justice book rather than a statute book). He includes the law of Dalarna in this category, but designates the law of Västmanland and the younger law of Västergötland as statute books, the result of 'omfattande bearbetning av den tidigare rätten' (comprehensive revision of the earlier law code). Holmbäck (*MELLNT*, xv note 4) leaves open the question of how many changes took place when the justice books were prepared from the recited law.

A glance at the table of contents of B 64 (taking into account the small differences between that and the text) reveals how unstructured *GL* is. Matters of civil law are interspersed with matters of criminal law, and provisions covering related topics appear at various points in the content. From the fact that, in the main, the chapters in the text agree with the table of contents at the start of the manuscript, and that the new provisions at the end of B 64 are not included in that table, it seems likely that the sequence of provisions is original. The arrangement of the content in the manuscript gives the impression of a document that records, somewhat randomly, what an individual or individuals remembered. Reading the body of the text gives a similar impression: there are omissions, repetitions and slight inconsistencies such as one would expect if memory were the chief source of the information. These observations militate against Steffen's suggestion that the text was written as an unrealised ideal, and it certainly does not have the characteristics of a theoretical work.

If one assumes that *GL* is to some degree practical rather than theoretical the opposing conclusions of Wessén and Holmbäck (i.e. that *GL* is either a statute book or a justice book) are equally worthy of serious consideration. Although *GL* as it is preserved has clearly undergone certain revisions, it does not seem to be a systematised set of statutes as Wessén contends. It is not organised into sections and chapters (Swedish *balkar* and *flockar*) in any logical manner and certainly could not be said to cover the whole legal process (Amira 1882–95, I, 711). Some chapters are relatively lengthy and unstructured, covering a number of different provisions (e.g. those on wounding and inheritance) whilst others (especially those towards the end of the text) are extremely short, frequently containing only one provision. The law relating to property is split across several chapters, scattered throughout the text (see *SL* IV, lxxiv–lxxv). *GL* could therefore be described as a more or less selective record by an individual or individuals of the law in force in Gotland at a particular moment, amended and copied at various times to give rise to the preserved manuscripts; in other words it is more nearly a justice book than a statute book.

B. *Legal system as reflected by* Guta lag

A discussion of the legal system contained in *GL* might usefully start with what is not included, since that is what distinguishes it most markedly from the mainland Swedish provincial laws. The most obvious omission is a section relating to the pledge of royal involvement in local law (Swedish *edsöreslag*, see p. xxxviii), and indeed there is no mention of the king at all in either *GL* or the town law of Visby. No fines are stated as payable to the king, and although taxes are referred to in *Guta saga* (*GLGS*, 64, 68), there is only an unspecific mention of them in *GL* (Chapter 53). There is no reference to Sweden, although it has been assumed by modern scholars that the non-Gotlandic people referred to in *GL* were residents of Swedish origin. Reciprocal arrangements between Gotland and Sweden are mentioned in *Guta saga* (*GLGS*, 64) and the forty-mark wergild, which is payable for non-Gotlanders, appears to be an import from the mainland provincial laws. Wessén notes that this same level of fine appeared in the Declaration of Artlenburg (see pp. viii, xii above) and considers that in this latter case it reflected the existing law in Gotland (see *SL* IV, lxxix–lxxxii).

Another omission from *GL* is any element of commercial or maritime law, despite the apparent importance of trade to Gotland; indeed Visby is named only once, and that in passing. Yrwing (1978, 105) suggests that this omission is explained by the existence, at the time of writing of *GL*, of special laws covering these matters, and cites the provision relating to the redemption by a foreigner of a captive Gotlander as an indication that this was the case (see Chapter 28, lines 54–58). Provisions relating to ships are included (Chapter 36) but these cover only the responsibilities of their owners to take due care to protect them from theft.

Although there are a number of provisions relating to the church (tithes, observance of the Sabbath, the duties of priests, etc.) there is no specific church law section covering the dedication, care and ringing of bells, forbidden degrees of kinship in marriage, trial by ordeal or bishop's visitations and courts such as appear in other Swedish provincial laws and in the Danish law of Skåne (*SkL*). The fact that arrangements for the bishop's visitation are described in detail in *Guta saga*, however, supports Wessén's contention (*LG*, xviii) that the latter is 'ett naturligt komplement till lagen' (a natural complement to the law) in that it includes relevant matter not present in *GL* itself.

A further example of *Guta saga* complementing *GL* may be noted. There is no reference in *GL* to the commission (*nämnd*), which forms an important element in mainland provincial laws. In *Guta saga*, however, an oath given by commissioners or nominees (*nemnda aiþr*) is described in reference to the failure of the islanders to send troops to the levy (*laiþingr*). Significantly it is stated in this context that the only such oath permitted is this particular oath to the king (*SL* IV, lxxix; *GLGS*, 69).

GL contains very few descriptions of the legal process itself, how assemblies were organised, their frequency and constitution. One institution that seems to have been absent from Gotland, however, is that of lawspeaker (*lagman*). This office was also lacking in the Danish legal system, whose law texts are similarly less structured than those of mainland Sweden. Wessén (*SL* IV, lxxxvi) suggests that there might have been a college of judges (*domerar*) in Gotland determining the legislative programme. One may infer that there were three or more (*þings*)*domerar* in each sixth (see Chapter 19, lines 120–21) and that a number of these were designated as *siettungsdomerar*. There also seem to have been a number of provincial judges (*lanzdomerar*), who had some legislative power. Such an arrangement is certainly implied by the second half of Chapter 61, the conclusion of the oldest section of the law text. On the other hand, Söderberg (1956, 12) thinks that there was a speaker at the general assembly, i.e. the *lanzdomeri*, who was the highest authority. He may have been the highest judicial voice, but one cannot infer that he was the sole lawmaker. The only instance of the word *lanzdomeri* in *GL* (Chapter 19, lines 7–8) suggests that there was at least one of these officials for each sixth (*siettungr*), possibly chosen from amongst the (*þings*)*domerar* or *siettungsdomerar*. A similar phrase later in the same chapter uses *domeri* alone, however, and Steffen (1943, 39 note 2) maintains that *lanzdomeri* referred only to the judge who presided over *land alt*, i.e. the general assembly.

In another contribution Steffen (1945, 229) suggests that a particular *lanzdomeri* might have been simultaneously a judge in lower levels of the judiciary. If the first manuscript of *GL* were written as a private document, the writer might have had in mind a specific situation in which the provincial judge was a local sixth judge when he wrote the provision. Yrwing (1978, 80–81) states that all the judges attended the general assembly and that until about the middle of the fifteenth century the three rural deans also attended. It appears at least possible that the redactor of *GL* was misled by this arrangement into thinking that all the judges attending the general assembly were designated *lanzdomerar*. It is also possible that the cited use of this word is simply an error, but if so it is an error common to all four manuscript traditions of *GL*. It is worth noting that there is no specific reference in *GL* or other contemporary sources to *þriþiungsdomerar*.

GL was a law designed for a closed, self-governing, farming community with a need to maintain estates at a viable size, despite the necessity of providing younger sons with a living and daughters with a dowry. Other classes were the lease-holding farmers who rented land, the landless, who were obliged to provide unpaid labour at harvest time, servants and slaves. Elsa Sjöholm (1976, 170–73) in her discussion of the date of origin of *GL* makes much of the importance of the Gotlandic aristocracy, but other scholars (e.g. Wessén in *SL* IV, lxxxiii) argue that there was, in effect, no aristocratic class in Gotland, and it is difficult to find evidence of such a class. Even the priests were answerable to the assembly of the people, and the power of parishioners in general seems to have been quite extensive.

As well as the native people, there was evidently a considerable foreign population (*ogutniskt fulk*) who were permitted to own land and who had their own rules of inheritance and their own levels of wergild.

This population is considered by most scholars to have consisted of Swedish people from other provinces, since the laws that relate to them coincide with the provincial laws of mainland Sweden, rather than those of Germany (*GGD*, 45 note 1; *SL* IV, lxxx). A similar expression, *vtlænsker maþer*, is used in this sense in the older law of Västergötland (*ÄVgL* Md 5 §§ 4, 5). On the other hand, Sjöholm (1976, 167) seems to argue that the group referred to was the population of Visby, or at least the (mainly German) merchants who lived there while visiting Gotland. She admits, however, that the lower level of wergild applicable to this group contradicts earlier agreements relating to compensation for travelling merchants.

Although information is sparse, at least three levels of judicial assembly are recognised in *GL*. The highest level was the general assembly (*gutnalþing*). This was thought, by tradition, to have been held at Roma, in central Gotland, although this is not mentioned in the Gutnish manuscripts of *GL*, and has now been called into question. It is possible, for instance, that the word *Rume* used in the German translation of *Guta saga* (*CIG*, 164) referred simply to an open space, possibly near Visby (see Steffen 1945, 246, 250; Söderberg 1956, 12). Steffen (1943, 37, 45–46) suggests that there might not have been a fixed site for the assembly, but that it was held at the farm of the presiding provincial judge. Yrwing (1978, 81 note 3), however, dismisses this as extremely unlikely in the early Middle Ages, although circumstances might have changed later (Wildte 1926, 212, 215–16, 219–21; 1931, 181; 1933–34, 171–72). The number of general assemblies held in the course of a year is not specified in *GL* but would seem to be more than one, since the 'assembly next following the Feast of St Peter' is specified in *Guta saga* (*GLGS*, 69). According to later laws, the frequency of assemblies varied between weekly and twice yearly province by province. The older law of Västergötland, however, like *GL* gives no details (Sjöberg 1969, 60, 81–82). By the end of the fifteenth century Visby was represented by burgomasters and local magistrates, an innovation by Gotland's Danish rulers. A place referred to in the sources as *Gutestue* in Visby was the occasional site of assemblies and of meetings between representatives of the town and the Danish crown (see Yrwing 1978, 80). Although King Hans I specified in 1492 that only one assembly a year was to be held, in 1618 there were four a year, one at *Gutestuen* and three at Roma.

The next level is commonly thought to have been the riding (*þriþiungr*) assembly. According to this theory, the island was divided into three ridings with an assembly for each, presided over by a judge (Tunberg

1911, 48–49, 135–36). There is no contemporary support for this (see p. xxvi), and Steffen (1943, 41) argues that the original ridings were purely ecclesiastical, each headed by a rural dean, and that the administrative function of ridings only came into being after 1645. Three of the four references in *GL* to the riding assembly appear, however, in the context of the redemption of lost or straying animals. The fourth reference is a general one to the maximum fine that could be extracted at the assembly:

(1) en þriþiungr til siex marka (Chapter 31, lines 11–12)

And the riding assembly up to six marks.

(2) þa skal hafa til tyggia þinga ok þriþia þriþiungs þings (Chapter 41, lines 3–4)

He is to take them to two assemblies and the third time to the riding assembly.

(3) þa hafi til tyggia þinga ok þriþia þriþiungs þings ok haiti upp um þry ar ok taki lausn eptir þi sum þriþiungr hafr fyr vana hapt (Chapter 42, lines 2–5)

He is to take them to two assemblies and the third time to the riding assembly and declare them for three years and claim a fee such as has previously been the custom for the riding.

(4) at tuaim þingum ok þriþia þriþiungs þingi um þry ar (Chapter 45a, lines 2–3)

(Must be declared) at two assemblies and the third time at a riding assembly for three years.

It appears to be difficult to deny, therefore, that assemblies for the ridings did have some judicial as well as an ecclesiastical function at the time *GL* was written, since these provisions seem to have no ecclesiastical significance (see Yrwing 1940, 108; 1978, 83 note 1). Pernler (1977, 186–89) reaches the same conclusion and observes at the same time that *GL* remained in force effectively until 1645, despite King Christian IV's attempt to introduce the law of Skåne to Gotland. This persistence, he infers, would hardly be likely if *GL* were a theoretical work by a cleric, with no practical application (see pp. xxii–xxiv above). Ecclesiastical matters that were not resolved at the appropriate riding assembly were referred to the general assembly (see *GLGS*, 68). Although there are no contemporary records naming the sites at which the riding assemblies were held, Lindström (1895, II, 482–83) suggests that these were at Tingstäde church for the northern riding, at Roma for the middle riding and at Suderting for the southern riding. Pernler (1977, 189) points out, however, that Suderting was actually in the middle riding. Suderting does not survive as a place-name, but it was situated in a property called Ajmunds (or Ejmunds), in the parish of Mästerby, southwest of Roma, and was an assembly site for the Hejde sixth (see Steffen 1945, 250–53).

Gotland was further divided into sixths (*siettungar*), which Lindström (1895, II, 480–83), Steffen (1943, 21, 22) and others consider to be pre-Christian in origin. The boundaries of these districts do not, however, exactly coincide with those of the ridings from which it was assumed they were created (see Steffen 1945, 236). Sixths seem to have had some administrative significance in that a number of judges were allocated to each. These judges apparently had the authority to adjudicate in cases in which the fine did not exceed three marks, but there is no reference in *GL* to an assembly for a sixth, which weakens Steffen's argument that such assemblies were part of the judicial structure at the time that *GL* was written. Yrwing's suggestion (1940, 107) that by this time the function of the sixth assembly had been taken over by the lower, district assembly seems in part to be supported by provisions elsewhere in *GL* relating to three-mark fines. He goes further, however, in a later article (1978, 83) to put forward the theory that sixths only became important as areas for taxation, and later the levy, under Swedish rule and did not have any judicial significance before Danish occupation. Pernler (1977, 188) supports Yrwing in this assessment, pointing out that the first unambiguous mention of a sixth judge occurs in 1511. He interprets the phrase *ann lanzdomeri af sama siettungi* to mean that there were judges who represented each sixth at the general assembly, rather than assuming that there were assemblies for each sixth. The Danish sixth assemblies and their judges were abolished when Gotland was recovered by Sweden in 1645 (see Yrwing 1978, 86 note 6).

The third level of assembly that is mentioned specifically in *GL* relates to a further division of the sixths into local districts or hundreds. The word *hunderi* appears in five contexts, in Chapters 19, 28, 31, 32 and Addition 8, but is not recorded in relation to Gotland outside *GL*. The word *þing* alone is used elsewhere in Gotlandic documents (see Yrwing 1978, 86–87). Tunberg has argued that the word *hunderi* in *GL* may be an import from mainland Sweden (Tunberg 1911, 138–39, 202–03; *SL* IV, lxxxiv–lxxxv). In *GL* it appears that each such district had a number of local officials, consistently called *raþmenn* (Chapters 19, 31, 32 and the *B*-text addition to 38). Steffen (1943, 41) questions the origin of the use of this word and suggests that it reflects a failed attempt to introduce the *nämnd*, alongside a system of local judges. Since the latter are not mentioned in *GL*, this theory lacks sufficient support and it seems more probable that the term *raþmenn* was used deliberately to distinguish local officials from those appointed to the riding assemblies. At least three *rapmenn* were chosen for each *hunderi* and it seems likely that they acted as local magistrates (see Addition 8 and Chapter 31). The terminology is, however, ambiguous and *rapmenn* might have just assisted a single *domeri*, appointed for the *hunderisping* (Amira 1882–95, I, 21; *SL* IV, lxxxv–lxxxvi, 280–81 note 1). Although Hegel (1891, I, 302), noting various three-mark fines payable by the parish, considers that the hundred was an administrative authority in Gotland, this interpretation is challenged by Yrwing (1940, 104). While other laws, for example the law of Uppland (*UL* Rb 1), mention *rætter pinxstaper* 'proper assembly sites' in relation to the hundreds, there is no indication of such fixed assembly sites in *GL*.

It might be inferred from *GL* that the lowest administrative and judicial body was at parish level. This body appears to have been of considerable practical importance, although Steffen (1943, 41) considers that it was, rather, the lowest level of ecclesiastical court, below the riding court and the consistory court. Certainly many of the cases referred to the parish were ecclesiastical in nature, or at least related to crimes committed in or near the church, but some of the duties of the parishioners were of a secular character. Examples are: (1) witnessing the freeing of a slave after his period of service (Chapter 16, lines 23–26), (2) witnessing the statement of a woman relating to a child born as a result of an illicit liaison (Chapter 20, lines 114–16) and (3) valuing a debt for which surety has been given (Chapter 30, lines 4–5). Yrwing (1940, 93, 95–98, 107) suggests that as the number of parishes increased and their importance developed, the power exercised by the sixth assemblies was passed to the parishes. These latter then became the local assemblies (called simply *ping*, see p. xxix), the manifestation of the so-called hundred assemblies (*SL* IV, lxxxii–lxxxviii, xc–xcviii).

Magnus Eriksson's national law for Sweden (*MELL*) was drawn up in the mid-fourteenth century to replace individual provincial laws prevailing in Sweden (outside the towns) with a single law. This replacement did not occur simultaneously in all parts of Sweden: the law of Hälsingland, for example, was still in force in 1436. In Gotland circumstances were such that *GL* remained in force until 1645 when Sweden finally recovered Gotland from Denmark. As noted above, in 1595 King Christian IV of Denmark ordered that all his subjects in Gotland should follow the provincial law of Skåne, but how far this was enforced is unclear and the attempt to replace *GL* seems to have been a failure (see Westman 1912b, 21).

C. *System of fines and non-monetary punishments*

The system of fines in *GL* is a complex one and in some sections seems to be confusing and contradictory: Appendix C sets out the monetary system used and Appendix D, table (ii) offers an analysis of fines imposed for different offences, showing the variations depending on the perpetrator and the victim. Wennström (1940, 74–95, 259–63) analyses the fines on the basis of the amount extracted.

Theft and adultery seem, to some extent, to have been regarded as more despicable crimes than killing, presumably because they were crimes that broke down trust in the farming community. An isolated killing resulting from a fight between two adult males, if admitted to and compensated for, might be forgiven or at least accepted. The danger came when compensation was not paid and a blood feud could start. One noteworthy aspect of the law relating to what might be called sexual harassment is that the woman appears to have been assigned some responsibility for protecting herself against unwanted advances, since fines for these diminished according to the intimacy of the advance. Such advances were clearly distinguished from straightforward indecent assaults, which were (as would only seem right to modern eyes) punishable in relation to the degree of exposure the woman suffered. This difference, so tersely described, gives us, perhaps, an insight into the prevailing relationships between men and women in thirteenth-century Gotlandic society. There are no similar provisions in other Swedish provincial laws for comparison, but one cannot infer from this that attitudes to women were therefore different.

The levels of compensation extracted for various criminal acts can be used as an indicator of the relative value of the goods involved. Wennström (1931, 25–26) suggests that a cow was worth nine *örtugar* of silver (⅜ mark) in thirteenth-century Halland. The definition of 'full theft', punishable by death or payment of wergild, in most other provincial laws is half a mark of silver (twelve *örtugar*), or alternatively a cow (see *ÖgL* Vb 32 pr, §1). In *GL* the limit for 'full theft' is one mark, and if this were equivalent to two cows or more, the full wergild of twenty-four marks would probably have been equal in value to the estate and movables of a considerable farm (see Note to Chapter 3, line 4). Only the very rich would have been able to afford to pay it; the remainder of the population might have had to forfeit their lives or liberty (see p. xxii). There is, however, an indication that this extreme was not always the case. In Chapter 14 we have the following:

Hittir maþr sakar at giera lerþr eþa olerþr, þa byti engin frammar firi annan, þan hans kustr vindr at.

If a man, whether ordained or not, commits a crime, no one shall be fined more for another than his resources can cover.

This provision appears to refer specifically to cases in which someone has inherited an obligation to pay a fine for another's crime, in particular the children of priests. Later in the same section there is an implication that the maximum that a person could be liable for was his or her personal share (*hafuþlutr*) of their inheritance. If these provisions applied more generally (and the rather disorganised nature of the preserved texts does not preclude such a possibility) then this throws a completely different light on the structure of compensation.

In comparison to some other Swedish provincial laws, there is little detail in *GL* concerning non-monetary punishments meted out to wrongdoers. Such punishments—excommunication, prolonged slavery, outlawry, loss of inheritance, branding, mutilation, hanging, and other capital punishments—were, however, inflicted in certain cases, particularly for theft, adultery and misuse of property. The circumstances in which they were applied are tabulated in Appendix D, table (i).

Where slaves had offended, they could not be expected to pay compensation themselves, and hence an alternative had to be found if the master were not to carry all the burden of restitution, as was usually the case. To extend the slave's period of bondage, or to execute the slave were the most obvious options, although in the latter case his or her owner would again be the loser. Where a killing (other than infanticide) was involved, the slave himself was offered as part of the wergild. In cases of infanticide and Sabbath-breaking (both considered to be ecclesiastical crimes), the period of slavery was extended, and for the rape of a Gotlandic woman the slave's life was forfeit, unless she preferred to receive compensation.

So far as residents of Gotland other than slaves were concerned, excommunication was imposed for damage to monastic property and as an interim punishment for violence during church festivals, until compensation had been paid. If compensation for a killing (including infanticide) was not paid within the specified time, the killer was outlawed, but this penalty is not mentioned in any other context. Selling one's farm illegally led to loss of one's inheritance and reduction in status to a non-Gotlander. If one misappropriated land worth three marks in rent, the punishment was even more severe: execution for a man and loss of her pew in church for his wife. Working in another man's woodland led to confiscation of one's tools, material and draught animal, which would have been a severe penalty.

Branding was the punishment for theft of an amount between two *öre* and one mark of silver. Theft of greater amounts (including land), or a second theft of a smaller amount, resulted in a shameful death by hanging. The other crimes leading to physical punishment were adultery, abduction and rape. The provisions were complicated, ranging from loss of a hand or foot for discovered adultery with an illegitimate daughter of mixed Gotlandic and non-Gotlandic parentage, to execution for the rape of a married woman. In most cases the woman could choose wergild or other payment as an alternative. No information is given in *GL* concerning the form of execution imposed, but as the neck is mentioned in at least one situation, it was probably death by either hanging or beheading (see Notes to Chapter 21, lines 15–20).

The complex provisions relating to killings, and the killer's circle of safety, seem to be unique to Gotland. They are described in detail in the Commentary to Chapter 13.

D. *Oaths*

In parallel with the punishments there was a system of oaths to be taken or arranged by the parties in a dispute. This system is summarised in the table in Appendix E, which shows that the person or group to whom the oath was given and the number of supporting witnesses or oath-takers varied considerably with the crime or misdemeanour involved. Oaths were in many cases sworn rather in the nature of character witnesses (see Note to Chapter 2, line 15).

E. *Laws of inheritance*

The inheritance provisions in *GL* have been justifiably described as extremely complex. Holmbäck (1919, 12–51, 219–41) has made a detailed analysis of them, particularly in relation to legitimacy and in comparison to other Swedish provincial laws. He sees, in the inconsistencies, evidence of an organic growth in the provisions and a gradual improvement in the position of women in relation to inheritance. *Guta lag* thus offers a valuable insight into the social history of the period not available in the mainland provincial laws (Holmbäck 1919, 48–51).

IV *Origins*

A consideration of the origins of the content of a legal text differs from a consideration of the sources of material in a narrative or poetic

work, whether historical or otherwise. Two questions that have to
be asked are (1) whether this law was influenced by any other law formulated earlier (which might assist with dating) and (2) whether this
particular redaction was a record of the law as it was enforced in a
particular place and at a particular time or was an idealised representa-
tion of how the redactor felt that the law should be. This latter issue has
been touched on to some extent in the preceding section, but in the case
of *GL*, the questions of origin and nature and those of date and authorship are so closely bound together that it is difficult to separate the
arguments.

Although an oral recited law (the older sense of the word *lagsaga*)
may be presupposed, according to Wessén (*SL* IV, lxxiii), the lack of the
office of lawman or lawspeaker in Gotland might be a counter-argument
to the suggestion that *GL* was a lawman's *aide mémoire* for his
oral discourse (see pp. xxii–xxiii above). It might still, however,
have been a private record prepared by a judge or some other person
involved in the legal process. Whatever their provenance, there must
have been some earlier form of the law than the written manuscripts that
have been preserved and, if Lis Jacobsen is correct in her assumptions
concerning the age of the language in the *A*-text (*GGD*, 13), there must
have been a pre-Christian law containing at least some of the material in
that manuscript. Despite the largely non-poetic language, there are many
alliterative phrases and some residual rhythmic passages. If there were
no single lawman reciting the law, then perhaps the duty rotated among
the elders, and *GL* originated as a result of a group of them agreeing
upon a text to be recited. This might explain some slight inconsistencies
and apparent repetitions, to be found within each of the manuscripts.

The opening words of *GL*, invoking Christianity and revoking
heathendom, provide us with a clue to the origin of the text. There are
remarkable similarities between these words and those of the older law
of Gulaþing (*GulL*), the oldest manuscript of which dates from about the
middle of the thirteenth century. The latter states:

> Þat er upphaf laga varra at ver scolom luta austr oc biðia til hins helga Crist ars
> oc friðar. Oc þess at vér halldem lande varo bygðu. Oc lánar drotne varom
> heilum. Se hann vinr varr, en ver hans. En Guð se allra varra vinr. Þat er nu þvi
> nest . . . (*NGL* 1, 3)

> This is the beginning of our laws: that we should bow to the east and pray to
> the holy Christ for good harvest and peace; and that we retain our settled land.
> And keep our liege lord in health. Let him be a friend to us and we to him. And
> let God be a friend to all. The next thing is . . .

It has been suggested that this similarity can be explained by assuming that the Christian section of the Gotlandic law was composed during a visit to Gotland by St Olaf in 1030 or thereabouts and his conversion of the Gotlanders to Christianity. Schlyter, however, who considers *GL* to date from the last quarter of the thirteenth or first quarter of the fourteenth centuries, suggests a later influence from Norway and this view is supported by Pernler (see *CIG*, vi–vii; Beckman 1920, 12–13; Wessén 1945a, 160; Schück 1945, 182; *SL* IV, lxxiii–lxxiv; Pernler 1977, 16–19).

A later borrowing of certain selected passages seems to be a possible explanation for the similarities, since the church laws in the older law of Gulaþing differ quite fundamentally from those (such as they are) in *GL*. Had St Olaf been involved in the initial development of the law in Gotland, the relevant provisions would surely have been more extensive. It is noticeable also that penalties for infringing church laws are much more severe in the older law of Gulaþing than they are in equivalent passages in *GL*. In particular, total forfeiture of property and banishment are frequently imposed as punishments in the former, whereas *GL* only implies banishment (but not outlawry) for a woman who cannot pay the fine for infanticide, i.e. as a punishment of last resort. The sections relating to the exposure of children in a number of Norwegian law texts begin in a similar manner to that in *GL* (Chapter 2, lines 2–3:

Þat er nu þvinest. At barn huert scal ala a lande varo er boret verðr (*GulL* 21; *NGL* 1, 12).

The next thing is that every child born in our land should be nurtured.

Ala skal barn huært, er boret uærðr en ængu spilla. Sina sæng for skal huær kona uita, oc lata barn til kirkiu bera (*EidsL* I (B-text), 1; *NGL* 1, 375).

Every child born shall be nurtured and none killed. Every woman must acknowledge her childbed and allow the child to be taken to church.

Ala skal barn huart, er boret er ok ængo spilla. Sinæ sængfor skal huar kona vita, ok lata barn til kirkiu bera (*EidsL* II (C-text), 1; *NGL* 1, 394).

Every child born shall be nurtured and none killed. Every woman must acknowledge her childbed and allow the child to be taken to church.

The older law of Gulaþing, however, contains the proviso that severely deformed children might be exempt, and detailed laws concerning baptism, completely absent from *GL*. On the other hand, the *B*-text of the older Christian law of Eiðsivaþing (*EidsL*) is particularly close to the text in *GL* (Beckman 1920, 11–12).

One of the greatest differences between Norwegian and Gotlandic society was the hierarchy that seems to have existed in the former. Below the king and two levels of aristocracy were three levels of free, landowning farmers. There is no indication in *GL* of any inequality between people apart from that between the free, slaves and non-Gotlanders. Admittedly, tenant farmers had different obligations from landowning ones, but there are no provisions that appear to have affected their status in any other regard. The conclusion would seem to be that, while the law makers might have borrowed phrases from other laws with which they were familiar, including those of Norway, the content of the law and the punishments applied were very much their own. This content was affected by the society to which the law was applied, as well as the priorities of the lawmakers, as is discussed below.

V *Date, place and circumstances of composition*

There are four principal theories concerning the date of composition of *GL* in written form. The first is that it was composed between 1220 and 1250 at the instigation of Andreas Suneson, the second that it was composed towards the end of the thirteenth century, the third that it was composed in the first half of the fourteenth century, perhaps as a response to the production of Magnus Eriksson's national law, and the fourth that it originated in the twelfth century or even earlier. This last is subscribed to by Hadorph (*Gothlandz-Laghen*, Introduction), Schildener (*G-L*, xxvi), Nordström (1839–49, I, vii) and Säve (*GU*, x). (See also *SL* IV, lxxiii note 1.) There is no concrete evidence to support such an early dating of a written law, although there is internal evidence to suggest that some of the individual provisions date from a period not long after the adoption of Christianity in the early eleventh century, and that others are pre-Christian in origin, as Jacobsen (*GGD*, 6–7) indicates.

Arguments for a dating in the second half of the thirteenth century, or rather later, were first put forward by Schlyter (*CIG*, v–xi) and have been supported by Maurer (1878, 168–170), Amira (1913, 98) and others. They are based principally on the existence of the provision relating to the inheritance rights of non-Gotlandic (i.e. Swedish) daughters in which two sisters received the same inheritance as one brother (Chapter 24d, lines 2–3). This must indeed have been included in *GL* after Birger Jarl introduced it into Swedish law, namely in 1260, at the time of the wedding of Valdemar Birgersson to Sofia, daughter of the murdered Danish king Erik Plogpenning (*SRS* I:1, 25, 86; *SRS* III:1, 5). The circumstances are referred to in *Erikskrönikan* (26, ll. 458–61). Schlyter takes this date as a *terminus post quem* for the first written version of *GL*, thus placing it in the last quarter of the thirteenth century. On the other hand, Wessén thinks that this particular provision, even though it appears in all four traditions, might have been a later addition, $*A_I$ on the stemma, first included in the manuscript group represented by u on the stemma. Accordingly, the first, 'original', manuscript of GL (*GL on the stemma) could have been considerably older (SL IV, lxix–lxx). Two further pieces of evidence in support of this theory are (1) the fact that the provision in question is to be found in the chapter concerning weddings, rather than in the chapter concerning inheritance, in which there are other specific provisions relating to females, and (2) that there appear to be slight differences (noted by Pipping; GLGS, xii–xiii) between the language of that particular provision and that in most of the rest of the A-text, suggesting that it originated from a different part of Gotland (see Läffler 1878, 288–89).

More recently an even later dating, namely the fourteenth century, has been forcefully argued by Elsa Sjöholm (1976, 170–73). She likewise argues on the basis of the provision relating to the inheritance rights of non-Gotlandic (Swedish) females, but an inconsistency in her argument is that she initially uses a different interpretation of the expression *ogutniskt fulk*, namely that it refers to the (mostly German) inhabitants of Visby (see pp. ix, xii–xiii, xxvi–xxvii above). In that context she points to the lack of any reference to maritime law in GL in order to place it in time after the separation of the town of Visby from the rest of Gotland in 1288 (see pp. xii–xiii above), by which date she considers that farmers were no longer seafaring merchants. The main thrust of Sjöholm's argument in the present context, however, is that the very fact that Gotlandic laws of inheritance differ from those of Magnus Eriksson's national law indicates that GL was written in order to emphasise Gotland's independence at the time of the development of a common Swedish law. This, she contends, was because any change in inheritance provisions would have led to a collapse of the social order in Gotland, which required that landholdings should not become excessively fragmented. She consequently dates GL, in what she calls 'seine endgültige Form' (its final form) (1976, 171–72), to as late as the second or third quarter of the fourteenth century, i.e. some one hundred years later than Schlyter's dating. Sjöholm's expression, which is similar to that used by Lis Jacobsen ('sin endelige Redaktion' (its final redaction); see GGD, 80 note 1) in reference to the date of GL, leads one to ask what Sjöholm considers the earlier forms of GL were and when they came into being. She appears to ignore the fact that there were in all probability written redactions of GL, as opposed to an oral law, earlier than the manuscripts that have been preserved, and it is the date of the first of these (*GL* on the stemma) that is of principal interest in the present context. Furthermore, since the oldest surviving manuscript (B 64) has been dated to about the middle of the fourteenth century, Sjöholm's argument would lead one to the conclusion that, in the manuscript B 64, *GL* was close to 'seine endgültige Form'. Inconsistencies and errors in B 64, however, and the fact that the text of AM 54 4to seems to represent an earlier form of *GL*, militate against such an assumption. On internal evidence, B 64 would appear to be a copy of an earlier manuscript, which was itself more consistent and did not contain as many errors.

It seems that there are equally strong arguments for the earlier dating proposed by Wessén (*SL* IV, lxxii) and several other scholars (Skov 1946, 114–16; Mitchell 1984, 151). They suggest that *GL* was composed in the first half, if not the first quarter, of the thirteenth century. The most recent challenge to Sjöholm's arguments comes from Dick Harrison of Lund University (2002, 164–69, 602). He summarises her arguments and those of Lindkvist (1989, 415–17) concerning the dating and nature of the provincial laws, and he concludes that the core of these laws must have been in existence prior to the laws of Magnus Eriksson, and that they reflected local conditions independently of centralised influence.

The fact that there is no mention of the king's person or rights, nor of the royal commitment (*konungens edsöre*) to punish crimes that threatened the general peace and that were regarded as too grave to be subject to fines alone, might indicate a date prior to 1280 (see Notes to Chapter 5, lines 7–9, Chapter 12, lines 9–10, Chapter 22, lines 2–3, Chapter 22, lines 26–28, Chapter 39, line 2). The law concerning *edsöre* was first set in place during Birger Jarl's regency (1250–66) and confirmed by Magnus Ladulås in the Statute of Alsnö (1280), which also freed from taxes those who undertook to bear arms for the king. The concept of crimes designated *edsöresbrott* only finally disappeared from Swedish law with a major revision in sentencing enacted on 16th February 1864 (Westman 1912b, 106; Hemmer 1928, 269–86; Yrwing 1940, 68; *KL s.v. Konungs edsöre*).

Part of the agreement relating to *edsöre* was that fines for breaking any of the relevant laws would be payable to the king in addition to or instead of to the victim and the relevant assembly. Sjöholm would no doubt cite the purpose she perceives in *GL* of upholding Gotlandic independence as a reason for the omission.

Another circumstance that suggests a date prior to 1300 for the first redaction of *GL* is the set of laws relating to slaves, particularly in the

B-text. The laws of Västergötland and Östergötland contain provisions relating to the sale of slaves, but the later laws of Svealand (e.g. the law of Uppland) forbid the purchase and sale of slaves. Magnus Eriksson abolished slavery in Västergötland in 1335 in the Statute of Skara (see Nevéus 1974, 158–59), and it therefore seems unlikely that *GL* would have originated after *c*.1300. Sjöholm's argument that the exclusion from the *A*-text of provisions concerning the sale of and theft by slaves supports the idea that *GL* in 'seine endgültige Form' post-dated the prohibition seems to be a circular one; it surely only indicates that the manuscript itself, or the one of which it was a copy, post-dates it.

Provisions relating to the children of priests (Chapter 5, lines 2–6, Addition 1, lines 1–7) must be considered in the light of the Synod at Skänninge in 1248 (see *GGD*, 32 note 4; *SL* IV, lxix). The papal legate, Cardinal William of Sabina, declared the marriage of priests forbidden, and that those currently married, with some exceptions, had to separate, thereby confirming the decision of the Lateran council of 1139. It is clear that this law did not come into force immediately, as is witnessed by provisions in the law of Östergötland relating to children of bishops. Furthermore, Lars, Bishop of Linköping, had to remind Gotlandic priests and people of the rules in a letter dated 18th June 1255 (*DS* I, 375, no. 426), and it was not until about 1280 that clerical celibacy finally became the norm in Sweden. The detailed nature of the provisions in *GL* makes it unlikely, however, that they were devised and written long after the synod (Hegel 1891, I, 300 note 5).

The case has been made by the present author for a date between 1220 and 1275 for the composition of *Guta saga* (see *GS*, xlix–liii). Since the language of the majority of the law text in B 64 appears to pre-date the language of *Guta saga* in the same manuscript (Pipping, *GLGS*, vii–xii), a date of *c*.1220 for the earliest manuscript of the law, as Wessén proposes, seems not unreasonable.

There is no direct statement of the place of composition of *GL*, but sufficient indirect evidence to suggest that it was actually written in Gotland. The principal indication is clearly the use of the Gutnish language. It is unlikely that this would have been employed had the text been composed in mainland Sweden. The opening sentence of *GL* contains the expression *i lagum orum* 'in our law'. This makes it highly probable that the writer was himself a native of Gotland. There are, moreover, references to circumstances peculiar to Gotland, such as the three churches of asylum for killers, in Farþaim (Fardhem), Þingsteþi (Tingstäde) and Atlingabo, which might not have been familiar to a non-Gotlandic writer. Frequent references to non-Gotlanders (*ogutniskt fulk*) are evidence that the redactor was aware that different laws applied to such people, but as he does not define who they were, he must have assumed that his audience would know to whom he referred. This also might be taken as an indirect indication that *GL* was written in Gotland for Gotlanders.

There is no external evidence of the authorship of *GL* as it is preserved, but if it is assumed that it was written at the instance of Andreas Suneson, it seems likely that a priest would be responsible. It cannot be ignored, however, that lack of a coherent church law section argues to some extent against a clerical redactor and the whole law has an element of earthy practicality that seems less clerical than one might expect if Bishop Suneson were responsible. It is possible, of course, that the writer in question was one of the last married priests in Gotland and that he deliberately wrote in this manner to emphasise his closeness to and feeling for the community as a whole. Indeed, the most emotive passages are those that refer to the dilemma of a priest's offspring having to take up a compensation case on behalf of his father and the painful choice between Christian forgiveness and honour that this duty implied.

What is clear is that the redactor (or redactors) was a Gotlander. This is manifested initially in the language, but also in the manner in which non-Gotlanders are referred to throughout: not disparagingly, but as a separate group. The closing sentences of the oldest section of the preserved text also suggest that it was intended to be a living document to be updated as circumstances dictated, rather than a fixed record at a particular time (but see pp. xxii–xxiv).

VI *Editions and translations of* Guta lag

A. *Previous editions*

The earliest printed edition of *GL*, covering only the *A*-text (including *Guta saga*), is that of Johan Hadorph in 1687, not long after the discovery of the manuscript B 64 in around 1680. The edition, *Gothlandz-Laghen*, is described in detail by Schlyter (*CIG*, xx–xxii). It contains certain errors and includes an introduction coloured by a romantic view of its subject matter, but it is important in that it raised awareness of *GL* at a time when the manuscript was in danger of being lost and has an index of statutes and levels of fine, together with a number of glossary entries.

The second edition is that of Karl Schildener in 1818, *Guta-Lagh das ist: Der Insel Gothland altes Rechtsbuch* (*G-L*), the main purpose of which was to present the text of *tyGL*. Schildener takes this from a copy of B 65 prepared by an unnamed German-raised and educated scribe ('[einer] in Deutschland erzogenen und gebildeten Litterator') and supplied to him by Lorenzo Hammarsköld (1785–1827), philosopher and copyist at Kungliga Biblioteket in Stockholm, who had supervised the work (*G-L*, vi, 89; *CIG*, xxii). Schildener includes, in parallel, a copy of Hadorph's reading of the *A*-text. The medieval German text is incomplete in that, although it contains the Danish statutes (see above, p. xvi), it lacks most of *Guta saga*, which is found in full in B 65 (see *CIG*, xxiii). Alongside these two texts Schildener gives a German translation. The derivative nature of the content, and the fact that the *A*-text has been presented in a sequence altered to match that of *tyGL*, makes this edition of less value than others.

In 1852 C. J. Schlyter published the first critical edition of all the major manuscripts of *GL*, *Codex iuris Gotlandici* (*CIG*), as the seventh volume of his series *Corpus iuris Sueo-Gotorum antiqui* (*CIS*). His edition contains a more or less diplomatic account of the *A*-text, with the *B*-text reading in footnotes. Schlyter also gives the full *tyGL* text from B 65, the *daGL* text from AM 55 4to and the Danish statutes from B 65 with alternative readings and the completion of the second statute from Holm C 81 4to. Each of these has footnotes indicating where equivalent statutes can be found in the others, and in the *A*-text. The edition contains a detailed description of all these manuscripts and the above-mentioned editions, a glossary (into Swedish and Latin) and an index of proper names of firstly the *A*-text and secondly *tyGL*. The textual apparatus is in Latin and there is a parallel translation into Swedish of the *A*-text. Schlyter's edition is consequently the most thorough available and his readings and translations have been accepted by most subsequent editors and commentators, often in preference to later editions. This preference is probably motivated by the fact that Schlyter edited all the Swedish provincial laws, thus facilitating comparison of them with *GL* by direct reference to his editions. Schlyter's comprehensive glossary, *Glossarium ad corpus iuris sueo-gotorum antiqui* (*CISG*), is particularly valuable, covering as it does all the Swedish provincial laws; this enables comparison to be made between their equivalent provisions and vocabulary.

In 1859 Carl Säve published his academic thesis *Gutniska urkunder: Guta lag, Guta saga och Gotlands runinskrifter språkligt behandlade* (*GU*). The text of B 64 is to a certain extent normalised without comment, but emendations are clearly noted. Major additions in AM 54 4to are given at the end of the text and differences between the two manuscripts appear in footnotes. Säve's introduction consists to a great extent of an analysis of the language of the manuscripts and inscriptions he has taken as his subject. He relies heavily on Schlyter's edition (*CIG*) but offers useful alternative readings in a number of instances, partly in footnotes and partly in a short commentary. Säve also makes comparisons with the contemporary Gotlandic dialect (*Gutamål*).

Some extracts of *GL*, less radically normalised than Säve's text, appear in Noreen's *Altschwedisches Lesebuch* (*AL*, 36–37), first published in 1892–94.

In 1901 Hugo Pipping published *Gotländska studier*, which contains a diplomatic account of the *B*-text of *GL*, followed by a short commentary and a detailed examination of some linguistic features of the text. This is the only complete edition of the *B*-text, and is therefore a valuable contribution. In 1905–07 Pipping published a diplomatic account of the *A*-text of *GL* and *Guta saga*, which includes apparatus showing the *B*-text variants and additions, a detailed study of the language and a complete glossary of the text. These two editions offer useful alternative readings of the manuscripts to those of Schlyter, Säve and Noreen.

A facsimile edition, *Lex Gotlandiae svecice et germanice* (*LG*), of B 64 and B 65, edited by Elias Wessén was published in 1945 in the series *Corpus codicum Suecicorum medii aevi* (*CCS*). There is no facsimile edition of AM 54 4to.

The most recent edition of *GL* is that edited by Tore Gannholm in 1994. The text is presented in a form close to a diplomatic reading of B 64, using some of the emendations suggested by Schlyter (*CIG*), but with a number of peculiarities (e.g. þ is rendered as *th* throughout). Gannholm also offers a parallel translation into Swedish, which clarifies some points left ambiguous in the translation by Wessén (*SL* IV), which he has used as a basis. The edition is useful in some respects, although the arguments in Gannholm's introduction do not always bear scholarly scrutiny.

B. *Translations*

The first modern translation of *GL* (as distinct from the medieval translations into German and Danish) is that which appears in Hadorph's 1687 edition (*Gothlandz-Laghen*, see above). While there are some inaccuracies and misunderstandings, the translation is serviceable.

Schildener's parallel translation into German (*G-L*) is described and evaluated by Schlyter (*CIG*, xxiii–xxiv) and he implies that it, too, contains some inaccuracies. Schlyter's own parallel translation into Swedish is vigorous and illuminating. It was the last translation into Swedish before the appearance in 1943 of the volume by Åke Holmbäck and Elias Wessén, the fourth in the series *Svenska landskapslagar* (*SL* IV). This latter translation, which covers the A-text, the additional provisions found in the B-text and the Danish statutes found in the other manuscripts, is clear and straightforward. It is supported by a full introduction and detailed notes and references, which have been useful for the present work. The editors analyse in detail the content and significance of the texts, with reference to the other provincial laws, and they also evaluate previous editions and translations (see *SL* IV, lxxxviii–lxxxix).

A further translation into Swedish of all the provincial, city and maritime laws, including some appendices not translated in *Svenska landskapslagar*, was published as an omnibus edition by Åke Ohlmarks in 1976: *De svenska landskapslagarna. I komplett översättning, med anmärkningar och förklaringar*. His translations are close to those of Schlyter, and Ohlmarks claims that, despite his use of more contemporary language, they follow the sense and vocabulary of the originals more closely than those of Holmbäck and Wessén. Ohlmarks's introduction discusses stylistic features of the laws and he includes a number of notes. Although his work is useful in many respects, his approach is not as scholarly as might be hoped and some of his translations are inaccurate.

The remaining translation is that of Lis Jacobsen into Danish. Her *Guterlov og Gutasaga* (*GGD*) appeared in 1910 and is largely based on Pipping's edition. In indicating Danish equivalents to Gutnish expressions, Jacobsen provides useful insights into the meaning of the latter and her translation is valuable for the interpretation of a number of otherwise obscure words and expressions. Jacobsen draws particular attention to the alliteration, rhythm and other poetic features found in the text, as well as including an index, and footnotes clarifying her interpretations.

C. *The present translation*

This is the first English translation of *GL*. It is a continuation of the work by the present author on *Guta saga* (*GS* 1999) and takes into account the two medieval manuscripts of the law in Gutnish. The presentation is broadly based on Pipping's edition of the A-text (*GLGS*), but uses his edition of the B-text (Pipping 1901a) to record further variant readings as indicated below.

Where there are possible differences affecting the accuracy of the text or the translation between Pipping's reading and the manuscript of the *A*-text, or the readings of other editors, this is indicated in a footnote and, as appropriate, discussed in the Commentary.

Since the aim is to produce a single, readable translation, the following criteria have been applied:

1. A difference only in orthography (e.g. final *j* for *i*, single final consonant for a double or vice versa), form or word order between the *A*- and *B*-texts is not indicated if it makes no semantic distinction in the translation.

2. Words missing from the *A*-text that can be inferred from the reading of the *B*-text are inserted in angled brackets, if they correct an error. If an alternative *B*-text reading is preferred to the *A*-text, this is presented in italics. In both cases a footnote shows the origin of the emendation and the *A*-text reading.

3. Editorial additions to the *A*-text (e.g. letters or words accidentally omitted by the scribe) not derived from the *B*-text are also inserted in angled brackets with a footnote showing the *A*-text reading. Editorial corrections to the *A*-text reading not derived from the *B*-text are inserted in italics with a footnote showing the *A*-text reading.

4. Editorial augmentations necessary for grammatical sense in the translation are inserted in square brackets.

5. Differences in reading of words or short phrases between the *A*-text and the *B*-text that have a bearing on the sense or accuracy of the translated text are indicated by the use of footnotes. The preferred reading is shown in the text and the alternative *A*- or *B*-text reading in the footnote, together with the readings of previous editors, if relevant.

6. Any words or passages missing completely from the *B*-text are recorded in a footnote.

7. Longer passages missing from the *A*-text but present in the *B*-text are recorded in a footnote and are presented as Additions, pp. 57–59, 60–63. Editorial emendations follow the conventions in 3.

8. Where there are extended differences between the *A*- and *B*-texts, the *A*-text reading is recorded in the translation with a footnote, and the *B*-text reading is presented as an Addition, pp. 59–60.

9. A number of provisions in the *A*-text are generally considered by all editors to be later additions, because of their language and orthography. These are indicated in a footnote.

10. Differences in the reading of the *B*-text that are considered by Schlyter and others to be scribal errors have not been noted.

11. Pipping's edition of the *B*-text differentiates between additions in the margin of AM 54 4to signalled by a dagger (†), and those by a caret mark (^). These marginal additions have only been indicated in a footnote if they differ from the reading of the *A*-text.

The chapter headings require special comment. They do not always agree with the table of contents, which in the case of the *B*-text is a later addition. Two tables of contents have been constructed (pp. 1–5), one for the *A*-text and one for the *B*-text. The *A*-text headings have been inserted in the translation, with details of the *B*-text chapter divisions and headings in footnotes.

The translation retains as far as possible the tenses and moods of verbs in the original. It also uses, if relevant, familiar legal concepts, where they reflect those of the original. The aim has been to include as much elucidation of the sense of the text as is possible in a translation. Where applicable, this elucidation, preceded by 'i.e.', has been included in parentheses. Punctuation and capitalisation follow modern English practice.

GUTA LAG

THE LAW OF THE GOTLANDERS

THE LAW OF THE GOTLANDERS
<Table of contents from B64>

<1> *See Introduction, xlv. The table is unheaded and the chapters unnumbered in the table in A.*

<32a> *A omits chapter in the text. See* Addition 7.
<38> **theft** *A*: thieves

List of regulated laws

\<62\>–\<65\> **\<Concerning bald patches . . . women's rights\>** *Table of contents in A omits these.*
List . . . laws *This heading comes from AM 54 4to.*

35 **Concerning women's rights** *This covers chapters 24b and 24c in A.*

55 **theft** *B*: thieves

<1> Here begins the law of the Gotlanders and it says firstly this

3   This is the first beginning of our law: that we should reject heathen ways and accept Christianity and all believe in one almighty God, and pray to him that he grant us good harvests and peace, victory
6   and health. And that we should uphold our Christianity and our proper faith and the province in which we live and that we should each day do, in our deeds and desires, those things that are to the
9   honour of God and which most benefit us, both in body and soul.

<2> Concerning children

Now the next thing is that each child born in our province should
3   be raised by us and not cast out. Every woman should know her own bed in which she is to lie in labour. She should call on two women to be witnesses with her, the midwife and a neighbour, to
6   witness that the child was stillborn, and that she had no hand in its death.

If a free woman is found guilty of having killed a child, then she
9   is fined three marks as soon as it comes before the parishioners, unless she has previously confessed her crime, and the priest bears full witness to it. Then she must complete her penance, and no
12 one has a right to claim compensation. If she denies the case, and it comes before the assembly members, then if she is found innocent, she shall receive three marks from those who charged
15 her, and an oath of rehabilitation from six men. If she is found guilty, she must pay three marks to the parish, if the parish can demand it. If the case comes before the assembly members, she
18 is to pay three marks to the assembly, and another three to the

---

1/1 **<1>** B: 1 *This chapter has no number in the table of contents in B. None of the chapters is numbered in the text of A.*
1/1–2 **and it says firstly this** B *omits.*
1/5 **and pray** B: and all pray
2/1 **<2>** B: 2 *Note that this does not agree with the table of contents in B.*
2/4 **in which** B: when
2/18 **another three** B: another three marks

rural dean, if she is found guilty. If the case comes before the general assembly, and if she is then found guilty, she incurs a fine of twelve marks to the general assembly. If she has no money to pay, then she must go into exile and every man is to be fined three marks who shelters or houses her, or gives her food. If she will not take an oath, she is nevertheless considered condemned in the case.

If those who have accused her abandon the case, and refuse to put down <money>, one should deem her to have no case to answer and clear her of the charge. The accusers should, however, confirm her honour by oath and remove the slander, which they laid on her. If she admits that she was the mother, and says that the child was stillborn, then they do not need to put down any money, if they disbelieve her, and if she did not have any female witnesses with her when she was in labour.

If such a case is brought against someone's female slave, no one is to lay any higher fine against her than six öre in coin. If she is found guilty, then her master is fined six öre in coin on her behalf, and six years are added after her time of slavery is complete.

<3> Concerning tithes

The next thing is that everyone shall have services and pay tithes, where he has taken part in building a church, or to [the church to] which his farm was allocated from the outset. The priest must carry out all Christian offices for him, whether he may demand them early or late. Thus all men are in agreement that every man should pay his tithe before the feast of the Annunciation (i.e. 25th March), both the part to the priest and the part to the church. Each

2/26 **If** B omits.
2/27 **<money>** B; A omits.
2/32 **any** B: two
2/35 **in coin** B omits.
2/36 **six öre in coin** B omits.
3/1 **<3>** B: 3 Note that this does not agree with the table of contents in B.
3/3 **has** B omits.

9   man must pay his tithes by the stook. Thus no one shall be able to
say that the tithe has not been threshed when Annunciation comes.
And after Annunciation, the priest is to make a declaration for
12 three Sundays, and lock the church door on the fourth Sunday and
withhold services from the parishioners until such time as all the
tithes are fully paid. And a three-mark fine is incurred by each
15 man who was not willing to pay his tithe previously. All should be
obliged to prosecute this and all should be party to it. The
parishioners should be entitled to a third, the church a third and
18 the priest a third. If a tenant goes from one parish to another with
the tithe unpaid, then he is liable to [pay] three marks to the priest,
the church and the parishioners, and still to bring back his tithe
21 (i.e. to his former parish), though it is late.

If someone wants to build himself a church for greater convenience than he had previously, he must do it from the remaining
24 nine parts. And the church shall receive its tithe and the priest
his, until the new one is consecrated. But afterwards, he is to
pay the tithe where he most recently built the church. He may
27 not later return to the previous church, if he has made another
new one. And he may not go from the previous church to the
new one later than the day on which the bishop consecrated it. If
30 disagreements arise between them (i.e. the person who moved
and the priest and people of the old parish) in the first or the second
year, then he shall himself declare with an oath, and with two
33 parishioners, whom his opponents wish to nominate, that he was
involved in the church-building and the consecration, and in all
things as other parishioners. When three years have passed or
36 more than three, then he shall have both parishioners' witness
that he was with them in the church-building, and the priest's own
witness that he has ever since paid him the tithe as every other
39 parishioner.

3/15 **previously** *B omits.*
3/20 **the church** *B omits.*
3/26 **the church** *B omits.*
3/34 **church-building** *B* building

If a man rents a field or a meadow from another parish, and there are no houses on it, he is to leave the corn-tithe in the place (i.e. parish) where the field was allocated, but take home hay or   42
hops with him, and give tithes from them to the priest whom he visits for services, and from whom he receives all Christian offices. If there are houses there, he is to leave everything behind.   45
The priest who is at the church there is to have tithes from it, and the church has its portion, as the priest his.

<4> Concerning sacrifice

Now the next thing is that sacrifice is strictly forbidden to all men, together with all those old customs that belong to paganism.   3
No one may pray to either groves or howes or heathen gods, nor to holy places or ancient sites. If someone is found guilty of this, and it is proved against him and confirmed with witnesses that he   6
has invoked something of this sort with his food or drink, contrary to Christian practice, then he is to be fined three marks to the parishioners, if they win the case. All should be obliged to prosecute   9
this and all should take a share in it: priest and church and parishioners. If suspicion falls on someone, then he is to defend himself with a six-man oath. If the parishioners do not win the   12
case and it comes before the assembly members, then he must defend himself again with a six-man oath, or pay a fine of three marks to the assembly. If it comes before the general assembly,   15
then <he> is to pay a fine of twelve marks to the authorities, if he does not win with the defence of a twelve-man oath.

<5> Concerning priests and priests' wives, and their children

Now the next thing is that priests and the wives of priests and their ordained children (i.e. those that are later ordained) are equal   3

4/1 **<4>** *B:* 3
4/9 **should be** *B:* should also be
4/10 **all should** *B omits.*
4/16 **<he>** *B; A omits.*
5/1 **<5>** *B:* 4 **priests' wives, and their children** *B:* priest's children

in the matter of assault and manslaughter and in all respects to
the children of farmers, but the lay children are treated in the
6   same way as the family of their mother.
If a man, whether ordained or not, commits a crime no one
shall be fined more on behalf of another, than his (i.e. the
9   wrongdoer's) resources can cover.

<6> Concerning holy days

Now the next thing is that all those days that the bishops have
3   declared holy, and which all men have accepted, should be
considered sacred by men. No one must do other work on Sundays,
or other holy days, but attend holy office, or hear God's service,
6   but he has permission to ride round his farm after mass has been
sung, or the holy office has finished. No one may have more on
his wagon on a Sunday than a lispound weight following a pair of
9   oxen, or half that following a horse. If he has more, one may
confiscate his load until he has paid six öre, and in addition he is
to pay six öre for Sabbath-breaking, unless an emergency arose
12 and the priest was asked. Then the latter may ascertain what is
necessary and give permission that he (i.e. the farmer) may travel
in his parish, so that he is not blamed or accused about it. If he
15 wants to travel further, then he must always seek permission from
the priest who has control of the church parish (i.e. the one he
wishes to pass through), if he wants to be unchallenged about it.
18 One has permission to ride to the marketplace with prepared food,
cheese and butter and all dairy produce, fish, fowl and those beasts
that one is to sell on the market square, with baked bread but not
21 with flour or barley, and not with other wares, without risking

---

5/5 **children are treated** *B:* children, they are treated
5/6 **mother** *See* Addition 1, *which also includes the following sentence.*
6/1 **<6>** *B:* 5
6/2 **those** *B omits.*
6/3 **men** *B omits.*
6/7 **have** *B:* transport
6/14 **blamed** *B omits* blamed *(but retains* or*).*
6/18 **ride** *B:* travel or ride

both the load and six öre. Half the fine goes to the one who apprehends him, and half to the priest and parishioners of the place where he was when he was apprehended with the goods. If a man is riding and carrying a burden (i.e. has a pack on the horse), one may not blame him or impose a fine on him for it, if he is sitting himself (i.e. he is riding the same horse). If the draught horse is in a train, or he is leading it with a pack, that pack may legally be seized, if it is more than half a lispound, and in addition a six-öre fine for Sabbath-breaking is incurred. If a free man or woman is found doing work on a Sunday or other holy day, then all the work is to be seized, which is found in their hands, and they are in addition to be fined six öre for Sabbath-breaking. Half of this is to go to the man who apprehended them, and half to the priest and church and parishioners. If a male or female slave is caught working on a holy day, their master is fined three öre for them, and they are to have their time of slavery extended by three years.

<7> Concerning monks' property

The next thing is that if someone is found guilty of felling [trees] in a wood belonging to monks, or knocking down boundary fences, or harming them, or their property, then he is to be excommunicated and pay a fine twice as much as that payable by one farmer to another. And he is to pay the fine before the first assembly next following. If he waits for the assembly, he is to pay a fine of three marks to the general assembly, and he is still to pay the fine to them as laid down in the law, although it is later.

If a man who is childless gives himself to the monastery, he retains authority over his property; he may neither sell nor transfer it during his lifetime. When he dies, one third remains with the monastery, but two thirds revert to his kinsmen. If he has children,

6/31 **woman** *B:* free woman
7/1 **<7>** *B:* 6 **property** *B:* rights
7/8 **still** *B omits.*
7/9 **to them** *B omits.*

he has command over his personal share. If <any> layman wishes
to leave property to the monastery or to a church, then he may
give a tenth of his property in land, but no more, unless his kinsmen
permit it.

<8> Concerning personal rights

The next thing is that an individual's right to peace and security is
in force on all those days designated 'holy days', from the time of
sunset on the eve of the day until dawn on the third day. Fourteen
days at Christmas are days of peace and security; seven weeks in
Lent, and the whole of Easter Week; three Rogation days; and the
whole of Whit Week. If you kill a man during these periods of
peace and security, the fine is three marks. If you wound a man,
the fine is twelve öre. If you strike <a man> with a staff, or an
axe hammer, the fine is six öre. If you manhandle someone,
or push him, or take him by the hair, or punch him with your
fist, the fine is three öre, if it is done in anger. If a slave is
involved, the fine does not exceed three öre, if he is made to
bleed. The fine is always to be paid where the deed was done,
and not where the perpetrator lives. The priest shall withhold holy
offices, and close the church door, to all those who have broken
the sanctity of God, for excommunication always follows Sabbath-
breaking. The ban shall subsequently be lifted immediately he
pays the fine stipulated, and the parishioners consider it advisable.
All are obliged to bring the action for the fines, and all should take
a share in them. Parishioners are to have one third of the fines,
the church another, and the priest a third, provided that fines
are not payable to the general assembly. But fines to the
general assembly are not payable for Sabbath-breaking, unless a
man is killed inside a church, in which case there is a fine of forty

7/14 <any> B; A omits.
7/16 in land B omits.
8/1 <8> B: 7
8/9 <a man> B; A omits.
8/21 of the fines B omits.

marks. This fine is paid to the general assembly. The rural dean
has three marks of this for pronouncing excommunication.   27
All churches in the province are equally sacred, if a man is
killed inside them. Three churchyards, however, are considered
in law to be the most sanctified. In these a fugitive should have   30
protection both on rectory land and in the churchyard. There is a
fine of forty marks if a fugitive is killed in this sanctuary. But of
all other fines, those that are smaller, and those that are not payable   33
to the general assembly, the parishioners are due one third, and
the church a second part, and the priest another. If you strike a
man in a church with a staff or an axe hammer, or wound him in   36
a churchyard, the fine for this is six marks. If you punch a man
with your fist or push a man or take him by the hair in a church, or
strike him in a churchyard with a staff, or an axe hammer, the   39
fine is three marks. If you punch a man with your fist in a
churchyard, or take a man by the hair, the fine is twelve öre for
Sabbath-breaking. The one who has desecrated the church shall   42
always be liable for the reconsecration, and cleanse that which
he has made unclean by a payment of three marks.

<9> Concerning the universal sanctity

Now there are, moreover, two other periods of peace and security,
which principally exist in order that one should observe an   3
individual's right to protection. In these cases there is no
excommunication and no fine to the bishop, unless the deed was
done on a holy day. This is the universal sanctity. It runs from   6
fourteen nights after Easter and five nights after Midsummer and
lasts for ten nights and ten days in each case; it both starts and

8/26 **marks** *B adds* or in a churchyard, in which case there is a fine of twelve
marks
8/32 **killed** *B; A:* captured
8/33 **not** *B omits.*
8/34 **due** *B:* always due
8/35 **another.** *B:* another part.
8/39 **or an axe hammer** *B:* or with an axe hammer
8/41 **churchyard** *B adds* or push a man
9/1 **<9>** *B:* 8

9   ends at sunrise. If you kill a man during these periods of peace
and security, the fine to the general assembly is as great a wergild
as he whom you killed is worth. No peace circle will protect you
12   before you have paid the fine. If you wound a man or strike him
during these periods of peace and security, the fine is three marks.
During these periods of peace and security no one may destroy
15   another's house or boundary fence, without being liable for a fine
of three marks.

<10> Concerning the springtime sanctity

Now there is then, in addition, the springtime sanctity. It runs
3   from a fortnight before the general sowing time, and lasts until a
fortnight thereafter. During that period of peace and security no
one may seize from another either horse or ox in payment of debt,
6   since a farmer needs these every day on his fields, without being
liable for a fine of three marks. If a debt is [outstanding] between
men and it is legally claimed, the one is to claim from the other
9   his house, cattle or possessions, and not his working beasts, which
he needs at the time.

<11> Concerning the assembly sanctity

Next there is in addition men's assembly sanctity. The assembly-
3   men must prosecute the action for [breaking] the assembly
sanctity. If you take a man by the hair, or punch him with your
fist, at the assembly, the fine is three marks for breaking the
6   assembly sanctity and in addition a legal fine (i.e. for the assault).
If you strike a man with a staff, or an axe hammer, or cause
injury, the fine is three marks. If you kill a man, or maim him, the

9/10 **is as great** *B:* is always as great
10/1 **<10>** *B:* 9
10/6 **these** *B:* both these
10/8 **it is** *B omits.*
11/1 **<11>** *B:* 10
11/2 **in addition** *B omits.*
11/7–8 **cause injury** *B:* cause a man injury

fine is six marks, unless the man was killed in revenge. A criminal 9
may not rely on the assembly sanctity, unless a universal sanctity
is in force.

<12> Concerning the homestead sanctity

Next there is in addition the sanctity of the homestead for all
men. If you kill a man at home on his farm, or maim him, the fine 3
is twelve marks to the general assembly, and another twelve to
him, and wergild in addition. If you strike a man with a staff or an
axe hammer, or cause him injury, the fine is three marks to him, 6
and three more to the community, and in addition the legal fine. If
a householder is struck at home on his farm, or more people, only
the one who is valued most highly is to take the fine for an attack 9
in the home, but no others. All should, however, receive legal
fines.

<13> Concerning manslaughter

The next thing is that, if the misfortune should occur through
the devil's agency that a man should happen to kill another, 3
his father, son and brother shall flee with him. If none of these
exist, then his nearest kinsmen should flee with him for forty
days to a church that all men have taken as a sanctuary, that is 6
Fardhem and Tingstäde and Atlingabo. There they shall have safety
and sanctuary, both on rectory land and in the churchyard.
And when that time has expired, he must ride to the place where 9
he wants to draw up his peace circle, and draw it around three
farms, and so far into the wood from the three homesteads that it
lies equidistant from other (i.e. from these and the other) 12
homesteads, which lie on the other side of the wood, if he has
(i.e. should he in any case have) permission from those who own

12/1 <12> B: 11
12/2 **in addition** B omits.
12/9–10 **fine for an attack in the home** B: case for homestead sanctuary
13/1 <13> B: 12
13/8 **and sanctuary** B omits.

15   the property. The circle may not be drawn around a place of assembly or a marketplace, nor around more than one church, the one in which he took refuge. Then he has sanctuary within his

18   circle, and someone else may negotiate compensation [on his behalf]. And he is always to draw it during the period of peace and security that is next after Easter, but until that time the peace

21   circle, which he drew up when he first put himself in danger, shall protect him. That is called the testified safety circle. No one may dispute any peace circle, which remains for a year, when a

24   year has expired. But a man has freedom to remain in his circle or go abroad on a pilgrimage to a shrine, to atone for his sins. He shall have eight days respite to take to his ship, and then travel in peace

27   on his pilgrimage. And when he comes back, he also has eight days to travel back to his circle in peace. If a man commits a crime (i.e. a killing) in his home parish, he must flee from there,

30   and draw his circle somewhere else, where neither mother nor daughter nor sister (i.e. of the victim) live. Meanwhile he must take himself to another church, since they must not both visit the

33   same church. Half the tithe is to go to the church he visits for services and half remains with the church to which his farm was allocated. If a man commits a crime at the homestead that he

36   himself lives in, then he is to flee immediately from there and draw a peace circle elsewhere, if he wants peace and security, since they may not both live in the same farm. If a non-Gotlandic man

39   kills another non-Gotlandic man, then he is to draw a circle in the same way as a Gotlander, if he lives on his own farm in Gotland.

    He (i.e. the killer) is to offer compensation for the man, if he

42   can afford it, when the year is past, and always leave a year

---

13/15 **the property** B omits.
13/24 **But a man** B omits. **has freedom** B: has then freedom
13/25 **to a shrine** Literally to the saints
13/29 **home parish** B: own home parish
13/34 **his** B omits.
13/36 **immediately** B omits.
13/39 **man** B omits.
13/41 B has a new chapter here: 13 Concerning the offering of compensation for a man

between, and offer three times in three years. And the other is a
man without dishonour if he accepts it the first time it was offered.
If he does not wish to accept it the first time nor at the second,   45
then he is to take it the third time, when three years have passed.
If he will not accept it then, then they (i.e. both parties) must be
taken to the assembly, before all the people. He (i.e. the plaintiff)   48
may still accept there, if he wishes. If he does not wish to, then
all the people take counsel over the money (i.e. distribution of the
money), but he (i.e. the defendant) is then free from guilt. If the   51
plaintiff says that the period had not expired, but the defendant
who is offering the wergild says that it had, then the one who says
that it had expired has the right to substantiate this, with the   54
evidence (i.e. corroboration) of three men who were with him at
the farm and offered compensation three times in three years.
And he is to confirm it with a twelve-man oath that there was   57
always a year's grace allowed between each. If a man does not
wish to offer wergild and all the time limits have expired, the
authorities shall deem him to be an outlaw, and liable to discharge   60
the wergild on a specified day after a period of a month, and
liable for six marks of silver to the plaintiff and another six to the
authorities. The same fine applies to him who does not keep within   63
his peace circle. There is no appeal against this [extra penalty]:
all of the fine will be extracted.

<14> Concerning inherited cases

But concerning claims for compensation (i.e. wergild) inherited
from father or brother or kinsmen, all shall negotiate compensation   3
until such time as they are able to offer wergild. But the plaintiff
can accept immediately, if he wishes, and not be dishonoured. If

---

13/43 **the other** B *omits.*
13/44 **time** B *omits.*
13/45 **time** B *omits.*
13/51 **guilt** B: shame
13/55 **with him** B: at home with him
13/59 **offer** B; A: pay

6   he does not wish to accept so quickly, then they must offer it three
times before the same time the following year, and then take it to
the assembly before all the people. He may, if he wishes, take
9   the offer there, or else the whole assembly decides the sum of
money, but they (i.e. the kinsmen) then become blameless.

If two or more conspire together and kill one man, then they
12 must all have the same peace circle until one of them admits to
the killing.

All those who will inherit a portion (i.e. with him) and wish to
15 do so [may] take revenge on behalf of a minor. Then it is [lawfully]
avenged if any one of them takes revenge for him, whether male
or female. That revenge is valid, just as <if> he himself took
18 revenge. They shall also take the wergild, if the inheritor is young,
when it has come to the time that the defendant who is involved in
the case can make an offer, and free himself from it.

21 If a Gotlander kills a non-Gotlander and can afford to offer
wergild, then he neither has to flee nor draw a peace circle. If a
non-Gotlander kills a Gotlander, then he is not protected by a
24 peace circle, unless he can afford to offer wergild.

If a minor causes the death of another, the fine is twelve marks
of silver.

27 If a pregnant woman is killed and her child also dies and men
can confirm with an oath that the child was alive in her womb,
then her husband is to swear to it, if he is alive. If he is <not>
30 alive, then the one most closely related to her shall bear witness
with three landowning Gotlanders from the same parish, and in
addition so many as to make up twelve men, all of equal birth to
33 her. Then the fine for the unborn child is twelve marks of silver,
but for the woman a full wergild.

14/6 **wish to** B *omits.*
14/8 **may** B: may still
14/11 **man** B *omits.*
14/14 B *inserts* A kinsman may take revenge, if he wishes, on behalf of a minor.
14/17 **<if>** B; A *omits.*
14/20 **offer** B: offer of money
14/29 **<not>** B; A *omits.*
14/32 **all** B *omits.*

<15> Concerning men's wergild

Further, there are now men's wergilds. A Gotlandic man is to be
compensated with a wergild of three marks in gold, if he is killed.   3
All other men are to be compensated with ten marks of silver,
except that a slave's wergild is to be four and a half marks in
coin. If a Gotlandic man marries a non-Gotlandic wife, her full   6
wergild compensation is to be paid for *her*, but the children are
treated in the same way as their father's family in the matter of
compensation. If a non-Gotlandic man marries a Gotlandic   9
woman, each keeps their own level of wergild compensation and
the children are treated in the same way as their father's family
in the matter of compensation.   12

<16> Concerning wergild within the peace circle

The wergild for a Gotlandic man within the peace circle is twelve
marks of silver; that of a non-Gotlandic man is five marks of   3
silver, and that of a slave is six öre in coin.

All are equal in the matter of fines, until maiming occurs. If
maiming occurs, then the hand or foot of a <non-Gotlandic> man   6
is to be paid for with ten marks in coin, and similarly all other
disfigurements, which are paid for with wergild.

If someone's slave kills a Gotlandic man, then the master is to   9
take the killer bound to the farm (i.e. the plaintiff's farm) within
forty days, and in addition nine marks of silver. If the killer cannot
be produced, then he (i.e. the master) is to pay twelve marks of   12
silver and no more. If a slave kills a non-Gotlandic man, then his
master is to pay two marks of silver for him and lead the slave

15/5 **is to be** *B:* is to be paid at
15/6 **full** *B omits.*
15/7 **her** *B; A:* him
15/8 **their** *B omits.*
15/12 **in the matter of compensation** *B omits.*
16/3 **is** *B omits.*
16/6 **<non-Gotlandic>** *B; A:* Gotlandic
16/14 **for him** *B omits.*

15 bound to the farm (i.e. the plaintiff's farm) within forty days. If
the killer cannot be produced, then he is to pay a fine of five
marks of silver. And swear (i.e. in all cases swear) him a six-
18 man oath that he neither advised nor caused the deed. If the master
cannot swear this oath, then he is to pay the full wergild, both for
a Gotlandic and a non-Gotlandic man. If a slave kills a slave, the
21 master cannot be compelled to give the killer in compensation, if
he offers four and a half marks in coin.

But a slave who has worked through his time of slavery is to
24 embrace his freedom at the church door with the witness of the
parishioners and then the slave is himself responsible for his
actions.

<17> Concerning unruly animals

A five-year-old uncastrated ox also carries a liability for com-
3 pensation of twelve marks (i.e. of silver) from the farmer owning
him, if it causes the death of a man. A horse must be tied up,
when one comes to visit a farmer, between the fourth pair of
6 fence supports from the entrance pillars, and four paces from the
man's door. Then he (i.e. the owner) is responsible for nothing
except for the near fore (i.e. if it kicks out), and its teeth, if it
9 bites. If you travel to a farm or to a storehouse, tie the horse to the
gable end or the back wall, then you will not be responsible for
more than stated above. A boar is the third (i.e. animal carrying a
12 liability), if it is over three years old and uncastrated. A dog is the
fourth. One is always responsible for everything, if it causes
damage, whoever owns it. Everyone is answerable for these four
15 dumb animals (i.e. if they cause a death) on their own farm to the
sum of twelve marks of silver.

If a dumb animal is the cause of the death of a man of lesser
18 value than a Gotlander, then two thirds of his wergild is written
off, but one third is paid by the owner of the beast. It is called
'wergild subject to claim' if a dumb animal causes the death of a
21 man or maims him in the limb. One shall demand the wergild

17/11 **boar** *B:* branded boar

(i.e. from the animal's owner) and not take revenge (i.e. upon the owner); [one shall] lay a legal claim to it like other debts (i.e. against the owner). If a dumb animal causes a man a wound or maims him, then two thirds of the compensation is written off, but a third is paid by the owner of the beast, apart from a dog bite; then each tooth-mark, up to four, is paid with two öre.

24

27

\<18\> If a man strikes a woman

If a man strikes a woman so that her unborn child is miscarried, and it was alive in her womb, then the fine is half a wergild. If she accuses someone, but he denies it, then she is to prove it against him with two witnesses, those before whom *she* declared herself on the third day after she was struck, or those who were present, who are also landowning men, together with the evidence (i.e. corroboration) of two women that the child was stillborn after she had been struck. And she must herself bear witness, with a six-person oath, that it had been alive.

3

6

9

A woman must take care of her child at every feast, put it in its cradle and have it by her, or have it in her lap, or lay it on the bed and lie down herself. In that way every woman shall provide care for her child for three winters. If any man causes the death by misadventure of the child during this period of care, he is to pay the full wergild. If a woman lays the child on the floor or in a chair unsupervised, or lays it on the bed, again unsupervised, then no compensation is to be paid for the child come what may. If a woman goes with a child into a bed in which drunken men are already lying and the child is smothered in the throng or by the bedclothes, then no compensation is to be paid for that child, even though the woman herself lay down.

12

15

18

21

17/26–27 **apart from . . . öre** B omits. See Addition 2.
18/5 **she** B; A: he
18/7 **who are also** B omits.
18/14 **for three** B: three
18/16–17 **in a chair** B: a chair
18/17 **lays it** B omits. **again unsupervised,** B omits.

<19> Concerning wounds

If a man wounds another, with one wound or several, a thumb-nail's breadth deep, then he is to pay half a mark for each thumb-nail's breadth, both in depth and in length, up to eight marks, and half less if it is not a thumb-nail's breadth deep, but still needs medical treatment. The man who received the wound shall get the witness of two magistrates in the same hundred and one district judge from the same sixth and himself swear with six men, with their evidence (i.e. the judges' corroboration) but not their oath, if the fine is more than three marks. If the fine is three marks or less, then it is a three-man oath. If he has more than one wound, then he may swear as he wishes, against one man or several, but the compensation is the same. All wounds that have penetrated the abdominal or breast cavity are compensated with a mark of silver. If one man wounds another with a knife, he is to pay two marks of silver. If a man throws a stone or some other object at another, who is wounded as a result, he is to pay three marks. If a man is wounded with a blow, which does not cause blood to be spilt, so that the blow is visible (i.e. leaves a visible mark), the compensation is half a mark for each blow up to four but with the same witness as for a wound (i.e. an open wound). If a man is wounded through his nose or *lip, the* compensation is two marks in coin and in addition for the facial defect, if it has healed over. If it is open so that it cannot heal, then the highest compensation is paid in full. But for an ear, the compensation is halved. If one can see a scar or facial defect from the opposite side of the road and a hat or hood does not hide it between beard and brow, the compensation is half a mark of silver. If it can be seen from right across the assembly, then the fine is a mark of silver and wound compensation in addition. A split scalp is paid for with one mark in coin. If the skull is visible, then the fine is two marks in coin. If the skull is indented or cracked, then it is a mark

19/1 **wounds** B: wounding
19/12 **wishes** B: rather wishes
19/22 **lip, the** B: (ver, þa); A has a scribal error (verþa).

of silver. If the membrane is visible, the fine is two marks of silver. 33

For each bone, which rings in the bowl, there is a fine of a mark in coin up to four bones. Each larger bone splinter, which can 36 carry an ell-long thread over a five ell-high beam, is subject to a fine of two marks in coin for each of up to four bones. Each finger, which is cut off, is subject to compensation of four marks 39 in coin. A thumb is <fined at> two marks of silver. If a finger is so stiffened that it has no holding power, then the fine is the same as if it were lost. If a man is damaged in one hand, but can still 42 hold a sword or a sickle but cannot lift the weapon, then the fine is two marks <of silver. If a man is incapacitated so that he cannot walk or run, then the fine is two marks> of silver. If he is damaged 45 in the sinew of the heel or neck, then the fine is also two marks <of silver. Each toe is fined at two marks> in coin, if it is lost. If a hand or a foot is lost or an eye is out, there is a fine of six marks 48 of silver for each of them. If a man assaults another and cuts off both of his hands, or both of his feet, or pokes out both of his eyes, and the man nevertheless survives afterwards, the payment is 51 twelve marks of silver for each. If a man has his nose cut off so that he cannot keep back his mucus or snot, the fine is also twelve marks of silver. If a man's tongue is pulled out of his head and 54 cut off, so that he cannot talk with it, then that also incurs a fine of twelve marks of silver. If a man is damaged in his genitals, so that he cannot father a child, then the fine is six marks of silver 57 for each testicle. If both are damaged, then the fine is twelve marks of silver. If the <whole> penis is cut off, so that the man cannot satisfy a call of nature other than sitting like a woman, 60 then the fine is eighteen marks of silver.

19/36 **up to** B: for each up to
19/40 **<fined at>** B; A omits.
19/44–45 **<of silver . . . two marks>** B; A omits.
19/46 **also** B omits.
19/47 **<of silver . . . two marks>** B; A omits.
19/51 **nevertheless** B omits.
19/59 **<whole>** B; A omits.

Each rib is to be fined at two marks, up to four ribs. Cutting off
63　or splitting a smaller bone in the hand or foot is fined at a mark in
coin. If a larger bone is broken in either foot or hand, the fine is a
mark of silver, if it heals without defect. If disability ensues, the
66　fine is two marks of silver. If a man has a visible mark from a
blow on the hand, and says that he has lost the use of it, then he is
to prove this with the same witnesses as for a wound. If there is
69　no visible mark from the blow, then the defendant has the right to
substantiate his denial. It is the least deformity in the hand, if one
cannot tolerate heat or cold as previously. That is fined at a mark
72　in coin and it is to be verified by self-witness.

If the hearing is struck out of a man's head with a blow leaving
a visible mark <so> that he can neither hear a dog on its leash nor
75　a cockerel on its perch, nor a man when he calls at the door, the
fine for that is twelve marks of silver and he is to prove this himself
with a six-man oath and with the same witnesses as for a wound.
78　If a man's hearing is damaged in one ear so that he does not hear
with it, if he covers the other, then the fine is six marks of silver.
If a man's ear is cut off, the fine is one mark of silver. But if the
81　ear is *damaged*, then the fine is two marks in coin. If you strike a
man's teeth from his head, then you are to pay a fine for each
tooth according to its worth: the two upper front teeth are fined at
84　two marks in coin each, the two next to them at one mark in coin
each, and then each at a mark in coin including molars and all.
But the lower teeth are all valued at a half less from first to last.
87　　If you take a man by the hair with one hand, you are fined two
öre. If you use both hands, you are fined half a mark. If you shake
a man, you are fined two öre. If you push a man, you are fined
90　two öre. If you throw ale in a man's eyes, you are fined eight
örtugar for the insult. If you kick a man, you are fined two öre. If

---

19/62–66 **Each rib ... two marks of silver.** *B rewords. See* Addition 3.
19/74 **<so>** *B; A omits.*
19/80 **one mark of silver** *B:* two marks of silver
19/80–86 **But if the ear ... first to last.** *B rewords. See* Addition 4.
19/81 **damaged** *A:* damaged damaged
19/91 **If you kick ... two öre.** *B omits.*

you punch someone with your fist, you are fined two öre. If you
admit to one blow, then he has the right to substantiate an accusation   93
of four blows. If you do not confess, then you have the right to
substantiate your denial as the defendant. If you strike a man
with a staff, the fine is half a mark for each blow up to two   96
marks. A man is not fined more from his property for a blow that
does not cause blood to be spilt, unless disability ensues. That is
the law of the Gotlanders.   99
A man's beard is subject to the same fines as other hair pulling.
For a bald patch on which one can put a finger, the fine is eight
örtugar. If you can put two fingers in it, the fine is half a mark. If   102
there is place for the thumb as a third, the fine is one mark in
coin. If the bald patch is so large that the flat of the hand can be
put on it, then the fine is two marks in coin. If all the hair is pulled   105
off, the fine is one mark of silver, but one does not pay more even
if each hair is pulled out. If a piece of scalp and hair is cut from
a man's head the fine is one mark of silver.   108
If you tear apart a man's clothing, the fine for outer garments is
one öre. The kirtle is two öre, undergarments eight örtugar, and
all the man's clothes are to be repaired and as good as they were   111
before. Undergarments are a man's vest and shirt, trousers and
hat. All cost the same, whichever is torn. If the skin is involved
and a wound is caused, you are fined both for the wound and the   114
clothing.
A man is to be answerable for open wounds for a year and a
day. If a man is wounded with a blow which does not cause blood   117
to be spilt, and he lies in the same bed and does not get up in the
interim, but still has full use of his senses, then he is to take the
witness of four landowning men and three district judges from   120
the same sixth and as many more as to make up twelve. If he

19/100 *B has a new chapter here:* 20 Concerning bald patches
19/100 **A man's beard . . . hair pulling.** *B omits these sentences at this point.*
19/105–08 **If all the hair . . . silver.** *See* Addition 5 *for differences in B.*
19/109 *B has a new chapter here:* 21 If you tear apart someone's clothing
19/116 *B has a new chapter here:* 22 Concerning open wounds and closed
wounds

does not have full use of his senses, then his heir has the
123 right of substantiation of the case, with the same evidence (i.e. corroboration). But if he gets up in the interim, the defendant has the right of substantiation of his denial.

126 If a man blocks another's way, grasps a horseman's bridle, or takes a pedestrian by the shoulders and turns him from his path, then he is fined eight örtugar for the insult. But if he does violence
129 to him and forces him to go further with him (i.e. in the opposite direction), then he is to pay him three marks for the violence and another three to the community.

132 If someone's slave fights with a free man, then if he (i.e. the slave) always receives two blows to one (i.e. against the other), then it is considered even between them. If the slave gets more
135 blows than two against one, then each blow up to four is fined at two öre. If the free man gets more blows than one against two, then each to him up to four is fined at half a mark. If the slave
138 gets a jerking or a shaking or a pushing, then the fines to him are always half those to the free man. If it comes to wounds, then the fines are the same as to a free man, up to three marks and no
141 more. No one pays fines for insults to a slave and similarly a slave does not pay fines for insult to anyone.

<20> Concerning all inheritances

If there are minors, who are young, after their father's death, and
3 also sons who are grown men, then the eldest must not part from the youngest, even if need may arise, before he (i.e. the youngest)

19/126 *B has a new chapter here*: 23 If someone blocks another's way
19/126 **horseman's** *B:* man's
19/131 **another three** *B:* three marks
19/132 *B has a new chapter here:* 24 If slaves fight
19/132 **if he** *B:* if
19/136 **blows** *B omits.*
19/137 **to him** *B:* blow
19/142 *The paragraph at 20/40–45 appears here in A, evidently misplaced, but in the correct place in B, although in the margin.*
20/1 **<20>** *B:* 25

is of age. They are to have enjoyment of everything undivided until he is fifteen years of age. Then he is to take his scrip and his scales and each have responsibility for himself, if they no longer wish to be together. If need arises, so that they have to part with land to buy food before they are all of age, an equal amount shall be taken in pledge from each, the eldest as well as the youngest, and <not> sell it outright. Should someone take the young minor as a ward, *however*, whether a male or a female, and feed him until he is of age, then he (i.e. the minor) keeps his portion, even if the others are forced to part with their land to buy food. If a father marries his son off and the son dies and leaves behind daughters, they shall remain in their grandfather's care and await their portion. If the head of the family dies and there are no surviving sons, the daughters and sons' daughters divide the inheritance according to their numbers. If the man has other sons, the son's daughters (i.e. the daughters of the deceased son) inherit their father's portion between them. In the same way inheritance is passed from the father's mother if she lives longer than her son. If an heiress has inherited land, then the one inherits from the other however many generations there might be, whether male or female, while her descendants exist. When the line has run out and has included two male descendants but not a third, then the inheritance reverts to the farm from which it first came. If it has included a third and all three follow each other, then it remains with the farm to which it has come, even if the line has died out. If an heiress has inherited her portion and leaves no sons, then the next of kin inherits. If both are equally close, a man and a woman, then the man inherits and not the woman.

If there are no sons on the farm, then the daughter inherits her maternal inheritance and her father's maternal inheritance after her father. If her paternal aunts survive, married or single, then

6

9

12

15

18

21

24

27

30

33

20/5 **They are** B: They are all
20/11 **<not>** B; A omits.
20/12 **however** A has a superfluous not here.
20/28 **it remains** B: remains
20/33 B has a new chapter here: 26 If the male line is broken

36 they take her father's maternal inheritance (i.e. a share in this inheritance). If some are unmarried, they take an eighth of the monetary value of the paternal inheritance (i.e. of their niece)
39 after debts have been paid.

If there are no sons on the farm, then the kinsmen each inherit *their* per capita share to the fourth generation. If it (i.e. the relation-
42 ship) is more remote, then they take an eighth part after debts are paid. A woman, however, is to take as much from the farm as *she* has put in, if it is written down in the first year. If it is not written
45 down, then the farm has the right of substantiation of its case.

If there is no male heir and a widow remains at the farm, then she is to have, as provisions at the farm for a year, a bushel of rye
48 and another bushel of barley each month, if she does not die or marry away. But as to the property that she brought to the farm, she is to take out of the farm that which she brought to it. If a
51 woman marries into several farms and has children in several, then all children inherit their maternal inheritance equally, both land and movables. And brothers receive for their full sisters,
54 whether they are married or unmarried. If a woman is married out of the farm with a dowry and has no male heir, then it (i.e. the dowry) reverts to the farm from which she married. If there are
57 no male heirs to the farm then the next of kin inherits, whether male or female, but in the case of a woman no further than the fourth generation. If they are both of equal degree, however, the
60 man inherits. It is also the law that a woman inherits consolation and provision from her husband. If she stays for a longer time on the farm with her sons <and> her sons die, leaving no male heir
63 after them, before eight years have elapsed, she is to take a mark

20/40–45 *This paragraph should be here, as indicated by the reading of B, where it appears in the margin. In A it appears at 19/142.*
20/41 **their** *A:* which *B omits.* **share** *B adds* with the daughters
20/43 **paid** *B adds* and the women's portions are discharged **she** *B; A:* he
20/45 **then** *B omits.*
20/53 **full** *B omits.*
20/60 **It is also . . .** *B has the words* Hogsl oc id ('Consolation and provision') *in the margin at this point, as a side heading.*
20/62 **<and>** *B; A omits.*

in coin for each year while her sons lived. But if she marries again while her sons are still alive, she is to receive consolation and provision and no more. A widow who is childless is to have 66 board and lodging, if she wishes, in the same farm into which she married. If she does not want this, she is to have half a mark in coin for each year <up to> sixteen years and receive it year by 69 year.

But in the case of female inheritance, a daughter or daughter's children inherit. If there are none of these, then the sister or sister's 72 children inherit. If there are none of these, then the father's sister or father's sister's children inherit. If there are none of these, then the next blood relatives down to the fourth generation inherit, 75 but no further. If there are none of these, the female inheritance remains in the farm estate with the kinsmen. If there are no male heirs and it has passed to the female line, whether it is through a 78 brother or a sister, and they are both equal in blood relationship, then they both inherit. Should both father and son be burned alive in the same house, both drown in the same ship, or both fall in the 81 same battle, then sisters are considered equal to daughters. If more than one son survives a man and the family grows from all of them, but one (i.e. if it happens that one) dies without sons, 84 then all (i.e. the others) are equally near in inheritance down to the fourth generation. Anyone who sells his ancestral home and disposes of everything within the farmstead will be separated 87 from inheriting with the kinsmen and brothers and will be assigned the wergild of a non-Gotlander. But his sons will remain within the line of inheritance and the legal entitlements of their kinsmen, 90 if they obtain land again worth three marks in rent.

No illegitimate son can obtain the right to inheritance unless it is the case that both his father and mother are trueborn Gotlanders, 93

20/69 **<up to>** *B; A omits.*
20/71 *B has a new chapter here:* 27 Concerning women's inheritance
20/72–73 **If there are . . . inherit.** *B omits.*
20/81 **both drown** *B:* or both drown
20/92 *B has a new chapter here:* 28 Concerning illegitimate children
20/92–93 **it is the case that** *B omits.*

and he confirms it with what is written in a genealogical table, to
the effect that three successive female ancestors are trueborn
96 Gotlanders. Then the son of the third in line can inherit with the
kinsmen. If a Gotlandic man begets an illegitimate child with a
Gotlandic woman and he has no (i.e. no legitimate) male heir and
99 he is survived by illegitimate children, sons and daughters, then
they divide their paternal movables according to their number with
the legitimate daughters, if there are any. If there are none, then
102 they divide their father's movables amongst each other according
to their number. But if a Gotlandic man begets illegitimate sons
with a non-Gotlandic woman, then he must support them until
105 they are of age. If they do not wish to remain with their father any
longer, then he is to give three marks in coin to each of them and
battle weapons and bedclothes, bedcover and under-blanket and
108 pillow and fifteen ells of broadcloth for walking-clothes. If he has
illegitimate daughters, then he must support them until they are
eighteen years of age; he has the right to give them in marriage if
111 someone requests it. But if they remain unmarried and no longer
wish to remain with their father when eighteen years have passed,
then he must give a mark of silver to each, and bed- and walking-
114 clothes and a cow according to his means. The entitlements of
illegitimate children must always be administered with the
corroboration of the parishioners.
117   If a Gotlandic man begets an illegitimate daughter with a non-
Gotlandic woman and if someone is charged with violation of
that illegitimate daughter, then he (i.e. the violator) is to give her
120 four marks as consolation, whether he <is> Gotlandic or non-
Gotlandic. If a man is found *in flagrante delicto* with this daughter,
then he must redeem his hand or foot with three marks of silver.
123 If a Gotlandic woman gets an illegitimate daughter with a non-
Gotlandic man, then she has the same rights as have just been
laid out.

20/102 **they** B omits.
20/116 **corroboration** B: witness or corroboration
20/120 **marks** B: marks in coin <is> B; A omits.

<20a> <Concerning men discovered in the act of illicit intercourse>

If a man is discovered *in flagrante delicto* with an unmarried Gotlandic woman, then he may be placed in the stocks and be captive for three nights and send word to his kinsmen. They (i.e. the kinsmen) are to redeem his hand or his foot with six marks of silver or he (i.e. the wronged party) [can] have it cut off if he (i.e. the miscreant) cannot afford to redeem it. If he is not discovered *in flagrante delicto* with her, but if a child is presented to him and the woman says that the child is his, but he denies it, then he is to take two resident men from the same parish as the woman was in when the child was conceived and swear, with a six-man oath, that they never heard word or rumour of the matter before the child was born. Then the right to substantiate his denial is in his favour, if he enlists two resident men. If he fails and does not get the right to substantiate his denial, then the woman has the right to substantiate her accusation with six men, all of equal birth with her, that he is father to the child. And he is then to adopt the child and take responsibility for the mother, if he is willing. If he does not wish to or cannot, then he is to give her full consolation, if she is a Gotlander. If a Gotlandic man is discovered *in flagrante delicto* with a non-Gotlandic woman, then she is to have three marks from him but only if he is discovered *in flagrante delicto* where her bed and home are. If a non-Gotlandic man is discovered *in flagrante delicto* with a Gotlandic woman, then he is to pay the same fine as a trueborn Gotlander. If he is not discovered in the act, but nevertheless begets a child with her, he is to give her eight marks in consolation and bring up the child himself. If the woman says the child is his but he denies it, then he is to defend himself with the same evidence (i.e. corroboration) as a Gotlander. But the child is to be raised by those who have the

3

6

9

12

15

18

21

24

27

30

20a/1 *B has a new chapter here:* 29 Concerning the discovery of illicit intercourse. *A has no heading, despite listing the chapter in the table of contents.*
20a/6 **are** *B:* are then
20a/17 **all** *B omits.*

right to collect the consolation, father or brother, if she is unmarried.
33 If a <non-Gotlandic> man begets a child with a non-Gotlandic woman, then he also is to give her consolation of three marks and raise his child. If he is discovered *in flagrante delicto* with her,
36 then he is also to give her three marks, even if there is no child.

<21> If a man commits adultery

If a man commits adultery, he is to pay three marks to the assembly
3 and six marks to the complainant. If a man, <whether a priest or> a layman, commits double adultery then he is to pay twelve marks to the authorities and another twelve to the complainant. If a
6 married man commits adultery with an unmarried woman, he is to pay her consolation. If a lawfully married woman commits adultery with an unmarried man, he is not to pay her consolation.
9 If a man, priest or layman, is discovered *in flagrante delicto* with another man's wife then he is liable for forty marks or his life and the complainant decides, however, which he would prefer, the
12 money or his (i.e. the defendant's) life. If a man seduces another man's daughter or one of his wards into betrothal without the authority of her father or kinsmen, then he must pay forty marks
15 to the complainant; of this the authorities take twelve marks. If a man takes (i.e. takes in marriage) a woman or maid by force or violence, without the authority of her father or kinsmen, then those
18 who prosecute her case shall decide between his neck or wergild, if the woman is Gotlandic; the authorities take twelve marks of the wergild. If the woman is not Gotlandic, then those who
21 prosecute her case shall decide between his neck and ten marks of silver; the authorities take twelve marks (i.e. in coin) of the wergild.

20a/32 **she** *B:* he *[i.e. the brother]*
20a/33 **<non-Gotlandic>** *B; A:* Gotlandic
20a/35 **with her** *B omits.*
21/1 **<21>** *B:* 30 **If a man commits** *B:* Concerning
21/3 **<whether a priest or>** *B; A omits.*
21/5 **twelve** *B:* twelve marks
21/10–12 **and the complainant . . . life** *B omits.*

\<22\> \<Concerning rape\>

If a woman is dishonoured in a wood or elsewhere and forced
into sexual intercourse, she must pursue the man with a shout, if   3
she does not want to endure the shame, and follow him to where
he goes. If someone hears her cry, he must provide her with full
and complete evidence, as if he had been present and was an   6
eyewitness. If no one hears her cry, she must declare her case
before witnesses immediately on the first day, in the place where
she comes to habitation and say the name of the man. She can   9
also benefit from their evidence, if their witness is valid. If she
delays and does not make an accusation, then it is best to remain
silent about it. The defendant has the right to substantiate his denial.   12
If a man is found guilty of such an offence and there is evidence
for the woman, then he is fined twelve marks of silver for a
Gotlandic woman but for a non-Gotlandic woman five marks of   15
silver and for a slave six öre in coin. If the case involves a lawfully
married woman, Gotlandic or non-Gotlandic, then he forfeits his
life or redeems himself with as much wergild as the woman is   18
worth. If the woman does not know the man, but declares her
case before witnesses on the first day after *she* has come to
habitation, and then claims to have known the man when a longer   21
time has passed, he can then defend himself with a twelve-man
oath. If she is pregnant and it happened at the time that she declared
her rape before witnesses, she has the right to substantiate her   24
accusation with a twelve-man oath and the witnesses before whom
she declared her case. If a man's slave commits such a crime with
a Gotlandic woman, it does not suffice that the master pays the   27
wergild penalty, unless she would rather the wergild than his life.

22/1 A *had no title for this chapter originally, simply an enlarged initial letter.*
Concerning the shaming of women *has been inserted in the margin. B:* 31 If a
woman is dishonoured on the road
22/15 **non-Gotlandic woman** *B:* non-Gotlandic
22/16 **slave** *B:* slave woman
22/20 **she** *B; A:* he
22/23 **oath** *B:* oath if she is not pregnant **at the time** *B:* at the same time
22/28 **rather** *B:* rather accept

\<23\> Concerning asaults on women

And concerning assaults on women, the law is as follows. If you
strike the headdress or wimple from a woman's head, in a way
that is not accidental, and her head is half-bared, then you are to
pay a mark in coin; if it is completely bared, you are to pay two
marks. She has the right to substantiate her accusation with the
witnesses who saw it, to say whether her head was completely
bared or half. An unfree woman, however, receives payment for
blows, and no more. If you pull the buckle or clasp from a woman,
you are to pay eight örtugar. If you pull both away, you are to pay
half a mark. If it (i.e. the garment) falls to the ground, then the
fine is a mark. If you pull the laces from a woman, the fine is half
a mark for each to the maximum fine. And you must give
everything back to her. \<She\> is to confirm herself when all has
been returned. If you push a woman so that her garments fly out
of place, compared to how they were previously, the fine is eight
örtugar. If they fly halfway up the shin, the fine is half a mark.
If they fly up so that one can see the kneecap, the fine is a mark
in coin. If they fly up so high that one can see both loins and
private parts, the fine is two marks. If you seize a woman by the
wrist, you are to pay half a mark, if *she* wants to lay a complaint.
If you seize her by the elbow, you are to pay eight örtugar. If you
seize her by the shoulders, you are to pay five örtugar. If you
seize her by the breast, you are to pay an öre. If you grasp her by
the ankle, you are to pay half a mark. If you grasp her between
the knee and calf, you are to pay eight örtugar. If you grasp her
above the knee, you are to pay five örtugar. If you grasp her still
higher up, that is an indecent grasp and it is called a madman's
grasp; no cash compensation is payable for it; most will endure it
when it has gone that far. If this happens to a non-Gotlandic

23/1 **\<23\>** *B:* 32 *A has rubric, exceptionally, in margin.*
23/6 **marks** *B:* marks in coin
23/11 **then** *B omits.*
23/14 **\<She\>** *B; A omits.*
23/18 **so** *B:* so high
23/21 **she** *B; A:* he

woman, you are to pay her half the amount for all assaults compared to a Gotlandic woman, if she is a free and freeborn woman.

33

<24> Concerning weddings

Concerning the wagon-riders' procession, no more than two shall travel in each wagon; but the ride of the relatives is abolished. The nuptial mass is to be sung where the bridegroom is and the wedding breakfast is to be held. The bridegroom shall send three men to his bride and the chief bridal attendant shall wait where the nuptial mass is to be sung and the wedding breakfast held. And the wedding feast shall be held with drinking for two days with all the people (i.e. guests) and gifts are to be given by everyone who wants to according to their inclination. But contributions by the guests to the wedding feast have been abolished. On the third day they (i.e. the bridal couple) have the right to invite the wedding hosts and the masters of the feast and their closest kinsmen to stay. As many toasts as the householder wants shall be drunk prior to the toast to the Virgin Mary. But after the toast to the Virgin Mary, then everyone has permission to leave and further ale is not brought in. Everyone who breaks this rule must pay twelve marks to the authorities. And whoever comes uninvited to a wedding or feast is to pay three öre.

3

6

9

12

15

18

<24a> <Concerning funeral feasts>

All funeral feasts are abolished. But those who wish to may give clothes and footwear to the parishioners in memory of the deceased.

3

23/32–33 **if she is . . . woman** B *omits.*
24/1 **<24>** B: 33
24/1 **weddings** B: the wagon-riders' procession
24/20 **öre** B: öre in coin
24/20 *See* Addition 6 *and* 63/14–17.
24a/1 **<24a>** B *has a new chapter here:* 34 Concerning funeral feasts A *has no heading, despite listing the chapter in the table of contents.*

\<24b\> \<Concerning fine woollen cloth\>

All fine woollen cloth and wall coverings of black cloth that exist are to be used, but no more are to be added to them once they are worn out, neither second-hand nor new.

\<24c\> \<Concerning riding clothes\>

Saddlecloths and riding cushions are not to be divided into smaller than quarters.

\<24d\> \<Concerning Gotlandic women\>

This is also stipulated concerning Gotlandic women: that each brother shall take responsibility for his sister's wedding. If he does not wish to do that, he must give her an eighth portion of his property to support herself under the supervision of \<his\> closest kinsmen and parishioners, so that she does not use her possession ill advisedly.

\<24e\> \<Concerning non-Gotlandic people\>

But concerning non-Gotlanders, then the stipulation is that two sisters should inherit the same as one brother. If the inheritance falls between siblings or the children of siblings, they divide it like their paternal inheritance or their maternal inheritance. If it goes to more distant relatives, then those who are closest in blood inherit.

24b/1 **\<24b\>** *B has a new chapter here:* 35 Concerning women's rights *and includes the majority of the first nine sentences from* 65/2–15. *A has no heading, despite listing a separate chapter in the table of contents.*

24c/1 **\<24c\>** *A has no heading, despite listing a separate chapter in the table of contents. B has the initial letter of* Reidkledi *('Saddlecloths')* enlarged and in red, indicating a new section.

24d/1 **\<24d\>** *B has a new chapter here:* 36 Concerning Gotlandic women *A has no heading, despite listing the chapter in the table of contents.*

24d/4 **her** *B omits.*

24d/5 **\<his\>** *B; A omits.*

24e/1 **\<24e\>** *A has no heading, despite listing a separate chapter in the table of contents. B has the first four words in red, indicating a new section.*

<24f, 64> Concerning travellers' pathways

And this is the law concerning travellers' pathways: if a man owns land which nowhere borders a right of way, he shall have the right himself to cross open ground (i.e. another's open ground) where the latter has a right of way. If he owns land bordering a right of way, that is open ground, he has no right of crossing over another's open ground. But if he has enclosed land, he has rights over another's open ground. If men wish to create grazing enclosures from grazing land by a road, they must leave a path fifteen paces in width (i.e. between the fences). In that way they may protect their enclosure, but not otherwise. If a man creates an enclosure across another's right of way, then he must create a gap for him and he is to have passage as before. If he fences across a path that is another man's lawful right of way, the one who owns the fence is to create the gap, but the one who owns the right of way is responsible for the gap (i.e. the security of the gap).

<25> Concerning disputes over woodland

If two men dispute about a wood, then one shall bring two types of evidence: the evidence of neighbours and evidence as to work. That one collected firewood in springtime, or cut fencing wood and laid it on stumps, or cut off branches and gathered them together and let them dry there until autumn, is sufficient evidence of work. He who has the stronger neighbours' evidence that work was done in the area has the right to substantiate his case. One of those who owns most shall present his oath first. If he does not wish to swear an oath, then his witness will not benefit either party. But concerning cultivated land one must also have two types of evidence: the evidence of kin (i.e. distant kin) and evidence

---

24f/1 **<24f, 64>** *B:* 37 *The chapter* Concerning travellers' pathways, *which in A appears after Chapter 63, should appear here, as in B and the table of contents in A. See also CIG, 61 note 56.*
24f/1 **travellers'** *B omits.*
25/1 **<25>** *B:* 38
25/6 **there** *B omits.*

as to work for three years. Those who own the neighbouring land shall provide the evidence as to work. If one owning neighbouring
15   property disputes this, those shall bear witness, who own the property next nearest. Kin witness is not borne by anyone nearer related than the fourth generation.
18   If cultivated land and woodland and marshland meet, then the cultivated land (i.e. the settlement containing the cultivated land) takes two thirds and the woodland and marshland (i.e. that
21   containing the woodland and marshland) a third (i.e. of the unclaimed land). Woodland and marshland then take half each of infertile land where they meet between stump and tufts of sedge.
24   And neither may witness concerning the other, not woodland with marshland and not marshland with woodland.

No man may give another leave to fell in shared woodland, or
27   cut down fen sedge on shared marshland without being liable for a fine of three marks to the injured party and another three to the community. No man may presume to work in another man's
30   woodland or marshland without that which he travels with being legally taken from him, building material and draught animal. But if he says that the other has seized it illegally, he is to prove it
33   with an eyewitness. When someone gets an injury (i.e. suffers a loss) in a wood or on other property, and wishes to suspect (i.e. accuse) someone of something, then no one can decline another
36   (i.e. the accuser) the right to conduct a search and inspection without [incurring] a fine.

Anyone who damages boundary land inside or outside the
39   enclosure is liable to a fine of three marks to the injured party and another three to the community. No man shall also presume to enclose shared property without being liable to [pay] three marks
42   to the injured party and another three to the community. Everyone is responsible for the enclosure that he has fenced in; the one who

25/18–20 *The words* **and woodland and marshland** *and* **then the cultivated land takes two thirds** *appear in the margin in A, possibly a 16th-century correction. See CIG, 62 note 15.*
25/19 **cultivated** B *omits.*
25/24 **witness** B *omits.*

owns the land bounding a road [is responsible] for the fence along
the road. But the one that does not own land bounding a road is   45
responsible for fences between fields or meadows. Everyone is
to redress the damage caused by the fence for which he is
responsible. If several keep a fence in a bad state, then all pay   48
damages who do not have a lawfully acceptable fence. No one
gets damages for his injury unless he himself keeps a lawfully
acceptable fence. No one may demonstrate damage on another's   51
bad fence unless he himself has a good one.

<26> Concerning shared fences

If someone asks another for a shared fence, then he must tell the
other with a neighbour or parishioner as witness. And the   3
parishioners shall decide each share within a week. You then
take your share yourself with the neighbours as witness, if the
other party does not wish to be present, and erect a fence in the   6
place you are given your share. And the other party then has a
year's grace (i.e. to erect his fence) from the day of division. If
farm animals (i.e. belonging to him) later get in, take them indoors   9
and do not release them before the other pays for the damage and
deposits half a mark towards the fence. He is to have the fence
made good within a fortnight and then redeem his pledge. If he   12
does not do this within a fortnight, then he loses his half mark and
you take another half mark as pledge until the work is done. He
must continue to pay for the damage as long as the fence is not   15
made good. For 'good fences make good neighbours'.

Whoever takes a creature indoors is to answer for the creature
until he has informed the one who owns it with the witness of   18
neighbours. If he (i.e. the owner) then does not wish to redeem
the creature, then he must himself bear the damage if the creature
is worse, or indeed dead. When all have been lawfully informed,   21

25/48 **keep** *B:* own or keep
25/50 **keeps** *B:* keeps or owns
26/1 **<26>** *B:* 39
26/7 **then** *B omits.*

the one who has the bad fencing is answerable for the damage. If someone has an unruly animal and it breaks in through a lawfully

24   acceptable fence, one must inform him with neighbours as witness and bid him tether his beast. If it subsequently does damage, then one must take the creature into the house, and he who owns the

27   creature is to pay for the damage. If an ox breaks a fully tied fence, even if it is not lawfully acceptable, then you are to pay for the damage. If it jumps over it, you do not pay unless the fence is

30   lawfully acceptable. An ox is lawfully tethered if it has a horn hobble around its hind foot and its horn. No fence is lawfully acceptable unless it is bound with two bands and is two and a half

33   ells in height to the upper band, but this nevertheless applies to those creatures that jump over, and not to swine or those creatures that crawl underneath. Each must take care of geese and pigs

36   themselves, provided that the fence (i.e. the neighbour's fence) is lawfully acceptable.

        If a man cuts down wood illegally in enclosed woodland and

39   travels there (i.e. to collect it), then he is liable to [pay] three marks to the <injured> party and another three <to> the community. But if he carries it home from the wood, then he is liable to a fine

42   of eight örtugar and complete restitution. If the wagon axle or other driving equipment breaks on the road, then a man may without penalty cut wood on another's land if he does not himself own

45   land so near that he can see yoke <and> wagon, or draught horse and cart [from it].

        If you tear up another man's fence so that you break the upper

48   tie, then you are to pay half a mark. But if you tear up a further fence section the fine is eight örtugar (i.e. in addition). If you tear up a third, the fine is four örtugar (i.e. in addition). If you tear a

51   wide enough gap to drive through, then you are liable to a fine of two marks and no more. And you are to make good his fence

---

26/33 **nevertheless** B *omits.*
26/38 B *has a new chapter here*: 40 Whoever cuts wood illegally
26/40 **<injured>** B; A *omits.* **<to>** B; A *omits.*
26/45 **<and>** B; A *omits.*
26/51 **then** B *omits.*

again, as good and long as it was before, and be responsible for
any damage during the time it was down.   54

If you take a man's firewood or fencing wood or timber in
his woodland, the fine is six öre. If the other (i.e. the owner)
has driven it to the road, then the fine is three marks, if one does   57
not leave one's own behind. And you are to give the other all his
own back, as good and as much, if you are found guilty of the
crime. He is to confirm himself by oath when all has been   60
returned.

<27> Concerning wells

A well is the responsibility of the one on whose farm it is, unless
a wheel or trapdoor covers it; then the one who goes away leaving   3
it open is responsible. If you dig a well in your meadow or [on
another part of] your land, you are to make the path and track as
good away from it as to it, or you are responsible for a man's   6
beast if it suffers injury.

<28> Concerning land purchase

No one may sell land unless pressing need arises. Then he is to
inform those kin most closely related and the parishioners and   3
the family members, and they are to test the need. But whoever
gives money for land without this test, has forfeited his money
and is to pay a fine of twelve marks to the authorities and another   6
twelve to the close-related kin, who are invalidating the agreement.
But property is never legally purchased without the discretion of
the assemblymen, and the kinsman's portion shall be offered for   9
a year. One shall pledge with the same witnesses as for purchase.
If men divide property, they are to declare the division to the
assembly, with both present. If someone disbelieves them, they   12
are to investigate in the same year. When the close-related kin
cannot purchase the property from the one who is forced to sell,
then kinsmen from another branch of the family are to buy it, or   15

27/1 <27> B: 41
28/1 <28> B: 42

family members (i.e. those more distant), with the same test as
laid out above. But land may never be bought out of the family. If
18   men, Gotlandic or non-Gotlandic, who are not in the same family,
have land (i.e. in common) and are forced to sell, they are to sell
to those who should inherit, if they are able. If they are not able,
21   then the land must be bought by the men of the hundred in which
the property lies. Whoever infringes against this, is to pay a fine
of twelve marks to the authorities. When a man more distant than
24   the nearest buys it, one must submit a kinsman's portion to the
hundred assembly in which the land lies and, before one submits
the portion, lawfully inform the one who is to take up the kinsman's
27   portion, and who is outside the assembly area, in the presence of
his own parishioners. If someone sells his land, then the kinsman's
portion is to be taken up both by men and women who would
30   inherit, but not those who share the use of the land with him. But
kinsmen (i.e. close kin), or men from another branch of the family
are to buy the land. If they do not wish to, then the female members
33   are nearer than men outside the family. If, however, a man sells
his land and buys other land of the same value to his benefit, then
the kinsman's portion is not extracted. Land is never free (i.e.
36   otherwise) of a kinsman's portion unless everyone makes a sale,
or it is forfeited as wergild, or land bringing a mark in rent as a
dowry is promised at the betrothal meeting, or it is forfeited as a
39   fine for theft. If there are a number of brothers or brothers' children,
or other close-related kin, and they have divided their inheritance
and several sell their land, then none of them is to take a kinsman's
42   portion from the other, apart from the one most closely-related
who retains his land.

     If someone is taken hostage and he ransoms himself with his
45   land or property, then his nearest kinsman is to redeem it, if he
wishes, and pay the money for it once the other comes home. If a
farmer's son is captive, or a minor, no one may ransom him for
48   more than three marks in silver, unless authority exists from his
father or kinsmen; and he is to receive (i.e. from them) a third for

28/44 *B has a new chapter here:* 43 If someone is taken hostage

himself in addition to the sum he put down, in the same currency. But he does not have the right to more than three marks of silver if there is a dispute about it. But he who has inherited land and is not a minor is to take up his own case as best he may. What he does himself, stands. It is the law between countries that a foreigner never ransoms a Gotlander dearer than three marks of silver, unless he has the authority of his father or kinsmen, and he is to take a third in addition, in the same currency he has put down. If a brother travels abroad with undivided property and falls captive, then his brother is to ransom him (i.e. with money) from the undivided property. If he travels with divided goods then he is to ransom himself. A brother must ransom another from captivity as long as the property has not been divided between them.

If some profit falls to one (i.e. one brother) more than to the other, or some find is made on his portion, then all should have a share, while it (i.e. their property) is undivided. If brothers possess undivided property and one of them kills a man, then each is answerable for his actions: the one who killed pays the fine.

No son of a Gotlandic father may have his portion from his father, although he ask for it, unless his father is willing or he marries with his father's consent. If he wants to make division, then he is to take his personal share in money after the drawing up of accounts, but his father is to keep his farm undivided and he is to give his son the land rent from it, as well as his personal share in money; and the son is himself to have the authority to go where he wishes. If they have several farms, then the son is to go to one of them at the drawing up of accounts, if he wishes, so long as the father does not prove to be unreasonable. If a non-Gotlandic man has married or unmarried sons, they are never to get a division of property from their father, unless the father proves to be unreasonable.

28/64 **some** B omits.
28/68 B has a new chapter here: 44 Concerning the sons of Gotlanders
28/68 **portion** B: property portion
28/70 **consent** B: counsel and consent
28/72 **is to keep** B: is then to keep

<29> Concerning debts

Whoever gets into debt ill advisedly forfeits his portion and no
3   more. And no one is to pay out a debt after his death more than his
own means can bear.

<30> Concerning surety

If you take surety from a man for a true debt, then you are to
3   summon him to the church or the assembly, and he is to redeem it
at the legal time, otherwise the parishioners or the men of the
assembly will make a valuation.

<31> Concerning assemblies

This is also agreed: that all assemblies shall commence before
3   midday. Magistrates shall judge at the hundred assemblies.
Whichever of them does not arrive by midday is to pay *three*
öre to the assembly. If none of them has arrived by midday,
6   they are liable to [pay] three marks to the first one to bring a
case forward and another three <to> the community. But
judgements may not be judged longer and oaths not taken later
9   than sunset. Whoever infringes this is to pay a fine according to
the level of the assembly. The sixth assembly may not impose
a fine of more than three marks, and the riding assembly up to
12   six marks and the general assembly up to twelve marks. If
the cases concern ownership, then anyone is lawfully dismissed
who does not come at the same time that the assembly is held.

29/1 **<29>** *B:* 45
30/1 **<30>** *B:* 46
30/2 **you take** *B:* a man takes
30/4–5 **or the men of the assembly** *B omits.*
31/1 **<31>** *B:* 47
31/4 **three** *A:* three iii
31/7 **<to>** *B; A omits.*
31/8 **longer** *B omits.*

<32> Concerning a money claim

If a claim for money arises between men, then neither gets a higher oath from the other than from six men if disagreement   3
arises between them. But it may be from up to eighteen men in respect of land disputes, if there is disagreement relating to as much as a mark in gold (i.e. land to that value), and similarly   6
even if more is involved. If they disagree (i.e. about the value involved), then the hundred's magistrates shall decide without an oath, if the disagreement concerns a mark in gold, and he (i.e. the   9
plaintiff) is now to take the initial summons with a month's grace from then. If he (i.e. the defendant) wishes to postpone this, he must postpone it within the first fortnight's <period and move it   12
by another fortnight's period> forward to the third (i.e. six weeks from the outset). When disputes concern less than a mark in gold (i.e. land to that value), then a six-man summons shall be taken   15
out initially for a fortnight. If he (i.e. the defendant) wishes to postpone this, then he is to postpone it before a week is up, and move it by another week forward to the third (i.e. three weeks   18
from the outset). But summonses may not be moved by more without the agreement of both parties.

<32a>

<33> If you buy an ox

If you buy an ox, then try it for three days. Two faults may be found with it (i.e. to warrant its return). One is if it does not pull,   3
the other if it breaks out.

32/1 **<32>** *B:* 48
32/10 **now** *B omits.*
32/12–13 **<period ... period>** *This text must be understood, by comparison with 32/18. It is missing from both A and B. Cf. SL IV, 282 note 5.*
32a/1 **<32a>** *B:* 49 *See* Addition 7. *A omits chapter, despite listing it in the table of contents.*
33/1 **<33>** *B:* 50 **If you buy an ox** *B:* Concerning the purchase of oxen

<33a> <Concerning the purchase of cows>

If you buy a cow, then test her for three milkings. Two faults may
3   be found with her. One is if she kicks so that she cannot be milked,
the other if she is lacking in milk.

<34> If you buy a horse

If you buy a horse, then try it for three days and lead it back with
3   the fault if you find one. Three faults may be found with a horse.
One is if it is moonblind, the second is if it bites, the third if it
kicks out with its forefeet. If you have it for longer, then the vendor
6   is not to take it back, even if faults are found, unless he himself
wishes.

<35> Concerning horses

If you take a man's horse at pasture or elsewhere, without leave
3   of him who owns it, and ride it or drive it, then you are to
pay three marks to the complainant and another three to
the community, if you are found guilty of being on the horse's
6   back, and [must] always return <everything> undamaged. If
you take a man's horse tied to a fence and do not leave one behind,
you are also to pay three marks to the complainant and another
9   three to the community, unless you have made a mistake and
left another one behind. If you have made a mistake, then you
are to pay eight örtugar and bring it back unharmed before the
12 third day.

33a/1 *A has no heading, despite listing a separate chapter in the table of
contents. B has the first three words in red, indicating a new section.*
33a/2 **then** *B omits.*
34/1 **<34>** *B:* 51 **If you buy a horse** *B:* Concerning the purchase of horses
35/1 **<35>** *B:* 52 **Concerning horses** *B:* If you ride another man's horse *A has*
hesti ('horse') *in the singular.*
35/3 **ride it** *B:* ride
35/6 **<everything>** *B; A omits.*
35/11 **back** *B:* back home

<36> Concerning the care of ships

And concerning the care of ships, the law is as follows: merchant ships, those that have thirteen ribs in them and three crossbeams, are to be cared for out on the beach. But a cargo vessel shall be fastened through a bollard or rib or through a plank to a house in which people are sleeping. There must be a padlock and a key, which the housewife or farmer carries. The chain is to be no more than three links in length and the fourth shall be an iron crosspiece. Each link shall weigh two marks or stretch over three ribs. And one is not responsible for the action of the sea. If someone finds an unattended small vessel out on the shore, then the one who has found it is to take possession of it, if the other (i.e. the owner) is not so near that he hears his shout, if he has shouted three times. A boat is not to be without supervision, otherwise whoever wishes may take it. If someone takes a man's boat, which is at the landing-place, and takes it out, then he is to pay a fine as if he had ridden another man's horse.

<37> Concerning house searches

If men come to a man's farm and ask to search the house, then no one can forbid the search. If he wishes to have his neighbours present, then they (i.e. the searchers) must wait for them, if they do not wish to do him an injustice. Each is to nominate a man to go inside. They are to go in loosely girded and coatless to perform the search. If someone denies another a search, then his door is not protected, and he receives no recompense (i.e. if someone forces their way in), even if no stolen goods are found inside. If something is found inside of that which they have a suspicion about, they are to enquire about its acquisition. If he confesses at once and explains his acquisition, the warrant for ownership must be traced (i.e. to the assignor) and his acquisition tested. If he gets full corroboration from the person to whom he first referred

36/1 <36> B: 53
37/1 <37> B: 54
37/3 **no one** B: no one else

15 (i.e. as assignor), then he is innocent in the case. If he acquired
the goods from another and did not know that they were acquired
<illicitly> then, if the one to whom he has traced the goods (i.e.
18 the assignor) takes responsibility, he himself is then free of
suspicion. If the other denies it, then he has to take evidence from
those who were there (i.e. at the purchase or receipt). This evidence
21 will condemn him (i.e. the assignor) if he cannot lawfully defend
himself. If someone carries stolen goods to a man's farm and
house, which has a lock, and means in that way to betray him,
24 then he is to forfeit everything that he carried in. And then he is to
pay wergild to him, as much as he to whom he took the goods is
worth, and in addition three marks to the assembly. *But if* he did
27 this to a Gotlandic man, then he is to pay a fine of twelve marks
to the authorities.

<38> Concerning the law of *theft*

And concerning the law of theft the legislation is this: whoever
3 steals two öre or less than two öre, is to pay a six-öre fine for
petty larceny. If he steals between two öre and a mark of silver,
he will be taken before the assembly and marked and be
6 committed to pay wergild (i.e. that of the victim). If he steals
again after he has been marked, even if it be less, then he shall be
hanged. If he steals as much as a mark of silver or more, then he
9 shall also hang.

<39> Concerning insults

There are four insults relating to a man: thief, murderer, violent
3 robber and murdering arsonist. And of a woman there are five:
thief, murderer, adultery, witchcraft and murdering arsonist. When

---

37/17 **<illicitly>** *B; A omits.*
37/22 *B has the first word of the sentence in red, indicating a new section.*
37/26 **But if** *B; A reading ambiguous here.*
38/1 **<38>** *B: 55 Both A and B have* thieves *for* **theft.**
38/8–9 *B omits the final sentence. See* Addition 8.
39/1 **<39>** *B: 56*

someone is subjected to such insults, then he is to travel to the farm of the one who has spoken the insult and lawfully summon   6
him to the church and request that he take back the words, which were spoken in the heat of the moment, in a quarrel, or in drunkenness. If he denies it, he is to swear with three men before   9
parishioners that he never said those words. If he cannot substantiate the oath, then he is to pay a fine of three öre and restore the man's honour with a three-man oath in church. If a   12
man abuses another with such insults before the whole parish or at the assembly or at a summons and does not get their veracity proved, then he is to pay a fine to the other of three marks and   15
restore his honour with a six-man oath at the assembly. This (i.e. this type of case) shall be prosecuted at the lawful time in respect of women as well as men.   18

<40> Concerning small <unbranded> livestock

If an unbranded small farm animal comes to someone, then he is to take it to church and to one assembly. If it is not recognised,   3
then he is to let it be valued and take an assembly fee in respect of it and the parishioners shall divide what is over.

<41> Concerning swine

If swine larger than piglets come to someone, branded or unbranded, he is to take them to two assemblies and the third   3
time to the riding assembly, and receive an örtug for each assembly. If they are not recognised, then the parishioners shall value them <and he (i.e. the finder) is to take an assembly fee from that   6
sum,> and the <parishioners> divide what is over.

39/13 **such** B *omits.*
40/1 **<40>** B: 57 **<unbranded>** B; A *omits.*
41/1 **<41>** B: 58
41/4 **each** B *omits.*
41/6–7 **<and he . . . that sum>** B; A *omits.*
41/7 **<parishioners>** B; A *omits.*

<42> Concerning tame sheep

If tame sheep come to someone, he is to take them to two
assemblies and the third time to the riding assembly and declare
them for three years and claim a fee such as has previously been
the custom for the riding. But any offspring shall go to the one
who has fed them.

<43> Concerning uncastrated unshorn rams

If an unshorn uncastrated ram comes to someone, he is to take an
örtug in redemption fine (i.e. from the owner). If it is not identified,
then he is to take a *fee* as for other sheep.

<44> Concerning uncastrated shorn rams

If a shorn uncastrated ram gets loose after the feast of St
Simon and St Jude (i.e. 28th October), up to the time that it
is usual to release them, then it has rendered itself forfeit
by wandering. But one shall nevertheless offer it back to
the one who released it with his parishioners as witness. If
he does not wish to redeem it, then the one who captured it
can have it, and put his brand on it, with his own parishioners as
witness.

<45> Concerning nanny- and billy-goats

<One> must declare billy-goats and nanny-goats for two years,
then they shall be redeemed: a nanny for six pence for each
assembly and a billy for an örtug.

42/1 **<42>** *B:* 59
43/1 **<43>** *B:* 60 **unshorn** *B omits.*
43/3 **fine** *B:* fee
43/4 **fee** *B; A:* fine
44/1 **<44>** *B:* 61 **uncastrated** *B omits.*
44/2 **shorn** *B omits.*
45/1 **<45>** *B:* 62
45/2 **<One>** *B; A omits.*

<45a> <Concerning cattle and horses>

Cattle and horses must be declared at two assemblies and the third time at a riding assembly for three years. If not identified   3
at the first assembly, they must be valued and then declared, and the finder is to have two örtugar for each assembly. Those cattle or horses that can be worked may be, with the knowledge   6
of the parishioners. But one is not to travel to Visby with them, but ride with them to the assembly, or lead them, and remove their saddle and tie them up, with all the animals that   9
are to be declared, so far away that one can see the assembly-site poles.

<46> Concerning *over-branding*

Whoever puts a brand <on> another's creature without having bought it or received it as dowry and is found guilty, he is to be   3
fined three marks.

<47> Concerning fields

If several men own a field between them and some wish to let it lie fallow and some to sow it, the ones who own more of it have   3
the say and are to declare, before the feast of the Annunciation, which they would prefer to do, allow it to lie fallow or sow it. If the tenants exchange farms, the one who moves away receives   6
six pence for each bushel-land, of those fields that he may not sow, from the one who comes in. And at haymaking time they are to make room, each for the other, space for as many hay   9
loads as the farmland is worth in marks.

45a/1 *B has a new chapter here*: 63 Concerning cattle and draught horses *A has no heading, despite listing the chapter in the table of contents.*
45a/7–8 **with them** *B omits.*
45a/10–11 **so far away ... poles** *B*: so far from the assembly-site poles that one may see
46/1 **<46>** *B*: 64 **over-branding** *B; A*: brands
46/2 **<on>** *B; A omits.*
47/1 **<47>** *B*: 65

<48> Concerning turnip fields

Every farmer who has arable land is to leave a bushel-land for
3 turnips every year. But those who have no arable land, but have a
house, must have half a bushel-land for turnips, and the one who
owns the land is to put it to the yoke. Everyone who does not
6 adhere to this is liable to a fine <of> three öre to the parish. And
every parish, which does not enforce this, is liable to a fine of
three marks when it comes before the assembly.

<49> Concerning shipwrecks

If a man finds jetsam on land, then he is to retain every eighth
3 penny of the find. If he finds flotsam at sea and it needs boat and
oars (i.e. to salvage it), or he finds it on the seabed and it needs
boat hook and grapnel, then he retains a third of his find. If he
6 finds it out of sight of land, then he retains a half of what he has
found.

<50> Concerning fire

If the misfortune occurs that injury results from a fire, which is
3 laid in the hearth or in the kitchen, and [which] flies to another
farm and does damage, the fine is three marks, if the damage is
up to three marks. If several farms are damaged, then they must
6 all be satisfied with those three marks.

<51> Concerning carried fire

When injury results from carried fire, then the one who carried
3 the fire is to pay half his own wergild. When this results from the
actions of a minor, then the one who sent him is to pay.

48/1 **<48>** *B:* 66
48/5 **land** *B:* field
48/6 **<of>** *B; A omits.*
49/1 **<49>** *B:* 67
50/1 **<50>** *B:* 68
50/3 **in the kitchen** *B:* the kitchen
51/1 **<51>** *B:* 69

<52> Concerning road repair

It is also agreed that roads shall be made good every year in all parishes. Every parish which does not make good its roads is to pay a fine of three marks to the assembly.   3

<53> Concerning tax

It is also agreed, if one must collect taxes for the requirements of the province, then they should be collected according to the value in marks, both of property and money and not of manufactured valuables.   3

<54> Concerning the watch

Everyone who is twenty years old [or over] shall sit watch and he shall provide himself with a weapon, and answer for all expenses, and pay the watch-money in Easter Week.   3

<55> Concerning houses and household servants

Anyone who raises a house without the permission of the parish is liable <to> a fine of three marks to the parish and is to pull it down the same year. Anyone who takes in household members, without the permission of the parish, is liable to a fine of three öre.   3

<56> Concerning harvesters

Each harvester who is in the pay of the farmer, and who goes away from the farm on a working day without the permission of his employer, is to pay back an örtug for each day of his hire and complete the day's work (i.e. for the missing day).   3

52/1 <52> B: 70 **road repair** B: roads
53/1 <53> B: 71
54/1 <54> B: 72
55/1 <55> B: 73
55/3 <to> B; A omits.
56/1 <56> B: 74

<56a> <Concerning those who have no arable land>

Each person who has no arable land in the parish has no excuse
3 for not harvesting seed for the farmer. And they are to receive six
pence for each bushel-land of corn and *five* pence for rye and
oats, and they are to feed themselves. And the farmer instructs
6 them with the right of law. Each one who refuses (i.e. to work) is
liable to a fine of three öre.

<57> Concerning squirrels

Anyone who catches a squirrel before the feast of St Simon and
3 St Jude and after the feast of the Annunciation is to pay a fine of
three marks. And no one is to catch a squirrel within an enclosure
without the owner's leave.

<58> Concerning hares

No one is to catch hares with a gin after the feast of the
3 Annunciation or before the feast of St Simon and St Jude without
risking a fine of three marks.

<59> Concerning tree-fruit

This is also agreed: that all tree-fruit shall be protected until
3 the feast of the birthday of the Blessed Virgin Mary (i.e. 8th
September). Whoever infringes this is to pay three öre to the
parishioners. Of this the one <who> brings the action takes half.
6 If a minor infringes this, the fine is less by a half.

56a/1 **<56a>** *B has a new chapter here:* 75 Concerning those who have
no arable land *A has no heading, despite listing the chapter in the table of contents.*
56a/4 **five** *A:* five five
57/1 **<57>** *B:* 76
58/1 **<58>** *B:* 77
59/1 **<59>** *B:* 78
59/5 **<who>** *B; A omits.*

<60> Concerning failure to say mass

It is also an ancient law that for every failure to say mass on a Sunday or other holy day, the priest is liable to a fine of three marks to the rural dean, and another three marks to the parish. If the failure to say mass be on a Friday or *on a* feast day on which nine lessons should be read or held, then the priest is liable to [pay] twelve öre to the dean and another twelve to the parish.

<61> Concerning gambling

Gambling is prohibited. Whoever gambles is liable to a fine of three öre to the parish. If the parish does not wish to prosecute, then the parish is liable to a fine of three marks to the assembly.

It is also agreed that this is the law, which is written here. All men should abide by this. If some occurrence should take place, which is not to be found here, then it must be decided by the majority of judges, and <they> are to swear that these are proper laws of the Gotlanders, and then they are to be written down here.

<62> Here is what was most recently adopted concerning bald patches

If the bald patch is more than the flat of the hand will cover, then the liability is a mark of silver. If every hair is gone, then the liability is two marks of silver.

60/1 <60> *B:* 79
60/5 **be** *B:* should be **on a** *A: and B:* other
61/1 <61> *B:* 80
61/4 *B inserts more here. See* Addition 9.
61/5–10 *The final sentences in this chapter constitute the end of B. They follow* Chapter 83 *in B. The words* Teth ier oc sempt sik: At *('It is also agreed that') are in red, with an enlarged initial* T*, indicating a new section.*
61/7 **here, then** *B:* herein
61/8 <they> *Supplied by GU, 30. Both A and B omit.*
62/1 *This chapter occurs only in A. It appears to be a later addition. The content appears in* Chapter 20 *of B. See* Addition 5.

<63> Concerning woodland

Whoever cuts wood in another man's woodland, within an
3 enclosure or without, and travels there, is liable to [pay] three
marks in coin and is to make full restitution. Whoever pulls down
another's fence to pass through it, is liable to [pay] three marks in
6 coin. Whoever passes illegally over another's property, is liable
to [pay] three öre. If someone tears an opening in another's fence,
he is liable to [pay] the same.
9 Concerning all land held in pledge: it is to be redeemed or taken
in payment (i.e. of the debt) in the same expiry period, or be
pledged again then. Whoever misappropriates land valued at three
12 marks rent, without coercion, has forfeited his neck and his wife
her place in church and she must stand at the back, in the belfry.

To in-laws and wagon-riders no more than three toasts are to be
15 drunk, and no vessel larger than a half bowl at the most is to be
used. And whoever abuses this, is liable to a double fine and twelve
marks to the authorities.

<65> Concerning women's rights

Concerning the rights of women it is also agreed that they should
3 take cattle up to five pairs, draught horses and sheep as many as
they brought to the farm (i.e. at their wedding). All gilding is
abolished except on buckles. Gilded copper shall be melted down
6 where it is found. Golden headdresses and satin ribbons, other

63/1 **<63>** *B: 82 This chapter appears to be a later addition in A.*
63/5 **to pass** *B:* in order to pass
63/9 **Concerning all land held in pledge** *B has these words in red, indicating a new section.*
63/14 *In B the closing words (61/5–10) follow here, together with details of Bilefeld's copy.*
63/14–17 **To in-laws . . . authorities.** *B does not have these two sentences at this point. See* Addition 6. *This provision belongs in the chapter* Concerning weddings; *cf. the note to* 24/21.
63/17 *A has the chapter* <24f, 64> Concerning travellers' pathways *here.*
65/1 **<65>** *B: 35 See the note to* 24b/1. *Concerning the two last paragraphs, see following footnotes. This chapter appears to be a later addition in A.*
65/4 **All** *B omits.*

than plaited laces, are all abolished. Old gilded vessels and belts are permissible, such as there are, but not to add to them (i.e. one is not to add to them by purchasing more). The dowry shall be   9 two marks in gold, and no more: no more may be given and no more requested. Wall coverings of blue cloth are abolished and wedding canopies, and nothing may be given between farms   12 except in white linen. Fine woollen cloth is also abolished. No one may buy fine woollen cloth, neither new nor old, and no one may at the time of the marriage exchange it between farms.   15

Silver bands and underskirt decorations are also abolished.

Buying on credit from town-dwellers is also forbidden. No one is to buy more than he can afford to pay for. Whoever infringes   18 any of this is liable to a fine of twelve marks to the authorities.

ADDITIONS

1. (*B:* Note to 5/6. Cf. Pipping 1901, 9–11; *CIG*, 104: Additamenta 1, 2.)

And then, furthermore, all the subsequent generations, both female and male, are always treated as Gotlandic families, unless he marries beneath him and so debases his birth (i.e. by marrying a   3 slave); and his rights are also the same as farmers or the children of farmers. If the lay *son of a priest* commits a crime or commits manslaughter, he must defend the claim for compensation himself   6 while he lives, whether he is at home or abroad.

If a man commits a crime, whether ordained or not, no one shall be fined more than his (i.e. the wrongdoer's) resources can   9 cover. If he (i.e. the wrongdoer) dies and an ordained man inherits the claim for compensation (i.e. wergild) after him, he is to offer

65/7 **vessels and** *B omits.*
65/12 **and** *B omits.*
65/13 **also** *B: entirely*
65/14 **neither new nor old** *B omits.*
65/15 **may at . . . the marriage** *B omits.*
65/15 *B adds* but keep it at the [original] farm *See also* Addition 6.
65/16 *B omits this sentence.*
65/17–19 *B rewords these three sentences. See* Addition 9.
Addition 1/5 **son of a priest** *B:* priest who
Addition 1/8–10 **If . . . cover** *This sentence also appears in* A Ch. 5/7–9.

12 compensation immediately, since no priest may negotiate compensation in a case, and the other may accept this at once without shame, if he wishes, since it is not right for him to kill an
15 ordained man, or to bear him ill-will. If he does not wish to accept compensation, he (i.e. the priest) must take the claim to the general assembly, where the other may accept it if he wishes; otherwise
18 all the people decide on the compensation, but he (i.e. the priest) shall then be free of guilt. If he (i.e. the plaintiff) should take revenge when it (i.e. compensation) has been offered, he is to pay
21 the full wergild, and forty marks to the general assembly.

If two brothers inherit a claim for compensation, the one ordained and the other not, and the ordained brother wants to pay
24 compensation and the other does not, then the ordained brother is to leave his personal share with a surety man, whom the general assembly shall nominate, and then be protected, and the other,
27 who did not wish to pay compensation, shall defend the claim. If wergild is offered, then each is to pay his personal share.

If an ordained man, who may not take revenge, inherits a claim
30 for (i.e. to receive) compensation, he must accept compensation immediately, when it is offered. If he does not want to accept compensation, but prefers to take revenge, then the other (i.e. the
33 defendant) must take it before all the people at the general assembly. There he (i.e. the priest) can still accept it if he wishes, otherwise they (i.e. the assembly members) shall be responsible
36 for the payment, and the man (i.e. the accused) shall be guiltless. If he does not want to offer the ordained man compensation, then the latter is to go before all the people at the general assembly
39 and there plead his case, saying, 'I am a priest, and ordained to the service of God; I may not take part in blows or battle; I will take compensation if it is offered, but I will not be put to shame.'
42 Then the people of the general assembly shall study it (i.e. the case), and compel the man to offer him compensation, just as he (i.e. the priest) would be forced to pay compensation to others,
45 since a priest can *neither* demand compensation, nor answer a

Addition 1/45 **neither** B: at what time, *which makes little sense.*

demand for compensation, without Christianity falling into disrepute.

2. (*B:* Note to 17/26–27. Cf. Pipping 1901, 23; *CIG*, 107: Additamentum 3.)

In respect of cattle and draught horses and swine, a man shall not be liable for more than the animal is worth, if it causes injury to someone. If it is an unruly animal and someone (i.e. the owner)   3
has been informed of this in front of the church door and before the parishioners, and it then does (i.e. damage) through carelessness, then the fine is twice as much as the case is worth.   6
If the damage is less than the creature is worth, then the fine is half as much. Dogs are the fourth creatures (i.e. carrying a liability): one is always answerable for it for everything, if it does   9
damage, up to half a wergild, whoever owns it. For a dog's bite, one is to pay a fine for each tooth-mark up to four, two öre each. If it causes a wound or maiming, then the fine is half the maximum   12
fine. One must demand the fine and not take revenge; lay a legal claim to it like other debts.

3. (*B:* Note to 19/62–66. Cf. Pipping 1901, 27; *CIG*, 39 note 50.)

Cutting off or splitting a smaller bone in the hand or foot is fined at two marks in coin. Each rib is to be fined at two marks in coin, if it is broken. If disability ensues, the fine is two marks of silver.   3
As many blows as are visible are each fined at half a mark in coin.

4. (*B:* Note to 19/80–86. Cf. Pipping 1901, 28; *CIG*, 41 note 63.)

But if an ear is damaged, then the fine is a mark of silver. A shinbone or a forearm is fined at two marks of silver if it is broken. If you strike the teeth out of a man's head then you are fined for   3

Addition 2/1 *The first letter of* Naut ('cattle') *is in red, possibly indicating a new section, although earlier in the manuscript the initial letters of some paragraphs are indiscriminately in red.*

the two upper and lower front teeth at a mark of silver. And then each is fined at two marks in coin, including molars and all.

5. (*B:* Note to 19/105–08. Cf. Pipping 1901, 28; *CIG*, 43 note 79.)

20 Concerning bald patches

If the bald patch is more than the flat of the hand can cover, the
3 fine is one mark of silver. If every hair is gone the fine is two marks of silver. If a man's scalp is cut, the fine is one mark of silver. A man's beard incurs fines as for other hair pulling.

6. (*B:* Notes to 24/20, 63/14–17 and 65/15. Cf. Pipping 1901, 40; *CIG*, 60 note 41.)

To in-laws and wagon-riders no more than three toasts are to be drunk, and none of them larger than half a bowl goes into at the
3 most. And whoever abuses this, is to pay a double fine and twelve marks to the authorities.

7. (*B:* Note to 32a/1. Cf. Pipping 1901, 51–52; *CIG*, 108: Additamentum 4.)

49 Concerning the purchase of slaves

If you buy someone's slave on your farm, then test him for six
3 days and on the seventh pay his purchase price or lead him back if he does not satisfy you. If the one who sold him will not take him back, but wants to hold you to the agreement that you should have
6 him and <not> lead him back, whether he satisfy you less or more, and if you have a counter-claim that you were permitted to lead him back within a period of grace, if he did not satisfy you, then
9 you, who lead him back and follow the law, have the right to

Addition 5 *The majority of these statutes occur in 62/3–5.*
Addition 6 *This statute occurs in A at the end of* Chapter 63.
Addition 6/1 *The first letter of* Magum *('To in-laws') is in red, indicating a new section.*
Addition 7/1 *A lists this chapter in the table of contents after* Concerning a money claim *but omits it in the text.*
Addition 7/6 **<not>** *Supplied by CIG, 108. B omits.*

substantiate your accusation. If you have the man longer, and
want to lead him back later, after the period of grace has expired,
and you say that you have made this agreement, then he who   12
made the legal sale has the right to substantiate his case: you
must pay him, and keep what you bought. But the vendor must
subsequently answer for three faults: epilepsy, and bed-wetting,   15
for which he is responsible for a waxing and waning, and if his
(i.e. the slave's) leg hurts, for which he is responsible for a year;
and then for an ownership claim for all time. If he (i.e. the slave) 18
is claimed while in your possession, you are to call to the vendor
and lead him (i.e. the slave) to him; he is then to defend your right
to the man, or give you back as much as you previously paid for   21
him. If there is a dispute between you, he (i.e. the vendor) saying
that he made the sale under conditions, you saying that you bought
with a firm purchase, then he who buys with a firm purchase, and   24
follows the law, has the right to substantiate his case.

8. (*B:* Note to 38/8–9. Cf. Pipping 1901, 55–57; *CIG*, 109:
Additamentum 5.)

If a man's slave steals an öre or less, then each owner is to pay a
fine for him of three öre, if the owner of the stolen goods discovers
the goods himself. If the stolen goods are worth more than an öre,   3
then he is in each case to get his property back, and in addition a
fine three times as much as the value of the goods. If several
slaves steal one öre, then each master is to pay a threefold fine   6
for his slave, if he does not discover the goods himself. If not all
the stolen goods remain, then the one who has lost the goods must
testify how much there was, but still only when house or lock   9
was broken into. If it was not taken from somewhere locked, and
neither bar nor bolt is broken, then he (i.e. the injured party) is to
take the slave and torture him, and not pay any compensation. He   12
(i.e. the accuser) is to bring him back to his master whole in bone
and breathing and not pay any money for him, even if he gets no
admission from him. If there is no material evidence, but simply   15

Addition 8/1 *The first three words in red, indicating a new section*

suspicion, then a deposit must be put down before the slave is tortured. He is to bring him back uninjured and pay a fine of six
18 öre for the wristbands <if he does not confess. If he confesses, and there is no material evidence, then he (i.e. the accuser) is still to pay a fine for the wristbands of> six öre. In need someone
21 forced says things [that] he has not done. If someone goes with evidence to a farm, and charges the man's (i.e. farmer's) slave with theft, then the master shall permit a house search and shall
24 himself bind the slave, and not stand in the way; then he is not liable to the triple fine. If the man does not wish to bind his slave himself, or permit a house search, and the stolen goods are
27 nevertheless found in the house, then he is to pay a triple fine to the owner of the stolen goods <that> he has now discovered. If the goods are so valuable that he cannot afford to pay a triple fine,
30 then the one who owns the stolen goods shall take the slave. He (i.e. the owner) cannot forfeit through theft more than his (i.e. the slave's) whole worth. If someone else, and not the one who owns
33 the goods, discovers the stolen goods, and takes the thief and binds him, he is to have a reward, an eighth of the value, both of the thief and the fine. If the slave is on the run, and has been
36 proclaimed at the church, or at the assembly, then he is a fugitive. And no one is to pay a triple fine for anyone who steals food for themselves, but each shall have their own back, if it remains. If it
39 has been eaten, then no one is to make amends for the fugitive. If a slave is recaptured, [someone must] redeem him again for two öre, if he is on land (i.e. Gotland), and for three öre if he has got
42 to a boat, and for half a mark if he has come out of the sight of land. The one who owns the ship is to redeem the slave, unless it was lawfully secured. If he has seized anything, then the slave's
45 owner is to return the things he has taken. If the ship was lawfully secured, or locked up, then the one owning the slave redeems the ship, and similarly all the things that he seized, but not more than

---

Addition 8/18–20 **wristbands <if he . . . wristbands of>** *Something is missing here. Cf. CIG, 110 note 24. The text in brackets is suggested by Wessén, SL IV, 284 note 10.*
Addition 8/28 **<that>** *Supplied by GU, 38. B omits.*

to the sum of three marks. If he flees in a ship, which was not 48
protected, or drowns in the sea, so that the owner of the slave
loses him, then the one who owns the ship is to pay for the slave.

If a man is bound in the absence of material evidence, then 51
three magistrates are to investigate, and hear his statement,
whether he is guilty or innocent. These three magistrates should
come from the same hundred, or the same sixth (i.e. as he does). 54
They shall witness what they hear, <whether> he is guilty or
innocent. And the same thing applies if there is material evidence.

9. (*B:* Notes to 61/4 and 65/17–19. Cf. Pipping 1901, 64; *CIG*,
112: Additamentum 6.)

81 Concerning purchase on credit from town-dwellers

Purchase on credit from town-dwellers is also forbidden. No one
is to buy more than he can afford to pay for. All property taken in 3
pledge should have a period of grace of three years for debts
more than a mark of silver (i.e. to be paid). One is not to give the
value in money, if the other does not wish, but in land, and he is 6
still to have a period of grace of three years.

Addition 8/55 **<whether>** *Supplied by CIG*, 112 note 29. *B omits.*
Addition 9/2 *The start of this chapter occurs in A*, 65/17–19.

NOTES

The chapter numbers in this commentary are those used for the text of B 64 in the present translation. They correspond largely to those used by Wessén in *SL* IV and earlier editors. Chapter breaks occurring only in the *B*-text are recorded in footnotes in the translation. The Gutnish chapter titles in the *A*-text are given, in angled brackets if the chapters are only distinguished in the table of contents. Note that 'Gutnish' (abbreviated to Gtn) is used throughout of the medieval language of Gotland whereas 'Gotlandic dialect' is used of the modern dialect(s), as recorded by the brothers Säve, Herbert Gustavson and others.

Table of contents

The table of contents in B 64 originally lacked numbering, although numbers have been inserted by a later hand, beginning with 'Concerning children' (*Af barnum*) as Chapter 1. Schlyter (*CIG*, ii and 3 note 2) considers these numbers to be from the fifteenth century, but it seems more likely, as Pipping (*GLGS*, 1 note 1) suggests, that they are in Bilefeld's hand, as are other notes and numbers in the same manuscript. Jacobsen (*GGD*, 21 note 1) suggests that the table of contents is older than the edition of *GL* represented by the *A*-text. She reasons that (1) more chapters are listed and they are more logically arranged; (2) the chapter concerning the purchase of slaves is listed; (3) the chapter concerning paths is in its original place and (4) the three later chapters and *Guta saga* are not listed.

The numbers have, to a greater extent, been erased from B 64 and a numbering system starting with the opening chapter has been adopted by most editors, though they all differ in minor respects. The chapter numbers adopted for this translation are shown in angled brackets in both the table of contents and the text.

The body of the text of B 64 lacks contemporary chapter numbers, but a sixteenth-century hand, probably Bilefeld's, has inserted them in the margin. The headings in the table of contents not represented by separate chapters in the text are indicated by suffixed letters in the numbering system. These headings are shown in the translation in angled brackets. The chapter 'Concerning travellers' pathways' (*Af farvegum manz*), which appears out of sequence in the text with respect to the table of contents, has been put in its proper place in this translation. Chapters in B 64 regarded as later additions and not listed in the table of contents have been given chapter numbers continuing the sequence established and titles shown in angled brackets in the table of contents.

The table of contents in AM 54 4to appears at the end of the manuscript and is numbered. These numbers match those in the body of the text, apart from the first three chapters. Even where the content corresponds between the A- and B-texts, chapter divisions are not always the same. These differences and the chapter numbers (and additional chapter headings) in the B-text are recorded in footnotes.

Page 1, last line. In B 64 chapter <24f> has been omitted either by the scribe or the writer of his original and appears following the later chapter 'Concerning woodland' (*Um skoga*). In AM 54 4to, this chapter appears in its proper place and this placing has been followed in the present translation.

Page 3/11 and footnote. The heading of the table of contents in AM 54 4to is in Danish and probably does not represent a heading from Bilefeld's original.

Page 3/13, 14. This incorrect duplicate numbering is present in AM 54 4to.

Chapter 1: *Hier byrias lag guta ok segia so at fyrstum*

1/3. The expression 'first beginning' (*fyrst upphaf*) appears to be tautological.

1/3–4. An account of the acceptance of Christianity and the influence of St Olaf is to be found in Peel (*GS* xxxvi–xlvi, 8–10).

1/5. The phrase 'good harvests and peace' (*ar ok friþr*) was a standard expression, which originated in the worship of Njǫrðr and Freyr. It combined concepts of material and spiritual well-being and similar phrases are found in *GulL* 1 (*NGL* 1, 1) and in *SdmL* Mb 36 (cf. Wessén 1924, 178–81).

1/7. The word *land* has a number of different senses, but here 'province' seems to be a reasonable translation. It is clearly Gotland as an administrative area that is referred to and it offers proof that the writer was a resident, writing for islanders. ModSwe *land* in the sense 'country, realm' is rendered by *riki*.

Chapter 2: *Af barnum*

2/2–3. A child was considered to be a possession of his father, who thus had the right to dispose of it, and exposure of children (especially females) seems to have been common practice from the earliest times. Lis Jacobsen suggests, however, that child exposure was regarded as shameful in Scandinavian countries even before the advent of Christianity (see *GGD*, 23–24 note 4). Banning the practice was one of the first changes in the law after the introduction of Christianity, but *GL* is the only Swedish-related provincial law to mention it explicitly. Jacobsen (*GGD*, 23 note 1) does not think that one can infer from the inclusion of this provision that parts of *GL* originated as early as the conversion. She considers that these customs took a considerable time to suppress and that an explicit prohibition could have been equally relevant in the thirteenth century. In *DL* Kkb 6 there is an implicit assumption that deformed children might be disposed of and this is also reflected in some Norwegian laws (cf. *BorgL* I 3 (*NGL* 1, 339)). Swedish provincial laws that incorporate provisions specifically forbidding infanticide are *ÖgL* Kkb 26 and *DL* Kkb 12.

2/4. Beckman (1920, 13) suggests that 'bed' (*seng*) should be changed to 'coming to bed, confinement' (*sengfar*), and cites *EidsL* I §§1, 3 (*NGL* 1, 375): *Sina sæng for skal huær kona uita* 'Each woman shall know [the time of] her coming to bed' and *Um sengfor kono* 'Concerning the coming to bed of women'. He interprets this as referring to the date of confinement and a need to make preparations, and suggests that the passage in *GL* was an inaccurate borrowing from Norwegian law. This certainly makes more sense than Schlyter's interpretation (*CIG*, 8 note b) that a woman should 'know her own bed', with the implication that she should give birth there and not elsewhere, in secret. Beckman refers to *tyGL* to support his proposal, but admits that it appears that the amendment there was made by the translator, while the original Gutnish text he was following had *seng* only. Jacobsen and Wessén have followed Schlyter in their notes. Both interpretations have attractions, but Schlyter's seems to match the context of the following provisions more closely.

2/5. The exact function of a *griþkuna* 'midwife' is not unambiguous; she was possibly a slave or a house servant, responsible for spinning hemp and washing (cf. Note to 2/34). In Norwegian laws a *griðkona* is a free woman without her own home, who has right of residence in another's home (presumably in return for work done) and sometimes designates a witness, in company with a *griðmaðr*, a man of similar status (cf. *GulL* 255 (*NGL* 1, 83–84); *BjarkR* 132 (*NGL* 1, 327–28)). In respect of the context in *GL*, one can compare

BorgL I 3 (*NGL* 1, 340): *Griðkonor oc grankonor skulu vera uið sengfor huerrar kono til barn er foðt* 'Free women and female neighbours shall be present at the confinement of every woman until the child is born'. In the Danish and German translations of *GL*, words corresponding to midwife (*iordemoder* and *hebemuter* respectively) are used (see *SL* IV, 245 note 3). Axel Kock (1918, 361–63) suggests that the person referred to should be a freeborn woman living on the premises, as opposed to a neighbour (*grankuna*) living nearby, but outside the family. The translators of *GL* would probably not have known the word (which occurs nowhere else in East Norse). Kock conjectures that *griþkuna* acquired the sense 'midwife' by association with a Gtn verb *graiþa* 'provide help during childbirth'. In *FrostL* II 10 (*NGL* 1, 134) the term *grið* is used, amongst other things, of the peace and security enjoyed during certain times of the year. Jacobsen (*GGD*, 24 note 2) states that *grið* is found in OldDan, but not *griðkone*.

The *grankuna* was a female neighbour. In *BorgL* I 3 and III 1 (*NGL* 1, 340, 363–64) there are provisions similar to those in *GL* relating to childbirth and the necessity for witnesses that a child was safely suckling before they left. Neighbours as witnesses of each other's veracity were frequently important in the legal process.

The two female witnesses together were both expert witnesses and witnesses as to fact. They had to be present at the birth and be knowledgeable in the matter of childbirth so that their evidence was reliable if anything went wrong with the delivery. Females were often specifically excluded from bearing witness, so this instance, which is the only one recorded in Swedish-related provincial laws, indicates a possible relationship between *GL* and the laws of Norway.

2/8. The expression *at þi san et* (*B*-text *ath thy san at*) used here was a common Scandinavian expression meaning 'found [unquestionably] guilty of'. On the change of sense of *sannr* from 'truth' to 'guilt' in this context, see Jacobsen (*GGD*, 24 note 4 and references). ModSwe retains the meaning 'truth' in *sanning*.

2/9. A fine of three marks in coin seems to have been usual for church law transgressions. Elsewhere in *GL* the word *penningr* is used to classify a mark as 'in coin' rather than by weight, usually of silver. If no qualification is given, as here, a mark in coin is usually intended, an exception being at 17/3. A mark of silver seems to have been equivalent to four marks in coin. This assumption is based on the fines for loss of and damage to an ear respectively (19/80–81).

The former is valued at one mark of silver and the latter at two marks in coin. The inference is that the latter was worth half of the former, since in most cases partial damage carries a compensation of one half of total loss (cf. *GGD*, 25 note 1; Wennström 1940, 239, 259–60, 287; *SL* IV, 245 note 4, 254 note 2 to Chapter 12). On the other hand a coining from Gotland in 1211 gave a norm of 4½ marks in coin to one mark of silver and King Hans of Denmark in his statute of 1492 suggests that there were 2⅔ marks in coin to a mark of silver (cf. Hauberg 1891, 9–10; *CIG*, 227). A mark in coin was presumably originally a silver coin with a weight of one mark, but a gradual debasement of the coinage occurred during and after the Viking period. The oldest evidence of difference between a *mark silfr* and a *mark penningar* is in *ÄVgL* Md 1 §3 where the phrase *hete þrer ok æru tuar* 'called three but is two' gives a relationship of 1:1½. The monetary system of *GL* is summarised in Appendix C.

2/10 The verb *skripta* used here carries the senses both of confessing and of submitting to punishment meted out by the church. It is related to English 'shrive', but that verb also refers to a priest's function as confessor and in giving of penance and absolution.

2/13. Jacobsen (*GGD*, 26 note 4) assumes that the assembly members (*þingsmenn*) referred to here are those of the local assembly, that is, all the mature men in the *hunderi*. This was the next level of jurisdiction above the parish, but the reference at 2/17 would suggest that the riding assembly was intended in both instances, and that the case passed directly there from the parish. See Note to 2/17.

2/13–14. The word *skir*, here meaning 'found innocent', is found as an element in Swedish *skärtorsdag* 'Maundy Thursday'. On this day, according to early Catholic rite, sinners who had undergone a course of penance during Lent were granted remission of their sins.

2/15. An oath of rehabilitation (*symdaraiþr*) was sworn by a group of people who had insulted another's honour by accusing them of a crime. The concept occurs again in Chapter 39/12. An analysis of the various types of oath sworn, and witnesses required, appears as Appendix E.

Jacobsen (*GGD*, 26 note 7) points out that the six men (or women) swearing the oath were not witnesses as to fact, but character witnesses as to the trustworthiness of the one of their number who was the principal in the case (see Notes to 3/36–38, 16/23–26, 19/6–8). In this instance the principal was the one who had accused a woman of infanticide and who was now retracting and apologising.

2/16. A *sokn* 'parish' was an area within which inhabitants had the right and duty to attend church services and receive ministrations from the priest. Parishioners were on their part obliged to pay tithes and other dues to the church and priest. Not all of Gotland's ninety-seven parishes had their own priest, and how many churches were built on private initiative is unknown. Chapter 3/22–24 mentions church building for the convenience of the lay people, and one can assume that there was at least some private input. Although the term *soknaþing* or the equivalent is not used in provincial laws, the concept is at least as old as those laws. It appears, however, that Gotland was the only province in which parishioners had judicial duties. Here the parish was able to pass judgements in a number of cases, including infanticide (Chapter 2), personal attack (Chapters 6, 8), fruit picking (Chapter 59), gambling (Chapter 61), unlawful house building or employment (Chapter 55). Road maintenance (Chapter 52) and oaths in respect of cases of dishonour (Chapter 39) were also parish matters. See Introduction, pp. xi, xxv, xxx.

Wessén (*SL* IV, 246 note 9) points out that the three-mark fine is a repetition of that recorded in 2/9, and suggests that it was divided between priest, church and parishioners.

2/16–17. The precise implication of the phrase *en sokn vindr sykt* 'if the parish can demand it' does not appear to have been considered by other editors. Since the main clause is a repetition, it probably refers back to the situation in which 'no one has a right to compensation', that is when the woman had confessed. In that case the parish (and presumably everyone else) lost their right to demand a fine. Three marks was also the maximum payable to the sixth assembly (31/10–11). See Introduction, p. xxx.

2/17. These assembly members must be the same as those referred to at 2/13, unless there is some text missing from all surviving manuscripts. Wessén (*SL* IV, 246 note 10) assumes that the riding assembly is referred to here, since the rural dean or archdeacon (Latin *præpositus*), of whom there was one for each riding, is also mentioned. The riding assembly received three marks and the dean another three, presumably in addition to the three that went to the parish. Similar additional fines, if a case were referred to a higher authority, are laid down in Chapters 4 and 7.

2/18–19. The fine for infanticide went to the rural dean rather than to the bishop, as did the excommunication fine for killing in a church (8/26–27) and that paid by a priest for failure in his duties

(60/3–4, 7). Bishops are only mentioned in *GL* in relation to church consecration and the designation of church feasts, although excommunication for killing on a feast day is referred to indirectly as a case for the bishop (*biskup sak*) (9/5). This suggests that rural deans performed at least some of the bishop's duties in Gotland for practical reasons.

2/20 The phrase *allir lyþir* used here is one of several used for (members of) the general assembly (*Gutnal þing*). Another phrase, *landar allir*, is used in the following clause, *allir menn* occurs in the following chapter (3/6) and elsewhere, whereas in Chapter 31/12 the phrase used is *land alt*. Twelve marks was the maximum, and usual, fine to the general assembly (see Chapter 31). Normally it seems to have been the severity of a case that determined whether it was heard first by the parish, the local (*hunderi*), the riding (*þriþiung*) or the general assemblies, but in this instance there seems to have been an escalating appeals procedure.

2/21. Allocation of fines to the countrymen (*landar allir*) of the wrongdoer as compensation for the inconvenience caused by bringing a case is mentioned on a number of occasions in *GL* and also in mainland provincial laws and in the national law (cf. *ÖgL* Db 1, 2; *ÄVgL* Md 5; *MELL* Tjb 4). In these latter fines were allocated to the crown, whereas in semi-independent Gotland the money was presumably used by the community.

The most frequent meaning of *fæ* 'money' in Scandinavian laws was 'property in general' and this seems to be the case in the laws of Iceland and Norway, the early Danish laws, *ÄVgL* and *GL* (see Ruthström 2002, 73–75). Jacobsen (*GGD*, 27 note 3) observes that the word, although used of money and other property, was never used specifically of livestock in *GL*, although it seems to have been on occasion in Danish and Norwegian laws. Ruthström (185–87), however, argues that the accepted etymology of *fæ* as deriving from a word for sheep is incorrect and that it derives from one meaning 'money' or 'property'. There are a number of instances in *GL* where *fe* is used unambiguously to refer to 'property in general', such as in the laws of inheritance (e.g. 28/58–59), and a number where it must be assumed that liquid assets are intended (as in this instance and elsewhere where fines and ransom are specified in terms of marks or other currency). There is also one instance in which there is an explicit distinction between *fe* as a designation for liquid assets and *aign* as a designation of 'real estate' in relation to disputes about property (32/2–6). See Ruthström (2002, 65–70, 85–90 and 240).

2/22–23. Although a woman who could not pay the fine imposed was forced into exile, and could not be fed or harboured, it does not seem that she was to be treated as an outlaw. There is, for instance, no mention of her being at risk of being killed (cf. Hasselberg 1953, 253).

2/23–25. As Wessén (*SL* IV, 246 note 13) points out, it is clear neither how an accused woman could defend herself against a charge of infanticide, nor how the charge was to be proved. In some cases, an oath would possibly not have been sufficient.

2/26–30. The accusers had presumably to put down a deposit, equivalent to the compensation due to a woman wrongly accused, before they could pursue their case, unless the woman concerned had no witnesses. If they did not wish to do this, they had to declare her innocent. Much stress is put on this: it is repeated three times in different wording.

2/34. An *ambatn* (OWN *ambátt*) was a female slave who did indoor work on a farm, varying from driving the mill to washing and spinning hemp (cf. Note to 2/5). Despite their low status, there is evidence that they were given time off after childbirth (*ÄVgL* Gb 6 §3).

2/35 and footnote. All but two instances of *oyrir* in *GL* refer to coin, either explicitly as here, or by implication. It was, however, a measurement of weight going back to the early Iron Age, the OWN equivalent being *eyrir*, plural *aurar*, related to Latin *aureus*. The standard weight given for an *öre* was 26.8 grams, very close to the Roman ounce (Latin *uncia*) of 27.29 grams and also closely equivalent to an imperial ounce of 28.35 grams (see Jansson 1936, 12). The equivalence of eight *öre* to one mark (whether in coin or weight) was universal in Scandinavia (cf. Notes to 53/3–5, Addition 9/5–6).

2/37. The word *mali* used here means 'a fixed period of time'. As Jacobsen (*GGD*, 28 note 6) remarks, the fact that slavery was not for life indicates that the system was in the process of dissolving at the time *GL* was written down (cf. *SL* IV, 260–61 note 11). The arrangement seems to have been unique to Gotland, as opposed to the rest of Scandinavia (cf. Nevéus 1974, 65–67). The relationship between levels of fine paid by the slave master and the number of extra years added to the slave's term suggest that slavery, in at least some cases, was a means for a defaulter to pay off a debt.

Chapter 3: *Af tiunt*

The date when tithes were first introduced to mainland Sweden is unknown, but it seems probable that the tithe in Gotland was organised independently, possibly at an early stage, since the rules there were different. Exhortations to pay tithes issued in the bulls of 1171–72 indicate that tithe payment was not at that date fully established in Sweden, but tithes were certainly being paid in Gotland by 1217 (Introduction, pp. x–xi). Jacobsen (*GGD*, 29 note 1) refers to this chapter as 'af forholdsvis sen Oprindelse' (of relatively late origin), and suggests that it could significantly postdate the introduction of tithes themselves.

3/2. The word *tiþir* meaning 'religious services' echoes the Latin *horæ canonicæ* 'canonical hours'. The monastic services were Matins, Lauds, Prime, Terce, Sext, None, Vespers and Compline; the non-monastic services differed slightly in detail, and were said privately by the parish priest; the laity only attended mass. A priest's obligation to say holy office is mentioned in several provincial laws, e.g. *ÖgL* Kkb 5, which records his duty to sing *ottu sanger* 'matins and lauds', mass, *aptunsanger* 'vespers' and all *tiþir*.

3/4. The word *bol* meant originally simply 'a property on which someone lived'. It later came to mean a farm of a certain size, valued at twenty-four marks of silver and taxed at twenty-four *örtugar* (cf. *GGD*, 29 note 3; Notes to 20/91 and 28/35–39; Introduction, p. xxxi).

3/5–6. The two main sacraments represented by the phrase *arla eþa siþla* 'early or late' were Holy Communion and Extreme Unction.

3/9. In Götaland, Skåne and Gotland (barley) sheaves were assembled into conical stooks (*röker* or *raukr*), one of a number of methods of stacking the harvest, perhaps after preliminary drying on racks (cf. *DL* Bb 22 §1). The number of sheaves in each stook varied; figures of thirty-two and forty are recorded, but in the beginning of the last century a *rauk*, in certain parts of Gotland at least, consisted of thirty sheaves. Every tenth stook was to be paid in tithe, counted while it was still standing, but threshed before it was delivered. This was done during winter and the time limit set by the Feast of the Annunciation (25th March) was thus a reasonable one since by then all the grain should have been processed (cf. *SL* IV, 246–47 note 4). The loft above the west porch in Garde church is fitted for use as a tithe barn and the large towers characteristic of many churches in Gotland and Öland were also used for this purpose. For example, in Etelhem church, a hoist mechanism in an opening in the west face of the tower, enabled grain to be raised to the first floor. In Alskog and Lye churches there are partitions, clearly medieval in origin, on the first floor of the tower, designed for grain storage. The fixing and payment of farm rents by Lady Day is clearly a remnant of this practice. Jacobsen (*GGD*, 29 note 6) suggests that the method of reckoning the tithe recorded here, which continued in Denmark until tenancy reforms, was very unfavourable to the farmer, but does not explain why she thinks that this is the case.

3/11–14. A lesser punishment, called *interdictum locale*, involving exclusion from church sacraments, except baptism and extreme unction, seems to have been more frequently applied than full excommunication. From the context, this punishment was clearly temporary and was discharged after appropriate payments were made (cf. Note to 8/17–19).

3/16–18. Wessén (*SL* IV, 247 note 6) observes here that it is fines (rather than tithes) that are referred to in the threefold division.

3/18. A tenant (*laigulenningr*) was someone who rented land. The sense is the same as *landboi* 'someone living on or using another's land on payment of a lease'. Wessén (*SL* IV 247 note 7) considers that the word is derived from the combination *leigu-land* 'land put out to lease' (cf. also Wessén 1932, 83–88). It is perhaps significant that the concept of legal moving days (*fardagar*), when a tenancy expired, does not occur in *GL*.

3/19–20 and footnote. According to Jacobsen (*GGD*, 30 note 2) and Wessén (*SL* IV, 247 note 8) one mark of the fine went to each of the priest, church and parishioners.

3/22–39. From the content of this paragraph it seems that the building of private chapels, equivalent to Old Norwegian *hægindiskirkjur*, was not wholly extinguished in Gotland, although it is not mentioned in Swedish provincial laws. The principle was that churches should be independent and self-supporting. Where new churches were built, 'for greater convenience', they seem to have been funded initially by a group of farmers and adopted in the sense that tithes were paid to them; they still had to be consecrated by the bishop. Only those who contributed to the building of a church could transfer their tithe duty to this new church and parish. As Wessén notes, there does not seem to have been an obligation on builders to apply first to the bishop (or the king) for permission, as was the case on the Swedish mainland (cf. *UL* Kkb 1 §1; *YVgL* Kkb 2; *ÖgL*

Kkb 1–2). This is less surprising in view of the fact that the bishop was not readily available for such consultation and also that he was not party to the division of tithes. It could also be that by the time the law was written, parish boundaries were finalised (cf. *SL* I, *ÖgL*, 21 note 1, 34 note 4; *SL* IV, 247 note 13 and references).

3/30. The disagreements referred to would have been between the parishioner and the priest in his original parish who was claiming tithe payments.

3/36–38. The witness borne by parishioners in the case was witness as to fact and that borne by the priest was almost in the category of expert witness. Witness as to the truthfulness of a plaintiff or defendant, but not as to fact was more frequent and there was also official witness to an act, for reference in the future (cf. Notes to 2/15, 16/23–26, 19/6–8).

3/42–43. As well as the barley (corn) tithe, there was a tithe of hay and hops. No mention is made of a tithe of livestock. It is worth noting that rye is not specifically mentioned in this context. Hops were used for flavouring ale and were the subject of tithes in other provincial laws (cf. *UL* Kkb 7 §5).

Chapter 4: *Af blotan*

4/2. The reference to sacrifice (*blot*) is unspecific, but seems to be an allusion to animal sacrifice followed by a pagan feast (4/7). There is no mention of human sacrifice in *GL*, although it is described in *Guta saga* (see *GS*, xxxii–xxxiii, 4/18–19 and notes).

4/2–5. Wessén (*SL* IV, 248–49 note 2) remarks on the rhythm and alliteration in the opening clauses of this chapter. Cf. also a similar passage in *Guta saga* (*GLGS*, 63 lines 20–23).

4/4. Legends and customs involving a *haugr* 'howe, cairn' occur frequently in Old Norse literature. The practices referred to here can be compared to those in the first chapter of the *U* redaction of *Hervarar saga ok Heiðreks*, which may refer to the public worship of heathen gods (cf. *Heiðreks saga*, 66–67).

The context in which *vi* is used, as one of five objects of the verb *haita* 'call upon', suggests that it might mean something more concrete and specific than simply a 'holy place', but no assumptions can be made from any archaeological finds (cf. Olsen 1965, 77–78, 84, 278–82). A summary of the theories surrounding the relationship between *vi* and the town name Visby is to be found in Peel (*GS* xlii–xliii, 43–45).

Prohibition of sacrifice, witchcraft and other heathen practices is laid down in *UL* Kkb 1, in *GulL* 29 (*NGL* 1, 18) and in *GulKrR* 3 (*NGL* 2, 307–08). It is forbidden in *EidsL* I §24 (*NGL* 1, 383) to have a *stafr* 'pillar' in one's house and another version of that law occurs in *GulL supp.* (*NGL* 2, 495–96), referring to a *skaldstong*, a pole raised as a totem. Kock (1912, 205–06 note) records that Lithuanian and Latvian have similar words to *stafr* meaning 'pillar' or 'image'. Sacrifice to a raised stone is described in *Kristnisaga*, Chapter 2. Whilst there are several instances of a *stafr* being forbidden by post-Christian laws, with the assumption that these were objects of worship, whether or not they were actually engraved with heathen images, the *stafgarþr* seems to have been a uniquely Gotlandic phenomenon. A full study of *stafgarþr* has been made by Olsson (1976; 1992) and a short résumé of his conclusions appears in *GS*, 28–29 note to 4/18.

4/8. The Gtn expression here, *sakr at*, means more precisely 'liable to a fine of'. Jacobsen (*GGD*, 32 note 3) observes that *sak* is generally used in provincial laws to mean 'fine', rather than 'legal case' (cf. its use in ModSwe) for which the word used is *mal*. Cf. also 9/5, 'fine to the bishop'.

4/13–14. Cases such as this, in which a defendant's provision of oaths was alone sufficient defence against a charge, still occurred when it was more usual to have an independent *edgärdsman*, someone who swore an oath as to the truthfulness of one of the parties (cf. *SdmL* Mb 5 §1; *UL* Mb 25 §1; *VmL* Mb 21 §1; Note to 13/54).

Chapter 5: *Af prestum ok prestkunum, ok þaira barnum*

5/1 and footnote. The reference to the wives and children of priests, and its implications for the dating of *GL*, are touched upon in the Introduction, p. xxxix. The omission of the majority of the relevant provisions from the *A*-text (although they are referred to in the chapter title and in the opening paragraph) suggests a date for the original of this manuscript later than for the original of the *B*-text. It could indicate (*GGD*, 32–33 note 4) that such children were not regarded as legitimate by the time that the former was written. Wessén (*SL* IV, 249 note 1) observes that *tyGL* and *daGL* follow the *A*-text.

5/4. Wessén (*SL* IV, 207, 249 note 2) initially translates *at allum lutum* 'in all respects' as 'i alla delar' (in all parts), but then explains this as referring to 'andra våldsgärningar' (other violent acts). It seems unnecessary to narrow the scope of the equality with farmers' families by limiting the sense in this way. A similar provision occurs in *ÄVgL* Md 5 §5.

5/7–9. The provision preventing fines being paid on behalf of another beyond what could be afforded, which occurs in both the *A*-text and the *B*-text, seems to be out of context. Its content may be compared to that of the provision in the *edsöreslag* (cf. Introduction, p. xxxviii; Note to 12/9–10): that no one was to be fined for the crime of another (cf. *ÖgL* Eb 9; Note to 29/3–4). Wessén (*SL* IV, 249 note 9) links this with the provision at Addition 1/27–28, that when compensation was offered, everyone was to pay his or her personal share. The *B*-text omits the phrase *firi annan* 'on behalf of another', which supports Wessén's suggestion.

5/9. The word *kustr* 'resources' is used in *GL* for both movable and immovable (24d/6) property. Whilst it was a term that, in the time of the provincial laws, was in the process of being replaced in Danish and mainland Swedish by *eghn* and cognates, the reverse seems to have occurred in Gotland. Ruthström (2002, 97–98, 173–74) explains this by pointing to the relative timings of links to the See of Linköping (and the Archbishop of Lund) and to Uppsala and the Swedish crown. Svealand retained *koster* longer than Götaland and Denmark. Having imported *eghn/aign* from the latter two areas during the conversion, Gotland then appears to have imported *koster* or *kustr* during the process of political integration. Alternatively, the two words might simply have been borrowed independently as functional terms.

Chapter 6: *Af helgum dagum*

6/3. Wessén (*SL* IV, 250 note 1) draws attention to the fact that the agreement of the population was to some extent sought in setting feast days.

6/5. The clause 'attend holy office, or hear God's service' (*tiþir at hafa eþa guz þianistu at lyþa*) is another instance of parallelism, which occurs quite frequently in *GL* (cf. *SL* IV, 250 note 2).

6/8. Schlyter (*CIG*, 287) and Pipping (*GLGS*, *Ordbok*) interpret *punz þungi* 'weight of a pound' here as a *lispund*, but Jacobsen (*GGD*, 36 note 3) suggests that no such assumption can be made. The *lispund* was a Baltic unit of weight, the Livonian pound. (Livonia extended roughly over modern Latvia and Estonia.) Although its actual weight varied from time to time and region to region, a *lispund* was usually between 6 and 9.5 kg, as opposed to a *skålpund* of 0.4154 kg (cf. Jansson 1936, 17–18, 23–24). This is a relatively moderate weight to be drawn by two oxen, even on a Sunday, and Schlyter queries whether twenty of these units are intended. A *skeppund*, used for cargoes, was equal to 24 (later 20) *lispund* and there were twelve of these to a (ship) load (see Jansson 1936, 23, 36). The *pund* was also a unit of capacity rather than weight, equivalent to 8 *spann* of 72 litres (12 *spann* in northern Sweden where the latter was smaller) and thus 16 *laupr* (cf. Jansson 1936, 17–18, 26–28; Note to 20/47–48). There were again twelve of these *pund* to a load, and it is possible that the weight of goods of that capacity was intended, although this seems less likely. *DS* II, 54–55, no. 970 (9/8/1288) refers to a *gotenense pondus*, which might indicate that a special *pund* was prevalent in Gotland. The *lispund* is recorded as a Scottish unit of weight, which was adopted in Orkney and Shetland for grain, malt and butter, varying from 12 to 30 pounds (5.44 to 13.60 kg) (cf. *SND* s. v. *lispund*).

6/8–9. The word *oykr* was apparently originally an adjective meaning 'capable of being hitched to', later developing into the noun for a pair (yoke) of oxen (see Bugge 1877–78, 274–75). Cf. Notes to 26/45 and 48/5.

6/10–11. It seems that the miscreant had to pay six *öre* to redeem his confiscated load and a further six for his crime, although as Wessén (*SL* IV, 250 notes 3 and 4) points out there is a certain ambiguity. See 6/27–30 and 6/30–33 for similar penalties.

6/11. Provisions relating to Sabbath-breaking (*helgisbrut*) varied considerably between the Scandinavian provincial laws. In Norwegian law, twenty-one feast days were subject to a six-*öre* fine if broken. In *YVgL* Kkb 52 the feast days especially mentioned number about twenty-four in all, in addition to all Sundays. The fine for breaking these was eight *örtugar* unless one presented a defence with a twelve-man oath. Exceptions were that one could transport hay and grain after the middle of the afternoon. *ÖgL* Kkb 22 has slightly different provisions, and more circumstantial descriptions of the times when holy periods started and ended. The penalty for striking anyone during these times was three marks (to the bishop) or again a defence with a twelve-man oath. *ÖgL* Kkb 23 records specific days that were subject to exceptional fines of forty marks, for instance if one struck or killed someone on the way to particular feasts. *UL* Kkb 16 (*VmL* Kkb 24) gives various exceptions. In addition fishing was allowed on feast days that did not fall on Sundays (in the fishing season), and spring and autumn work could be done after mass on such days when appropriate (*UL* Kkb 14 §9). *SdmL* Kkb 17 allowed work up to sundown on the afternoon of the eve of certain feast days during sowing and harvest seasons (otherwise the fine was three *öre*), but working on a feast day itself incurred a fine of three marks. All these fines fell to the bishop. *GL* seems to represent a more liberal (and possibly older) situation in which laymen had a right to suggest which days were to be included, and were allowed more latitude in what could be done. Cf. *GulL* 10, 15–18 (*NGL* 1, 7–8, 9–11), where there are similar dispensations.

6/18 and footnote. Jacobsen (*GGD*, 36 note 4) and Schlyter (*CIG*, 270) translate *kaupung* as 'by' (town) rather than 'handelsplads' (marketplace), but this interpretation is rejected by Wessén (*SL* IV, 251 note 6 to Chapter 6), following Björkander (1898, 36 note 1). The word *kaupungr* for 'marketplace' is older than in the sense 'town' (*UL* Mb 8 pr). The only town in Gotland was Visby, but there were certainly more marketplaces, some possibly having a temporary existence. Under Magnus Ladulås, trade became concentrated in the town, although remote areas were permitted greater freedom. Conflict between the inhabitants of Visby and the farmers of rural Gotland, which culminated in 1288 with the building of Visby town wall, was possibly occasioned by this freedom (cf. Introduction, pp. xii–xiii). In *GL kaupung* more closely relates to a *marked*, a local market for produce and barter. Cf. Note to 13/16.
The *B*-text has a parallelism here: 'travel or ride'.

6/18–20. The goods that one was permitted to take to market on a Sunday were those that were perishable, or which had been prepared in some way.

6/18. The *torg* was the area where the market was actually held, the 'market square'.

6/21. Barley (*korn*) was the most common bread grain and was also used for malting. Gotland must sometimes have been short of grain because in 1276 Magnus Ladulås (*PRF* I, 1) gave Gotlanders the right to import grain from Sweden except in years when there was a general export ban.

Chapter 7: *Af munka aigum*

7/2. The provision here is one of a number relating to cutting timber (cf. 25/26–37; 26/38–46; 26/55–61; 63/2–4).

7/4–5. Concerning the clause 'he is to be excommunicated' (*liggr hanum viþr bann*), Jacobsen (*GGD*, 38 note 1) points out that *liggia viþr* originally referred only to fines and meant 'to be subject to (a fine)'. Here the sense has been extended to excommunication as a punishment in respect of stealing or damaging monastery property.

7/5. Excommunication (*bann*) was not a punishment laid down in the earliest provincial laws, although it was later applied alongside other punishments. Fines to the bishop were the more common punishment for breaking church law. Elsewhere in *GL* the word *bann* is used only where the *interdictum locale* appears to be intended (cf. Note to 8/17–19).

7/5. The Gtn *halfu mairi* meant literally 'half more', but the actual sense was 'twice as much', the 'half' referring to the relation of the initial amount to the final amount (cf. Addition 2/6).

7/9. Delay in paying the fine did not result in an additional penalty. See 3/21 in relation to tithes.

7/11. The strong noun *aign* is the one most commonly used in the *A*-text, although not in the *B*-text, for 'property in the form of land'. The weak feminine *aiga* is used occasionally, whereas *land* and *iorþ* do not occur with this meaning. Ruthström (2002, 77, 96, 97–98) provides evidence that *aign* was in the process of being replaced by *kustr* in the sense of possessions in general, as opposed to land (cf. Note to 5/9).

7/13–17. Wessén (*SL* IV, 251 note 7 to Chapter 7) examines the significance of the inheritance arrangements following the death of a man who has entered a monastery in adult years. If he divided his property with his sons, taking one per capita portion for himself, it is possible that on his death the whole of that could have been inherited by the monastery. This would seem to imply that a man with one son could give a half, and one with two sons one third of his property to the religious house. Wessén considers the former, at least, unlikely and that in that case the limit of one third still applied. Jacobsen, however, translates *þa valdi hafuþlut sinum* as 'da raade de over deres Lod' (then they had control over their personal share), referring to the children. This gives no hint as to the division of the personal share of their father.

7/14. Wessén (*SL* IV, 250 note 21) defines *hafuþlutr* as 'så stor del av ett arv, som uppkom, om det delades i lika delar efter huvuden (per capita)' (as large a part of an inheritance as would be obtained if it were divided equally per capita). The same word is used in

Chapters 4 (*B*-text only), 20 and 28, all in relation to inheritance (cf. Iuul 1941, 103, 106; Note to 20/40–41).

7/16 and footnote. Jacobsen (*GGD*, 38) incorrectly gives 'en Tredjedel' (a third) for *tiunda lut* 'tenth part', obviously influenced by the previous paragraph. Wessén notes that Pope Gregory IX in a letter dated 23/1/1230 (*DS* I, 258, no. 257) confirmed a previously prescribed limit on donations to a religious house of one tenth of one's liquid assets. *UL* Kkb 14 and *SdmL* Kkb 11 have similar limits, but *ÖgL* Kkb 24, *ÄVgL* Äb 9, *YVgL* Äb 13 and *SkL* 38 (*CISk* I 37) differ (cf. *SL* IV, 252 note 8 to Chapter 7 and references). Note that the *A*-text here, and here only, clarifies the property referred to by specifying *iorþaign* 'property in land' (see Ruthström 2002, 97). The *B*-text does not specify 'land'.

Chapter 8: *Af mannhelg*

8/2. The concept of *mannhelg* 'personal rights' is closely linked with that of *friþr* 'peace and security'. The origins of the laws on 'peace' or 'truce' are not absolutely clear. It is possible that they developed from the periods during cult festivals when no one took up arms (cf. Tacitus 1914, 51) and were later connected with markets and trade. They might, on the other hand, have originated in the twelfth century under the influence of Pope Hadrian IV (Nicholas Breakspear). The word *mannhelg* occurs almost exclusively in law texts. It referred to the 'human rights' (a translation suggested in conversation by Helle Degnbol at Copenhagen University) of free men and women (but not slaves) under law. That is, the protection a citizen had for the personal rights of life, liberty and honour, particularly during periods when there was an enhanced respect for these rights (cf. Grønbech 1955, 2: 104–08). Mainland provincial laws have similar provisions (cf. *UL* Kkb 17 pr, 22 §1; *SdmL* Kkb 18 pr). Temporary loss of these rights, short of full outlawry, could result from certain infringements (cf. *FrostL* IV 7 (*NGL* 1, 159–60); *MLLL* IV 11 (*NGL* 2, 56–58)).

8/3–4. As Jacobsen (*GGD*, 38 note 7) points out, holy days lasted for two nights and a day. Reckoning such days from sunset on the eve of the feast seems to have its origin in Jewish practice, when the Sabbath started at sunset on Friday. It was customary, in any event, to count days from one evening to the next.

8/5–6. The 'seven weeks in Lent' include Holy Week, the week immediately preceding Easter. The Gtn *paskavika* must therefore be Easter week, the week following Easter Sunday. The word 'påskvecka' in ModSwe means Holy Week, and this is the translation that Wessén (*SL* IV, 210) uses. Pipping (*GLGS*) does not translate the whole word. Schlyter (*CIG*, 287), on the other hand, translates it as *hebdomas paschalis v. festum paschae proxime antecedens* (the week after (literally the seventh day of) Easter, or immediately before the Easter feast) but simply as 'veckan näst efter påsk' in his (later) concordant glossary (*CISG*, s. v. *Paska vika*). He was clearly not initially sure of the meaning. Söderwall (*OSMS* II, 200 s. v. *paskar*) cites Old Norse *páskavika*, which is translated as 'Easter Week' in Cleasby Vigfusson. There remains an ambiguity, however, since in Chapter 9/7–8 *aldra manna friþr* is said to last from fourteen nights after Easter for ten days. Is this from fourteen nights after the end of the Easter peace, or is it from fourteen nights after Easter Sunday, i.e. seven nights after the end of the Easter peace? The latter seems to be more likely, but it is not certain.

8/6. Rogation days (*gangdagar*) were the days on which penitential processions were held carrying crosses, icons and censors around the community, and prayers were said. The three principal Rogation days were the Monday, Tuesday and Wednesday following the fifth Sunday after Easter, that is the days leading up to Ascension Day. These were called *síðari gangdagar* in OWN, as opposed to *gangdagher litli* or *fyrri*, the feast of St Mark on 25th April (cf. *GulL* 18 (*NGL* 1, 10)).

8/7. Although Schlyter (*CIG*, 264) thinks that *helgudagavika* 'Whitsun week' in the text is an error for *þingizdaga vika*, Wimmer (1887b, 63–64 note 3) points out that it was a specific Gotlandic dialect word for Whitsun, which also appears, albeit in a corrupt form, in the runic calendars (Lithberg and Wessén 1939, 15 note 20). Thomsen (1870, 135) draws parallels with Finnish-Lappish *heluntai* f. 'Pentecost', Swedish-Lappish *helutagh*, noting that *hela* f. was a pre-Christian Finnish festival.

8/8. The three-mark fine, and subsequent ones in this chapter, were clearly additional to the normal wergild or other compensation payable.

8/12. The proviso that the action was done in anger (*i raiþi*) rather than accidentally seems to have applied only to cases in which no weapon was involved.

8/12–14. The limit here on the compensation for injuring a slave contrasts with the provision in *GulL* 215 (*NGL* 1, 73) where a slave is to have board and lodging while wounded, be given leech treatment, and his master is to have compensation for loss of labour. See also 19/137–141, where in certain cases a slave is paid half compensation and in other cases his compensation is limited. 8/14–15. The provision stated here is a general one and the reason for it becomes clear when one reads that the parishioners, church and priest of the injured party all shared the fines paid (cf. Note to 8/21–23).

8/17–19. The *bann* 'excommunication' referred to here is most probably an *interdictum locale*, as defined at 3/11–14. The provisions also seem to allow certain latitude and to permit the excommunication to be revoked as soon as the fine outstanding was paid to the satisfaction of the parishioners. This appears to be another example of the relative independence of the parish priest in Gotland, since a fine was paid to him for the ban, rather than to the bishop (cf. *SL* IV, 252 notes 8 and 9 to Chapter 8). It is not clear if 'excommunication always follows Sabbath-breaking' (*e fylgir bann helgisbruti*) refers only to violence during periods of church feasts recorded in this chapter, or if it also covers other forms of Sabbath-breaking listed in Chapter 6.

8/21–23. Division of fines in this threefold way was unique to Gotland. Wessén (*SL* IV, 252 note 10) refers to further examples in Chapters 3 and 4.

8/25–26. There are five occasions on which a fine of forty marks in coin is referred to in *GL*, apart from as wergild for a non-Gotlander. In three cases (1–3 below) the fine was payable to the general assembly (presumably in addition to the applicable wergild) and in the remaining two to the complainants: (1) for killing in a church as recorded here; (2) for killing a fugitive in sanctuary (8/31–32); (3) for killing a priest who had already offered compensation (Addition 1/19–21); (4) for discovered adultery with a married woman (21/9–10); (5) for forcing an unmarried girl into marriage without her parent or guardian's consent (21/12–15). There are two opposing theories relating to the origin of the forty-mark fine: Wennström (1931, 86–88; 1940, 294–300) and Schwerin (1941, 484) suggest that it was a later introduction, which came into being as a result of devaluation and the increased severity of fines, whereas Hjärne (1929, 102 note 4; 1947, 17, 18–21) and Hafström (1949, 190) contend that it was an old Swedish fine connected with the levy (*ledung*, Gtn *laiþingr*). In defence of the latter theory it can be mentioned that this level of fine occurs in Article 1 of the old Russian law *Pravda Russkaia* (*MRL*, 26), which, it has been suggested, was subject to early Swedish influence. In any event, the forty-mark system eventually replaced the three-mark system in Swedish law (cf. *ÖgL* Db 1; *UL* Mb 9 §2; *VStL* I 9 pr, §1). Hasselberg (1953, 217–18) also considers the forty-mark system to be foreign to the Gotlandic system of justice (cf. Björling 1893, 113; Note to 11/6). Wessén (*SL* IV, 253 note 11) agrees that in the case of *GL* this level of fine was almost certainly imported from the Swedish mainland, where it was the standard wergild. In a similar situation in the following chapter (9/9–11) the extra fine to be paid to the assembly was the wergild value of the man killed. The question then arises whether these provisions have been inserted (or revised) at a later date than the first written edition of *GL*. The fact that one reference (3) occurs in a passage found only in the *B*-text (with its presumed earlier origin) would seem to argue against this supposition, in that particular case at least, although the *B*-text as it is preserved may itself have been subject to later influences. What links all instances of the forty-mark fine is the fact that an alternative punishment was explicitly, in case (4), or might originally have been, death, bearing in mind the severity of the crime and the element of betrayal involved (cf. Note to 21/9–12). A gradual move from capital punishment and revenge killing could have been accompanied by the importation of levels of fine from the mainland.

8/26–27. For the most serious crime in a church, killing, the rural dean rather than the priest received the excommunication fine.

8/28–30. Wessén (*SL* IV, 253 notes 12 and 14) considers the first sentence of this paragraph to belong to the preceding paragraph, but this does not seem to be a necessary amendment. The opening sentence seems simply to be an introduction to what immediately follows (an excursus relating to the killing of sanctuary seekers in sanctuary churches). The three churchyards are those of the parish churches of Fardhem (*Farþaim*), Tingstäde (*Þingsteþi*) and Atlingbo (*Atlingabo*), referred to in Chapter 13.

8/31. The OldSwe *kirkiugarþer* denoted both the area immediately surrounding the church and the fence that enclosed it. The area was used both for burials and as a place for preaching, marriages, meetings and trials.

The rectory land or glebe (*prestgarþr*) was the holding from which a priest fed himself (and his family). In some Swedish provincial laws the extent of it is defined in detail. In *GL* it was included within the compass of the sanctuary provided at the three sanctuary churches, in addition to the churchyard. The dimensions of several rectory grounds in Gotland have been preserved in parish records; some had an imposing entrance arch. Although *garþr* was originally a word for an enclosing fence, then the area enclosed (as here and at 13/8), it came to include all the buildings within a farm's fence. Both residential and working buildings lay within the enclosure. These might have included buildings for several families, but in Gotland and mainland provinces, farms were isolated and not situated in villages.

8/32 and footnote. The *A*-text reading given by Pipping is *fangin* 'captured', but as the word has been almost obliterated other readings are possible. Schlyter (*CIG*, 21 note 43) gives *vengin*. The *B*-text reads *vegin* 'killed', which Jacobsen (*GGD*, 40 note 2) points out must be the original reading, both from the context and from the fact that the German and Danish translations both have expressions meaning 'killed'.

8/32–35. The distribution of fines seems to be a repetition of the earlier provision at 8/21–23, as an introduction to additional punishments for assaults in churches and churchyards (cf. *SL* IV, 252 note 10).

Chapter 9: *Af aldra manna friþi*

9/8–9. Jacobsen (*GGD*, 41 note 1) notes that periods of universal sanctity run from morning to morning in contrast to the sanctity in force on holy days described in the previous chapter. That they had no association with the church is clear from the fact that penalties laid down in the previous chapter did not apply. Wessén (*SL* IV, 253 notes 1 and 2 to Chapter 9) suggests that these two periods of sanctity might have coincided with general assemblies, although the wording at 11/10–11 indicates that there was also a separate assembly sanctity. The timing of the first period, a fortnight after Easter, would have placed it at or shortly after the time of the new moon, when small local assemblies might have been held. The timing of the second period of peace, five days after midsummer, places it immediately after the final day for sailing on the levy (*laiþingr*), 29th June (see *GS*, 59 note to 14/8). Several interpretations might be placed on this timing: (1) that it would have provided ten days of protection for the families of those taking part in the levy from opportunists who had not been called up; (2) that if the levy did not get called out at the end of June, or no favourable wind came, the provision would offer protection from armed men who had become frustrated with waiting and might have been looking for trouble; (3) that any killing or assault done while the levy was out would inconvenience and endanger the province proportionally more than at other times. It seems unlikely, despite Wessén's suggestion, that the general assembly would have been timed to coincide with the departure of the levy fleet. In *KrLL* Rb 8 it states that one of the assembly times must be between Walpurgis Night (30th April) and Midsummer Day.

9/10–11. The word *vereldi* 'wergild' does not occur elsewhere in Scandinavian legal sources, but it is related to *wärold*, in *HL*, with the same sense. There are equivalents in other West Germanic languages and the first element of the word is related to OWN *verr* 'man'. The second element is related to OWN *giald*, OldSwe *giäld* 'payment'. Wessén (*SL* IV, 250 note 20) suggests that both *vereldi* and *wärold* were loan words from a West Germanic language. The usual word in Swedish provincial laws is *manböter* and cognates, although *arvabot* is frequent in *ÄVgL*, whereas OWN has *vígsbœtr*. It was a means by which a wronged family could obtain satisfaction from wrongdoers without resorting to a blood feud. Swedish provincial laws demonstrate how the latter was gradually replaced by a system of compensation. Levels of wergild are defined in Chapters 14 and 15.

9/14–16. The additional provision relating to the destruction of property seems particularly to suggest that protection of the vulnerable was intended. This would apply both to times when people were absent at a local assembly and when their able-bodied men were away on the levy.

Chapter 10: *Af varfriþi*

10/2. The spring peace (*varfriþr*) might have had Christian origins. The 'general sowing time' in Gotland was St Urban's day on 25th May (Lithberg and Wessén 1939, 62), so the springtime sanctity lasted from 11th May until 8th June. It coincided with the period during which men might be making ready for the levy, but before the first departure date (see *GS*, 59 note to 14/8). Similar arguments apply to those suggested in Note to 9/8–9 concerning its purpose. Other provincial laws have periods of sanctity in spring: *ÖgL* Bb 22, *UL* Rb 14, *VmL* Rb 24, *SdmL* Rb 11, *HL* Rb 14.

10/5. The Gtn verb *virþa* appears to have two meanings. One is 'seize in payment of a debt, claim [something] from [someone]' and this is the meaning here, at 10/8, 63/9–10 and Addition 9/5–6. The other meaning is 'make a valuation', as at 30/5, 32/8, 40/4 and in similar contexts. Cf. Notes to 30/4–5, 63/9–11 and Addition 9/5–6.

10/6. The word *bondi*, meaning both 'husband' and 'farmer', is the only one in *GL* used of a group of free farmers, apart from *landboi* (cf. Note to 47/6). *Bondar* owned their land and made up the majority of the population of Gotland outside Visby during the thirteenth century.

10/7–8. The word *gield* is commonly used in provincial laws meaning a legal debt or contractual obligation between two parties. The party who was owed the goods could lay a legal claim (he could *lagryþia*), but the debtor also had protection (cf. Amira 1882–95, I, 32–39).

10/9–10. A distinction is drawn here between stock kept for food (*soyþir*) and those for draught (*ortasoyþir*). The latter were not included in the property valuation for the purposes of settling a debt, since their confiscation would affect the ability of a farmer to run his business. Both oxen and horses were used for draught in Gotland.

Chapter 11: Af þingfriþi

11/2. The assembly peace (*þingfriþr*) was directly related to (heathen) cult and market and was ancient in origin. Assembly sanctity as described here applied at the place of the assembly and for its duration. Increased compensation for personal injury during an assembly is otherwise mentioned in *Grágás* I §56 (*LEI* 1, 99) and the severity of breaking the sanctity is stressed in *ÄVgL* Urb §1 (cf. Almquist 1942, 61–62). A three-mark fine, in addition to the usual compensation, applied to insults offered at the assembly (Chapter 39).

11/6. The legal fines (*laga bytr*) for an offence were distinct from the additional fine for breaking the peace. According to Hemmer (1928, 67 and note 1, 74 and note 7, 247–49), *GL* shows a transitional stage in which movement from a system of wholly private compensation to one including community fines was starting to take place. There were still no fines to the crown. Fines were in marks of gold, of silver ($\frac{1}{8}$ mark of gold) or in coin ($\frac{1}{4}$ mark of silver). The original pattern of fines clearly had a three-mark basis and the occasional forty-mark fine lay outside the usual system (cf. Note to 8/25–26).

Hasselberg (1953, 217 note 47) dismisses assumptions made by Wilda (1960, 445–46) and Amira (1882–95, I, 372–73) that community fines were imposed in all cases where the fine was three marks or more, even if it was not stated explicitly. Delin (1926, 258–59) takes a similar view. German medieval laws seem to have included fines to the community either separately imposed, or as part of the total fine (see Hasselberg 1953, 218–26).

11/9. The exclusion of revenge killing (*hemd*) from this provision demonstrates that the substitution of compensation for blood revenge was not complete by this time (cf. Note to Chapter 13; *KL* s. v. *Hämnd*).

11/9–11. The final provision implies that certain assemblies were held during the periods of universal sanctity referred to in Chapter 9. These would possibly have been held after Easter, rather than after midsummer (cf. Notes to 9/8–9, 10/2).

Chapter 12: *Af haimfriþi*

12/2. The concept of home peace (*haim(a)friþr*) seems to have originated in pre-Christian times and to have been connected with a homeowner's 'high-seat'. An attack on a man in his own home was deemed to be a *níðingr*-crime in Norway, punishable by outlawry and loss of all property (cf. *GulL* 178 (*NGL* 1, 66)). Such crimes were considered to be particularly shameful and could not be atoned for by compensation to the victim. An attack in the home was apparently regarded much less seriously in Gotland and mainland Sweden.

12/3–5. The householder received additional compensation for an attack in his home, while the remaining members of the household had to be content with their normal compensation (12/7–11) (see *GGD*, 42 note 6). The total fine payable for an attack on a Gotlandic man in his own home was ninety-six marks in coin (three marks of gold), plus twelve marks (to him) plus twelve marks (to the general assembly). This gives a total of 120 marks in coin, which was three times the usual Swedish wergild of forty marks. This triple fine was usual in Swedish provincial laws in such cases (cf. *UL* Mb 12 §1; *SdmL* Mb 27 pr; *VmL* Mb 11 §1). The equivalent for a non-Gotlandic free man was forty marks plus twelve marks plus twelve marks, giving a total of sixty-four marks in coin. Hemmer (1945,

235) suggests that community fines payable for injury to the house-holder were a later addition to the *laga bytr* (cf. Note to 11/6) payable to all injured parties. As Wessén (*SL* IV, 254 note 2 to Chapter 12) observes, similar additional fines were payable in cases of double adultery (Chapter 21) and selling land without going through the required procedures (Chapter 28). See also Björling (1893, 112–13) and Hemmer (1928, 74 and note 6).

12/7. In *GL*, Schlyter translates *mogi* 'community' as 'hela (gotländska) folket' (all the people (of Gotland)), and it seems always to be used in a similar context to the general assembly, otherwise called *land* (*alt*) 'the (whole) province' or *þing firi alla lyþi* 'assembly of all the people'. Hasselberg (1953, 217 note 48) agrees with Holmbäck (*SL* IV, xciii note 1), however, that it referred only to members of the assembly relevant to the context. The translation 'community' has been chosen to distinguish this usage. Neither *alþing* nor *Gutnal þing* is used in *GL*.

12/9–10. The word *haimsokn* covers only harm caused in a person's house or its immediate neighbourhood (in *GL* and *ÄVgL* Md 9 the house only), the crime thus being a specific form of attack on a person's *haimfriþr*. In the laws of Västergötland, anyone attacked in his or her own home could, without fear of penalty, kill the attacker in self-defence. The extent to which the original intent of the perpetrator had to be criminal in this instance is uncertain. In *ÖgL* Eb 1 §1–4, 6 there has to be criminal intent for the crime to come under the *edsöreslagstiftning* (laws relating to the oath taken by the king to punish certain crimes that threatened the general order); if there were no intent, the milder provincial law applied (cf. Introduction, p. xxxviii). Self-defence killing or wounding applied more widely in *ÖgL* than in *ÄVgL*. *Haimsokn* was originally considered to have been a group crime, but in some provincial laws it was extended to include an attack by one person.

Chapter 13: *Af mandrapi*

In the Early Middle Ages *drap* 'killing' was seen not just as a crime against the person killed, but also as dishonour against the family of that person, one that could only be countered by blood revenge. Immediate right of revenge continued until there was a formal reconciliation, which formed the basis for attempts to replace personal revenge with a legal process. The concept of *drap* originated in circumstances of battle, but later expanded to include all situations resulting in the admitted death of another and incorporated special rules relating to involuntary killing and conspiracy. In *GulL* 156 (*NGL* 1, 61) and the oldest section of this chapter of *GL*, only two possible choices exist for the family of a victim: revenge or compensation. Norwegian provincial laws put a much heavier stress than Swedish laws on revenge, which could be taken for a considerable number of crimes (cf. *GulL* 152, 171 (*NGL* 1, 60–61, 65); *FrostL* prologue 8 (*NGL* 1, 123)). In *GL* there is clearly an attempt to steer the wronged party away from taking revenge and towards a judicial solution. In this way it differs markedly from *SkL* 85–121 (*CISk* I 84–118) (see *SL* IV, 66–69). A number of scholars, principally Wilda (1960, 495) and Amira (1922, 27, 30), suggest that anyone committing a murder or other crime punishable by death automatically made himself an outlaw and thus liable to be killed himself. This view has been disputed by, for instance, Hemmer (1928, 39–45) who sees a clear distinction in later laws between crimes resulting in outlawry, which could be rescinded, and indefensible crimes (OldSwe *orbotæ mal*) for which compensation could not be paid (cf. Wennström 1936, 274). The concept of charging a dead man with a crime that rendered the killing justified and thus not subject to compensation (*obyttr*) does not occur in *GL* (but see Note to 18/16–22) and was no longer in force by the time of *MELL* and *MEStL* (see Wallén 1958, 246–49). To avoid being accused of hidden murder (*morþ*), which was often punishable by death, the killer had to declare the act at the assembly (cf. *UL* Mb 19 §3). In *GL*, however, the term *morþingi* is used only in the provision relating to insults, and in *ÄVgL* the word does not occur at all. See Wessén (*SL* IV, 254–56 and references) for a summary; also Hasselberg (1953, 270–74) and Note to 15/3.

13/4. A number of Swedish provincial laws, although not *GL*, gave the right to the relatives of a murdered man to charge a number of people in connection with the killing (cf. *ÄVgL* Md 1 §1, 3 §2 and notes). It is possible that this arrangement was a means of dividing responsibility in the same way as the responsibility of paying fines was shared between family members (cf. *YVgL* Db 8, where it is relationship with the killer, rather than presence at the crime, that is the deciding factor). In *GL* this law might be reflected in the fact that, when a man who had committed a killing drew up his security circle (*banda*), he was to take his nearest available male relatives with him. From this one could infer that they might be considered to be at risk of accusation as well.

13/7. Of the three listed churches, *Farþaim ok Þingstepi ok Atlingabo*, Farþaim (now Fardhem) lies in the southern riding, Þingstepi (now Tingstede) in the northern and Atlingabo in the middle riding. They were centrally situated in each third and therefore convenient places of asylum. The churches at Atlingabo and Farþaim are mentioned in *Guta saga* (*GLGS*, 66 lines 18–19) as respectively the second and third parish churches to be built in Gotland. Þingstepi is not referred to in this context, either as a place or a parish. Wessén (*SL* IV, 256 note 2) thinks that the forty days for which a killer had to take refuge constituted the period of time during which blood revenge could be taken and that the case was subsequently subject to legal process. Chapter 16/9–11 has a similar provision concerning killing by a slave. The concept of a holy place as a refuge for criminals was at least as old as Graeco-Roman culture and is mentioned in the Pentateuch (cf. Exodus 21 v. 13; Num. 35 vv. 6–8, 11–15; Deut. 4 vv. 41–43, 19 vv.2–4; Olsen 1965, 64–65). Mosaic asylum laws applied only to manslaughter (killing 'unawares' of someone not previously an enemy, as clearly intended in this context) and not to premeditated killing. Medieval asylum rights were linked to church law, but their origin might have predated the introduction of Christianity. The resemblance between provisions in *GL* and the later *VStL* might be as a result of a common concept, rather than a direct influence, but *GL* was certainly the most advanced of the laws of Götaland (cf. *VStL* I 36 §2; Wennström 1946, 188; Hasselberg 1953, 277). While a wrongdoer was in a prescribed holy place, he was under the protection of the church until it was decided whether he was to be handed over for lay justice or be dealt with by the church authorities.

13/7–8. Jacobsen (*GGD*, 43 note 5) considers 'safety and sanctuary' (*helg ok heli*) to be an example of the parallelism common in the *A*-text, the phrase as a whole meaning 'a place of sanctuary'. Since the *B*-text, which it has been argued represents an earlier stage, omits the second half of the phrase, this seems a reasonable assumption. On the other hand, the *B*-text has parallel expressions not found in the *A*-text at 6/18, 25/48 and 50 and at 28/70 (cf. also Notes to 19/33, 21/16–17, 25/48 and 50, 60/6). The word *helg* originally meant 'that which brought luck', but the normal sense of the related Gtn adjective *hailigr* is 'sacred, protected'. It is possible, considering the concept *þinghelgi* in OWN, that *helgi* originally had religious connotations. De Vries (1957, I, §240–42) notes that *heil* means 'whole' and that *heilagr* and *helgi* are related concepts.

13/9–22. The singular provisions in *GL* relating to peace circles may find echoes on the Swedish mainland. There is evidence from a tenth-century runic inscription that certain places in Östergötland had rights of asylum (cf. Holmbäck 1919, 10–11; Delin 1926, 258–64; Nordén 1931, 346–49; von Friesen 1933, 152–53). The procedures for drawing up a peace circle and the area that it could cover are not entirely clear in *GL*, but the boundary presumably lay equidistant between each of the farms included and those bordering them, in the uncultivated land between.

13/13. The sense of the expression *annanveg skogs* in the *A*-text is made clearer in the *B*-text's *annan wegh til schogs* 'on the other side of the wood'.

13/13–15. The clause 'if he has permission from those who own the property' (*en hann loyfi far af þaim sum aign aigu*) refers to the preceding clause: 'and draw it around three farms' (*ok dragi um haimþorp þry*). That is, a killer had to obtain permission from farm owners to include their land in his circle at all, rather than just in respect of its precise limits.

13/16. Jacobsen again translates *kaupung* as 'by' (town), but it seems likely that 'marketplace' was intended (cf. Note to 6/18). The intention behind the prohibition against including an assembly site, marketplace or more than one church in a peace circle was to avoid the possibility of the killer and the family of the victim meeting. Cf. the provision in *SkL* 97 (*CISk* I 96).

13/19–20. The 'period of peace and security that is next after Easter' (*friþr sum nestr ier eptir paskar*) is either that referred to in Chapter 8/6 or, more probably, 9/6–7.

13/22. The' testified safety circle' (*vatubanda*) was a provisional legally witnessed or testified safety circle, later replaced by a more permanent one drawn up during the general period of peace following Easter. Of the provincial laws, this word occurs only in *GL*. Schlyter (*CISG*, 695) thinks that *vatu-* must be the genitive of *vatn* f. 'water', since this form appears in other combinations, but he does not suggest what its meaning might be here. Wessén (*SL* IV, 256–57 note 9) agrees with Kock (1918, 364–68) in finding this derivation unlikely. Kock suggests a relationship with Norwegian *våtta* 'take notice of; suffice', giving *vatubanda* as 'a circle of safety that one took notice of', or which 'sufficed for the time being'. Wessén thinks that a more likely root is a Gtn *vatta* or *vata* f. with a meaning related to OldSwe *vat*, *vatt* f. 'the twelve men collectively swearing an oath; the oath itself' or *vatter*, *vætti* m. 'one of the twelve witness; the witness statement itself'. Cf. *vattum minum* and *vattum sinum* in *ÄVgL* Md 1 §2, 3 pr; Gb 7 and *YVgL* Kkb 3; Tjb 1. The *vatubanda* was therefore a 'witnessed safety circle' since the provisional circle would presumably have been confirmed by witnesses, pending the declaration at an assembly of an official peace circle, although this is not specifically stated. Amira (1913, 238) draws parallels between *GL*'s *vatubanda* and Icelandic *fjǫrbaugsgarðr* 'lesser outlawry', and there are certain similarities between the provisions. In the case of the latter, a miscreant had three years in which to arrange a passage abroad from Iceland, during which time he was confined to an area that offered a limited protection, provided he abided by certain rules (cf. *Grágás* I §§51–53 (*LEI* 1, 92–95)). In *GL*, however, a killer was not truly outlawed while he was in the peace circle, but was given three years in which to offer compensation and close the case. Only if he refused, or left the peace circle, was he outlawed.

13/23–24. The word *atmeli* 'period of a year' does not occur elsewhere in the provincial laws. Schlyter (*CISG*, 51) thinks that it is possibly a contraction of *ater mali*, meaning 'the return of the time', referring to the time elapsing between the same season one year and the next. The concept is similar to that in *iemlangi* (cf. Note to 14/6–7).

13/25. In 1171 Pope Alexander III issued a bull to the Swedish church prescribing penance of a pilgrimage to Rome for patricide, amongst other crimes, but the pilgrimage suggested here seems to have been of a more general nature. From about the end of the seventh century, a pilgrimage was often prescribed as penance by a shriving priest for a grave crime, particularly a killing.

13/28–33. A killer must not attend the same church as the family of his victim, for obvious reasons. Wessén (*SL* IV, 257 note 11) queries whether the mother, daughter and sister mentioned are those of the killer or the victim, but it seems more likely that they are the latter, since the killer is elsewhere enjoined to take his family with him.

13/38–40. The non-Gotlandic man referred to is most likely Swedish, rather than German (cf. *GGD*, 45 note 1; Introduction, pp. xxiv, xxvi–xxvii). Wessén (*SL* IV, 257 note 13) considers that this provision belongs more logically with those in the following chapter at 14/21–24.

13/41 and footnote. The *B*-text has a new chapter (13) here.

13/41–42. Of the clause 'if he can afford it' (*en hann orkar*) Wessén (*SL* IV, 257 note 16) rightly points out that there is no indication of what action was taken if a killer could not afford to pay compensation. It is probable that the killer was permanently subject to blood revenge in this case, but judging by the situation regarding a slave woman committing infanticide, exile seems to be another likely option (2/21–23). The circumstance where he did not wish to pay is covered at the end of the chapter (13/58–65). The *B*-text variant *bella* for *orka* was current as the verb *bälla* in, e.g., the dialect of Jämtland, at least in the early part of the last century (cf. *ÍO* s. v. *bella*[3]).

13/42–43. In the expression 'always leave a year between', Pipping (1904, 3) argues that *ai* here means 'always, each time', rather than 'not'.

13/44. The statement that a person accepting the first offer of compensation is 'without dishonour' (*oskemdr*) is evidence that there had previously been a certain stigma attached to immediate acceptance and that blood money was still a doubtful form of compensation. In *VStL* I 36 §2 a similar phrase, *ane laster unde ane scande* 'without blame and without shame' is used and the initial procedures involved are the same, although the subsequent ones are much simplified (cf. Hasselberg 1953, 274, 276–78). In other provincial laws, the killer has to swear an oath of parity (Swedish *likställighet*). Although in principle the provision of compensation took away the right of revenge, it seems that it was still possible for a wronged party to take revenge: in the laws of Götaland as an alternative to compensation, and in the laws of Svealand provided he paid the king's and province's part of the compensation himself.

13/49–51. The phrase 'then all the people take counsel over the money' (*þa raþin allir lyþir firi fe*) is not unambiguous. Jacobsen (*GGD*, 45 note 5) translates: 'da skal Tingfolket træffe Bestemmelse om Bodens Fordeling' (then the assembly members shall reach an agreement on the division of the fine). Schlyter (*CIG*, 28) and Wessén (*SL* IV 213) both translate: 'råde allt folket över böten' (all the people shall take counsel concerning the fine), without further comment. In Addition 1/17–19, relating to priests, there is a similar phrase, which Schlyter expands as 'D. ä. folket tage boten' (That is, the people take the fine). It seems likely that the same provisions applied in the present case and that the fine rejected by the claimant was nonetheless collected and distributed by agreement. 13/51 and footnote. Once payment was made the defendant was 'free from guilt' (*mandr osakr*), or, in the *B*-text, 'shame' (*mad'r oschemd'r*). Delin (1926, 261–62 note 1) interprets the law in such a way that a killer always had the right to pay the community for his crime with wergild. He considers this to result in the strange concept that the community valued each of its members only at their wergild price, and that any killing could be compensated for simply by a standard payment. He thinks that this was unlikely to have been acceptable to the relatives of a victim and that the right to revenge must still have been retained. On the other hand, wergild must have been a significant deterrent to the farmers of Gotland, amongst whom there were probably none sufficiently rich and powerful for the sum to be inconsequential. Wessén (*SL* IV, 257 note 19) comments that the three-year movement restriction placed on a killer was in itself a form of punishment. He also thinks that Delin has missed the point that in all probability the provisions concerning circles of safety applied only to accidental killings or manslaughter, and not to premeditated murder.

13/54. The 'right of substantiation' (*vitorþ*) was the right in particular to bring forward witnesses to prove one's case, whether as plaintiff or defendant. It was regarded thus rather than as a 'duty', and only one of the parties had this right (see *GGD*, 45 note 8). If a case was more or less clear, the plaintiff had the right of proof, whereas in other cases it was the defendant. The defendant was found guilty if either the plaintiff brought sufficient witness or the defendant failed to do so. By the time most of the Scandinavian provincial laws came into being, this one-sidedness had disappeared. The system, known later as the *edgärdsed*, had led to criminals escaping justice by gathering like-minded witnesses. A papal letter of 1218 from Honorius III to the Archbishop of Lund (*DS* I, 196, no. 176, 28/5/1218) refers to this situation as a 'pestilence that militates against all justice' (cf. *SL* I, xxv–xxxii). In *ÖgL* there is early evidence of oaths being taken by both opposing sides. Gradually, proof through means of a *nämnd* 'body of nominees' replaced the *edgärdsed*, but it was several centuries before this was universal and there were a number of intermediate stages (cf. Note to 4/13–14).

In *GL*, although the old system was clearly still current, *vitorþ* had also come to mean 'right' in a more general way, for example the right to return an unsatisfactory slave (Addition 7/9–10).

13/58–65. This is the only place in *GL* where being outlawed (*friþlaus*) is mentioned as a punishment, although banishment is prescribed for an infanticide who cannot pay her fine. A killer who failed to offer compensation within three years was given a month to pay the full wergild for the victim and, in addition, a further half wergild (twelve marks of silver), divided between the claimant and the community. The same additional penalty applied to anyone breaking the terms of his or her restriction of movement. There was no appeal against these fines and if they were not paid the outlawed person was more or less ostracised from society; revenge taken against him could not in turn be avenged by his relatives. It was, in fact, a means of putting a stop to family feuds and the purpose was to encourage the wrongdoer to offer compensation. *GL* does, however, still seem to recognise the right to self-judgement in certain 'inherited' cases (14/14–20).

13/60. Hasselberg (1953, 252–53 note 26) questions the generally accepted translation of *utretta* here as 'claim, demand', or 'exempt'. The verb is not known from medieval Swedish law texts, or in the sense given by Schlyter elsewhere in Old Swedish. The Middle Low German verb *utrichten*, which occurs in the equivalent passage in *tyGL*, does not have either of these senses, but rather means 'pay, discharge' (cf. 20/43 footnote). The *B*-text reading *wt reyda* suggests a connection to OldSwe *reþa*, which has the same meaning. Hasselberg suggests that this offers a more acceptable grammatical construction in which the verb *dyma* governs all three elements of the judgement, rather than the first and third only. It also follows the general rule in *GL* that wergild could not be demanded, but had to be offered. This suggestion has been followed in the present translation.

13/62. Although the mark was a weight of silver (or gold), the means of paying was more frequently in other goods: homespun, cattle or other property up to the required value. It is difficult to be certain of the value of these in precious metal at any particular time. In *ÖgL* (Db 16 §2; 21) ninety-six ells of ordinary homespun are equivalent to a mark of silver, whereas in *Grágás* (I §78 (*LEI* 1, 126)) six ells of marketable homespun, new and unused, are equivalent to an ounce or *öre* ($\frac{1}{8}$ mark). This implies either that Icelandic homespun was twice as good, or the mark half the value of the Swedish equivalent. The *öre* equivalent of homespun with russet stripes, clearly of better quality, was only five ells. Elsewhere (*Grágás* II §246 (*LEI* 2, 207)) two skins of old tomcats were worth one *öre*, six shorn wether skins were worth an *öre*, and so on. The concept of marketable means of payment is also laid down here. For a cow to satisfy the requirements it had, amongst other things, to be between three and ten years of age, capable of bearing a calf, in milk, horned and free from defects. Jacobsen (*GGD*, 25 note 1) thinks that these and similar conditions, although not stated in *GL*, would have been current throughout Scandinavia.

Chapter 14: *Af lutnum sakum*

As Jacobsen (*GGD*, 46 note 4) remarks, this chapter refers specifically to cases in which wergild was due to be paid and where the killer died before the claim had been fulfilled. In this case the relatives (presumably those who fled to sanctuary with him) inherited the obligation to pay compensation, which was probably already being negotiated on his behalf (13/17–19). Responsibility both to pay and demand compensation was inherited (cf. *YVgL* Add 11 §4, 17–18). As is frequently the case in *GL*, information is limited and the full process involved is not clear. In fact only the first and third paragraphs refer to this situation. The remaining paragraphs belong either with the previous chapter or refer to particular instances of killing (see *SL* IV, 258 note 1).

14/2–5. The process for negotiating a settlement is not stated, but the implication seems to be that relatives of the killer should not be forced to pay more in compensation than they could afford. Furthermore, they were to be given time to accumulate the money required. Again, the relatives of the victim could accept what was offered without shame. The fact that this is stressed on several occasions implies that it was not the customary attitude at the time.

14/6–7. Three offers were to be made within a year and a day (until the day was the same length (*iemlangi*) as the one on which the first offer was made). Jacobsen (*GGD*, 46 note 7) observes that there is a similar expression (*dagh oc iamling*) in *JL1* I §9. This provision differs from that in Chapter 13/41–43 where the killer was given three years to make his three offers of compensation.

14/11–13. This paragraph presents a difficulty, noted by Jacobsen and Wessén, in connection with the sense of the word *bani*. In previous scholarship this has led to translations meaning (1) 'until someone admits to the killing' (Delin 1926, 267; Hadorph *Gothlandz-Laghen*, 11); (2) 'until one [of them] takes in the killer' (Schlyter *CIG*, 29–30; Jacobsen *GGD*, 47) and (3) '. . . one accepts the charge of murder' (Schlyter *CIG*, 379; *CISG* s. v. *bani*). The present translation follows Delin and Hadorph but the alternative, 'admits to being the killer', would retain the usual sense of *bani* as 'killer'. Elsewhere in *GL* there are several instances in which the literal translation of *bani* as 'killer' would result in clumsy English and an alternative has been used. It is worth noting in connection with this provision that no mention is made of extra compensation for killing (or wounding, Note to 19/11–13) by a group of people. This principle, common from Germanic law, distinguishes *GL* from Swedish provincial laws and from *VStL*. The difference is so marked that Westman (1902/1905, 50–51) thinks that *GL* must represent a different legal system in which the family as a whole was not held responsible for an act by one of its members (cf. Delin 1926, 291–94; Gædeken 1934, 105–07; Hasselberg 1953, 198–99; *SL* I, *UL*, 120–21 note 43; *SL* II, *DL*, 42–43 note 32; *SL* III, *SdmL*, 194 note 155; *SL* V, *ÄVgL*, 44 note 47, *YVgL*, 266 note 22).

14/14 and footnote. The first sentence of this paragraph in the *B*-text does not appear in the *A*-text, *tyGL* or *daGL*.

14/14–17. Schlyter (*CIG*, 30 note f) interprets this passage as 'om de som, jämte öfvermage, taga sådant arf, hvarom här är fråga, vilja hämnas å hans vägnar . . .' (if those who (together with the minor) take such an inheritance as is in question here want to take revenge on his behalf . . .). Wessén (*SL* IV, 258 note 9), following Delin (1926, 264), offers the interpretation 'om någon av dem som, jämte omyndig närmaste arvinge, ha att taga del i arvet, vill hämnas på hans vägnar . . .' (if one of those who (together with the minor nearest heir) have the right to take part in the inheritance wish to take revenge on his behalf . . .). There seems to be little material difference between the two interpretations, although Wessén remarks upon it. This passage, together with Addition 1, stresses the right to revenge more than is done elsewhere in *GL* (cf. Note to Chapter 13).

14/14–20. Jacobsen (*GGD*, 47 note 5) cites these sentences as an example of the more expansive style of later provisions in contrast to the earlier, terser style.

14/15. According to most Swedish laws, the age of majority was fifteen years (cf. *YVgL* Add 7 §29; *ÖgL* Eb 15 §1, Vb 15 §3; *UL* Kkb 19 §2, Mb 2 pr, Jb 4 §5; *SdmL* Mb 18 pr; *BjR* 14 §20; *GL* 20 pr; *MELL* Jb 8, Eb 32, Db (II) 13, Sb (I) 17 pr; *MEStL* Db (II) 10, Sb (I) 19; *KrLL* Jb 8 §1). On the other hand, in *SdmL* Kkb 11 pr, it seems that children over the age of twelve, but who had not received their inheritance, were treated differently in some respects from those who were younger. Minors (and in certain circumstances women) had considerable protection from the full force of the law in many cases: they could not be outlawed or hanged and were subject to lower fines in cases of theft (cf. *KL* s. v. *Myndighedsalder*; *Úmagi*). See also Note to 20/6–7.

14/18–20. The relatives of a minor who was claiming compensation had to pursue his portion of the wergild, as well as their own, once the killer was able to pay the claim (i.e. after a year had passed) (see *GGD*, 47 note 6).

14/22–24. This must refer to a non-Gotlander having property in Gotland of sufficient value to pay the wergild (cf. Wessén *SL* IV, 259 note 12).

14/25. Killing by a minor was valued at a half of the standard wergild, the same as for death caused by a dumb animal (Chapter 17). Contrast this with damage by fire (Chapter 51) where payment was made by the responsible adult, presumably at the full price.

14/27. 'Alive in the womb' (*quikt i quiþi*) was a standard expression, indicating that a woman was pregnant with a live foetus.

14/33–34. A pregnant woman was valued at 1½ standard wergilds. It is implicit that a Gotlandic woman is referred to here.

Chapter 15: *Af vereldi manna*

15/2–6. As in several other provincial laws (*ÄVgL* Äb 22, *JL1* III §12) one mark of gold is equivalent to eight marks of silver in *GL*. This is not stated explicitly, but may be inferred from parallels between 15/2–6, 16/2–4 and 22/13–19, where it is clear that twelve marks of silver are equivalent to 1½ marks of gold (half the wergild of a Gotlander). Here marks of gold, of silver and in coin are mentioned in the same context and this is the first instance in the text of the qualification *markr penninga*, clearly inserted to avoid confusion in relation to the slave's wergild, since even 4½ marks of silver would be less than the wergild of a non-Gotlander.

15/3. The Gtn phrase *at dauþum drepin* (perhaps equivalent to 'done to death') implies that the verb *drepa* might not mean 'kill' in every instance. The noun *döþsdrap*, 'killing', occurs in *UL* Mb 2 §1, *SdmL* Mb 2 §1, *VmL* Mb 2 §1, Tjb 15, *HL* Kgb 10, Mb 10, *BjR* 14 §16 (*CIS* VI, 123 note 6) and *MELL* Rb 21 §2. Hellquist (1980) notes that the original sense of the verb in other Germanic languages was 'hit, strike, come up against'. He suggests that the uniquely Scandinavian meaning 'kill' developed from the original sense either directly, or via a form with a now lost prefix. Schlyter (*CISG* s. v. *Dræpa*) gives 'strike' as the first meaning and cites this instance in *GL* and those in *SdmL* and *VmL*. The Danish translation (*daGL*) reads *slagin tiil dödz* here.

15/4. The lower level of wergild for non-Gotlanders should be considered alongside the principle stated in *ÄVgL* Tjb 12 §2: *Þylik lagh ok ræt, sum utlænskir mæn göra os, þylikæn vilium vir þæm göræ* 'The same law and right, which foreign men render to us, the same would we wish to render to them'. Gotlanders could not therefore expect their own higher levels of wergild in Sweden.

15/6–12. There seems to be an ambiguity over the wergild to be paid for a non-Gotlandic woman married to a Gotlandic man. The expression *at vereldi sinu* 'her wergild' most probably refers to the ten silver marks she would have been worth if unmarried, but the addition of *fullu*, which occurs only in the *A*-text, could mean that three marks of gold is intended, under the assumption that marriage had given the woman the status of a Gotlander. The principle that the male partner in a marriage could raise the status of his wife, but not vice versa, is common. On the other hand, the fact that a Gotlandic woman married a non-Gotlander did not prejudice her own status, although her children were treated as non-Gotlandic. The equal rating of men and women so far as compensation is concerned corresponds to concepts of gender equality elsewhere in Scandinavia, although these did not extend as far as laws of inheritance (cf. *SL* IV, 259 notes 3 and 4).

Chapter 16: *Af banduvereldi*

16/2–4. The wergild payable for a man killed within his peace circle (*banduvereldi*) was, for both Gotlander and non-Gotlander, half that normally payable. For a slave, only six *öre* in coin was payable. This was one-sixth of the normal wergild payable (4½ marks in coin, i.e. 36 *öre*). In respect of the element *banda* in *banduvereldi*

Pipping (*GLGS*, *Ordbok*, 9) refers to OWN *vébǫnd* n. pl. 'ropes surrounding the assembly or court'. The concept in *GL* is again of a prescribed area. Details of how the assembly area was set up and the fines for trespass within it are listed in *GulL* 91 (*NGL* 1, 44–45). The fines were: three marks to the king, twelve *öre* to a jarl, six to a baron, three to a *hauldr* (landowner of a class slightly higher than that of a freeman), 1½ to a freeman, one to the son of a freedman and to a freedman (cf. *FrostL* I 2 (*NGL* 1, 127–28); *MLLL* III, 2 (*NGL* 2, 34–35)).

16/5–8. Jacobsen (*GGD*, 49 note 4) remarks that this clause is obscure. The wergild payment was frequently used as a unit of fine; half the standard wergild was a common level. Jacobsen finds Schlyter's interpretation (that compensation was to be ten marks in coin for all occasions on which full wergild would normally have been paid) unsatisfactory, as the last phrase would then be misleading. Wessén agrees with this objection and notes that the rubric *Af banduvereldi* only refers to the first paragraph of the chapter. He thinks that the next paragraph refers to maiming (*lastr* or *lestr*) in general and that the purpose was to state that in all cases where compensation was based on a proportion of the wergild for a Gotlander, the same proportion applied for a non-Gotlander (he cites one quarter for a hand as an example). He points out that it is not clear what action was taken in cases where the fine in relation to a Gotlander was two marks or less of silver, i.e. one twelfth or less of the wergild. If maiming did not occur, all (*allir*) were treated equally. The paragraph should form the end of Chapter 19 (cf. 19/47–61; *SL* IV, 260 note 4; Hasselberg 1953, 218 and references).

16/6 and footnote. The *B*-text reading seems to be the correct one here.

16/9–13, 13–17. If the slave in question had been killed or had fled then half the wergild was to be paid, both for a Gotlander and a non-Gotlander. This provision places a value on the slave himself of three marks of silver (twelve marks in coin), since nine or two marks of silver respectively were to be paid if he could be handed over. This valuation must be compared with the wergild for a slave of 4½ marks in coin, only three-eighths of that amount.

16/17–18. The oath was obviously to be taken in both the stated cases.

16/23–26. This paragraph is not directly relevant to the chapter rubric. It makes clear that a slave usually had a limited period of slavery, after which he was publicly granted his freedom. The witness borne by the parishioners in this case was for use in the future (i.e. that the slave had been freed on such a date) rather than in connection with a past event or a person's truthfulness. The witnesses were acting in a more or less official capacity (cf. Notes to 2/15, 3/ 36–38, 19/6–8).

Chapter 17: *Af osoyþum*

The prefix *o-* in *osoyþr*, literally 'a bad creature', is not the usual negation, but pejorative, as in Swedish *otyg* 'witchcraft, nuisance' (cf. Note to 39/8). For related provisions, albeit less detailed, see *SkL* 102, 105 (*CISk* I 100, 103).

17/2. The word *fastr* in the sense 'entire, not castrated' is still used in Gotland (see *GO* s. v. *fast*). Jacobsen (*GGD*, 50 note 7) notes that, at the time she wrote, the word was used with this meaning in Jutland. The normal OldSwe word for 'castrated' is *snopr*, from a verb meaning originally 'insult'.

17/5–6. The Gtn word *staurgulf* originally seems to have denoted the central space between the rows of supporting columns of a hall, as opposed to the aisles between these columns and the walls of a building. The word could also be used to denote the space between two of the columns, making room for a place to sit or a bed, the best being the 'high seat' (OWN *stafgólf*) (cf. *KL* s. v. *Skåle*). In *GL* the meaning is either the space between a pair of uprights in a fence, or else the pair of uprights themselves (cf. *CIG*, 33, 66; *GGD*, 50 note 9, 85 note 4; *SL* IV, 261 note 3 to Chapter 17). The former sense is still current in Gotland, with various dialect forms (see *GO* s. v. *stör*). Wennström (1936, 357–61) argues that in the context of *GL* the sense of *staurgulf* must be 'the space between a pair of uprights'. A horse, certainly, would not be tied up to a pair of uprights, but rather to a horizontal rail between them. In provisions relating to damage to fences *staurgulf* denotes a section of fencing between uprights (26/49).

17/6–7. Wessén (*SL* IV, 261 note 3 to Chapter 17) suggests that *ok fiugur stig* 'and four paces' could be an error for *eþa fiugur stig* 'or four paces', making the inference that the average distance between the uprights in a fence was about a stride (one metre) and if no such fence existed, four strides would give the same safety margin. This would certainly be a reasonable practical assumption and would merely be another example of parallelisms common in

GL. The distance between supports in a lawful fence in *FrostL* XIII
21 (*NGL* 1, 246) is three ells, about 1.5 metres.

17/7–9. Horses were and are handled mainly from their left (or near) side.
The owner was thus only responsible for his horse's reactions to the
normal actions of tacking up and mounting when performed by others.

17/9. The word *kleti* for 'food store' occurs only here in Scandinavian
sources. Säve (*GU*, xxx–xxxi) considers it most likely to have been
introduced to Gutnish by Swedes resident in Estonia. He assumes
that they borrowed the word, not from the Finnish-speaking Esto-
nians, but from Lithuanian or Latvian speakers and cites the forms
klêti in Lithuanian and *klêts* in Latvian, meaning 'grain store'. The
word might, however, be an error for *klefi*, for which there is an
OWN equivalent with a similar sense.

17/17–19. Although half the wergild was paid for a Gotlander killed
by an animal (17/2–4 and 17/14–16), as if the creature were a
minor, only one third was paid for a non-Gotlander (i.e. 3⅓ rather
than five marks of silver). This discrepancy seems unusual in that
the proportion of wergild payable for injury to a non-Gotlander
was commonly the same as for a Gotlander (cf. Note to 16/5–8). In
respect of wounds and maiming by animals, the proportion seems
to have been the same for both classes of person, however, at one
third of the ordinary rate (cf. 17/25).

17/19–21. Compensation demanded for death or injury that was to
be pursued as a normal debt and could not justify revenge was
called *krafarvereldi*. Wessén (*SL* IV, 261 note 10) points out that
the word is used both for killing and for maiming, implying that a
proportion of the wergild was paid for injury (cf. Note to 16/5–8).

17/23. The word *gieldeti* 'debt' appears only in *GL* and seems to
refer to the responsibility for a debt (see Lidén 1911, 273–77).

Chapter 18: *Ber maþr kuna*

The title strictly refers only to the first part of the chapter, and then
only to pregnant women who lose their children as a result. The
content of the second half is, however, related in that it deals with
the proper care of small children.

18/3. Half the standard wergild seems to have been the usual amount
payable for an unborn child (cf. 2/21, 14/32). The amount would
possibly have varied depending on whether the father was a Gotlander
or not, although this is not stated. What is also not specifically

stated is the level of wergild for a minor (under fifteen), although it seems that the full fine was paid from the time that they were born (18/16). Minors committing crimes, however, sometimes paid half the normal fine (cf. 14/25, 59/6).

18/5. The phrase 'two witnesses' is the first use in the text of *vitni* without qualification referring to a personal witness as opposed to an abstract concept. Witnesses might, but did not need to be, eye-witnesses. In this case they were named as those who were to be called by a woman immediately after she had been the victim of an attack, in order to declare that she was telling the truth.

18/5–6. The verb *skirskuta* (OWN *skírskota* 'appeal', literally *skuta* 'wipe away' plus *skir* 'clean') is used reflexively in *GL* in the context of either a plaintiff or defendant calling witnesses, as opposed to an earlier usage in the context of a defendant attempting to prove innocence (cf. *GGD*, 52 note 7; *SL* IV, 262 note 4 to Chapter 18 and references, 272 note 2 to Chapter 22). The verb was common in Scandinavian laws (cf. *ÖgL* Eb 26; *SL* I, *ÖgL*, 51 note 39; *SdmL* Kgb 6 pr; *SL* III, *SdmL*, 58 note 28). It is also used in *GulL* 37, 40, 266 (*NGL* 1, 22–24, 24, 86–88) with the preposition *undir* to indicate the formal calling of witnesses.

18/8. This is the second occasion in *GL* on which two female witnesses are mentioned. As the evidence they were to give was in respect of a miscarriage, it seems likely that they were the same witnesses that the woman would have called to witness a birth (cf. Note to 2/5).

18/10. It is also significant that the expression *þiauþa aiþr* 'person oath' rather than *manna aiþr* is used of the six witnesses confirming the woman's statement that the child was alive before the attack. This seems to imply that some at least of those witnesses could be female. These six oath-takers were clearly neither the same as the two witnesses referred to at 18/5, nor the two female witnesses. A similar distinction is drawn in the case of a woman falling pregnant to a rapist (see 22/23–26).

18/14–15. Jacobsen (*GGD*, 53 note 4) takes *vaþi* 'by misadventure' as meaning a deliberate act, but with unforeseen consequences, rather than an unintentional, accidental one, and the full compensation payable justifies this assumption. Swedish provincial laws clearly differentiate between *vådaverk* and *viljaverk*: the latter were acts of deliberate malice and the former more or less unintentional, although culpable. There is no mention of the former in *GL*, although reduced fines for killing by a minor (14/25) or a dumb animal (17/ 2–4; 17/14–16; 17/17–19) might be considered to reflect a view of these acts as accidental. Amira (1882–95, I, 711) regards the lack of provisions for accidental acts as evidence that *GL*, as preserved, is incomplete (cf. Introduction, pp. xxii–xxv).

18/15–16. 'He is to pay the full wergild' (*þa bytir hann vereldi fullu*). It appears from this that the half wergild was only applicable in certain cases and that if the child itself were subject to (albeit unintentional) violence it would be apportioned full compensation, provided that the mother had taken all necessary precautions.

18/16–22. The concept of a dead person as *obyttr* 'not subject to compensation' usually applied in cases in which they could be said to have committed a crime warranting their death (cf. Note to Chapter 13). In this instance, however, it is the mother who forfeits her right to a claim through her own negligence.

Chapter 19: *Af sarum*

Apart from the section on inheritance, this is the most complex section of *GL*. There are a certain number of inconsistencies, which are noted below, but otherwise *GL* is notable for the variety of levels of compensation and the absence of an explicit concept of OldSwe *full sar* or *fullsæri* (a major wound requiring treatment and subject to full, i.e. maximum, compensation). This concept appears in several Swedish provincial laws as well as in *VStL* and in Norwegian laws (cf. *ÄVgL* Sb 1; *GulL* 195 (*NGL* 1, 69–70)). There is, however, an implicit equivalent in *GL*, see following Note. Appendix D (ii) tabulates the various fines exacted for different acts of wounding.

19/2–6. The measurement of a *mundr* (a thumb's width or notional inch (2.54 cm)) for the depth of a 'full wound' is used in *VStL* I 13 §1. It is not absolutely clear how the calculation of compensation was made, but evidently two dimensions (depth and length) of each wound were taken into account and compensation paid in respect of the total, up to a maximum of eight marks in coin for sixteen *mundr* (or more) of wound at least a nail's breadth in depth. If the depth was less than a nail's breadth, but treatment was still needed, the maximum fine was four marks (cf. *GGD*, 54 note 2; *SL* IV, 262 note 2; Hasselberg 1953, 285–86). An analysis of fines that would have been payable based on the sum, as opposed to the product, of the two dimensions makes it seem more likely that the former would have been used. According to this formula only the very largest and deepest wounds would lie outside the eight-mark range and these would probably have resulted in permanent disability or been fatal, in which case other compensation provisions would apply. Eight marks in coin (two marks of silver) were equivalent to one twelfth of the wergild for a Gotlander. This was also the fine for any knife wound and for injuries resulting in four bone fragments of a certain size having to be removed (see Notes to 19/15–16, 19/36–38).

19/5. The expression 'half less' (*halfu minna*) means simply a half (see also 19/25, 23/31, 59/6, Addition 2/8).

19/6–8. The choice of witnesses on this occasion, two *raþmenn* 'magistrates' and a *lanzdomeri* 'district judge', suggests that they were official witnesses to a legal process (cf. Notes to 2/15, 3/36–38, 16/23–26).

19/7. The hundreds (*hunderi*, equivalent to *hundaren* in Svealand or *härad* in Götaland) were entities for legal, defence and military activities, but *Guta saga*, where the levy is described, does not use the word and *GL* uses it only in respect of the *hunderis þing* as a legal entity. The term *raþmaþr* for a local judge at a *hunderis þing* is unique to Gotland (cf. *GGD*, 91 note 7; 31/3; Addition 8/ 51–54). The structure of the legislature and judiciary is further described in the Introduction, pp. xxvii–xxx.

19/9. As Wessén (*SL* IV, 262 notes 3 and 4) indicates, officials were only asked to bear witness to the nature and extent of the wound itself. The perpetrator was charged by the injured party and his peers.

19/11–13. The number of assailants did not affect the compensation payable, which depended on the wounds themselves (cf. Note to 14/11–13).

19/15–16. The maximum fine was always payable for knife-wounds. Several Swedish provincial laws prescribe increased fines for knife injuries (cf. *SL* IV, 262 note 7). Presumably the extent of the wound was in this case irrelevant, as in the case of a wound involving internal organs (*hulseri*).

19/16–17. The fine for throwing a stone at someone and wounding them was three marks in coin, equivalent to the fine for a wound of about six *mundr*.

19/18. 'A blow which does not cause blood to be spilt' (*lukahagg*). Schlyter (*CIG*, 278 s. v. *lukahagg*) suggests that the first element is the same as OWN *lúka* 'flat of the hand'. In that case the meaning would be a slap, but this hardly seems to apply to this provision. The provision is missing from *tyGL* and *daGL* (cf. *SL* IV, 262 note 9).

19/23. The word *litvan* 'facial defect' is known only from *GL*. Although Rydqvist (1850–83, V, 243–44, VI, 272), following Hadorph (*Gothlandz-Laghen*, 16), has suggested *likvan* 'bodily disfigurement', Tamm (1883–84, 311) in his review of Rydqvist's work considers that the form in the *A*-text can stand and that it refers to facial disfigurement, the element *lit* occurring in several words relating to the face (cf. ModSwe *anlete* 'countenance'). Wessén takes the first element as *litr* m. 'colour, appearance and the second element as a noun derived from OWN adjective *vanr* 'lacking'. The extra compensation to be paid for such disfigurement is laid down at the end of the provision. If no healing took place, the full two marks of silver was paid for a nose or lip and half that for an ear.

19/25–30. The criteria given here for judging the severity of a facial disfigurement, whether it could be seen across the road or across the assembly and whether it could be masked by a hat or hood, are similar to those in several Swedish provincial laws, the Old Danish laws and *VStL* (cf. *VmL* Mb 21 §1; *SdmL* Mb 5 pr; *SkL* 95 (*CISk* I 94); *JL1* III §29; *VStL* I 15 §6–7).

19/30. The phrase 'and wound compensation in addition' (*ok þau sara bytr*), indicating that compensation for the initial wound was additional, applies to both the preceding criteria (cf. *VStL* I 15 §§6–7; *SdmL* Mb 5 pr).

19/33. The Gutnish text has *himin eþa hinna* for 'membrane'. Schlyter (*CIG*, 379; *CISG*, 274) considers *himin* 'membrane' to be a scribal error, corrected by the scribe to *eþa hinna*, but Pipping (*GLGS*, 24 note 2) and Wessén (*SL* IV, 263 note 14) argue that the two expressions supplement each other. Cf. the parallelisms noted by Pipping at *GLGS*, 58 line 17 and 68 line 5 (in *Guta saga*), which are also taken by Schlyter (*CISG*, 415 and 273) to be scribal amendments, and the Notes to 13/7–8, 21/16–17, 60/6. There are further examples from *B*-text at 6/18, 25/48, 25/50 and 28/70.

19/35–36. The singular method of measuring the size of a bone fragment by dropping it into a bowl and hearing if it rang (*i skalu skieldr*), seems to have been common in Scandinavia. It also occurs in the Frisian laws (see *SL* IV, 263 note 15). Similar regulations appear in *ÖgL* Vb 19, *Eriks SjL1* Text 1 II §39, *GulL* 185 (*NGL* 1, 67–68) and *FrostL* IV 49 (*NGL* 1, 172). These last two read respectively *Eyri firi bein hvert er ór leysir, ef skellr i skalom* and *er bein leysir or sári manns, þó at alllítit se oc skellr á skilldi, þá scal eyrer uppi.* Larson (1935, 139 and note 11) translates the first as 'an *öre* for every [bit of] bone that has to be removed if the silver rings in the scales' and interprets this as meaning that the 'money is ready for payment'. This, however, seems to be a misunderstanding, since the word 'silver' does not appear in the original text. Similarly, in *FrostL*, Larson (1935, 277 and note 11) translates *oc skellr á skilldi* as 'and [the coins] rattle on the shield' with a footnote that this means that 'the money is ready for payment'. Again, this does not seem to be the correct interpretation. Both instances seem to refer to the bones themselves rattling in a receptacle as a measure of their size.

19/37. The form *eln* 'ell' is recorded on a standard (half) ell measure found at the church at Stånga, a parish in the southeast of Gotland: *hitta ier ret gota eln* 'this is the true ell of Gotland'. The length of an ell varied from time to time and place to place, but the ell at Stånga is about 55.36 cm. Two further ell measures from the same part of Gotland, at Havdhem and at Hemse Church, are similar in length, but there is evidence of a shorter ell (52.1 cm) in use in the twelfth century (see Jansson 1936, 44). In 1863 the last recorded Swedish ell measured 59.38 cm (about 23⅓ inches). In England an ell was 114.3 cm (45 inches), approximately double that measurement.

19/36–38. This stipulation is obscure and may be corrupt. There is no record elsewhere of a similar method of measuring larger bone shards than those in the previous sentence. The German translation, *tyGL*, provides the interpretation that the shards had to be so large that with an ell-long thread attached, they could be thrown over a five-ell (2.75 metre) high roof beam. Säve (*GU*, xxx) suggests that *ri* 'pillar' or 'beam' is a loan from Estonian, transmitted to Gotland by the Swedish population of Estonia's western seaboard and islands. See *SL* IV, 263 note 16 and references.

19/38–40. Wessén (*SL* IV, 263 note 17) points out that *iiii markum penninga* equates to a mark of silver and this is the fine quoted in *daGL*. In *tyGL*, which mistakenly gives one mark in coin as the fine for a finger, it states that a thumb is equal to all the other fingers, instead of counting it as equivalent to two fingers. If the fingers of both hands are included, valued at one mark in coin each, the total would be eight marks in coin, or two marks of silver as in *GL*. Loss of a thumb was thus valued at one third of a hand (19/48–49), as opposed to a half in the majority of Swedish provincial laws (cf. *ÄVgL* Sb 4; *ÖgL* Vb 18 pr).

19/43–47 and footnotes. Pipping (1904, 10–12) provides detailed commentary on these lines. The thrust of his argument is that Schlyter (*CIG*, 38–39 and notes) has made an error in saying that the Gtn for 'toe' is *ta* (written in error as *þa* on occasions). Pipping argues that neither is correct and that *tia* is the correct form. By a careful comparison of the *A*- and *B*-texts, Pipping shows convincingly that the scribe of the former has omitted two separate phrases, which are found in the latter (and so identified in this translation), by skipping from one occurrence of an abbreviation of *marcum* to the next. This supposition, supported by Wessén, removes any objection to the word *ok* 'also' in line 46, since the fines concerned are both two marks of silver (cf. *GGD*, 56 note 9; *SL* IV, 263 notes 20 and 22). It also renders unnecessary Schlyter's change of the preceding *þa* to *ta* in the disputed sense 'toe' and replaces the emendation that gave rise to it. The *B*-text form *thia* follows a practice common in that manuscript of writing *th* for *t* as well as for *þ*. Wessén points out additionally that although loss of use of a finger was considered as serious as its being cut off, only one third of the compensation was paid for disablement of a hand or foot as for its complete loss, for which one quarter of a wergild was due (cf. *SL* IV, 263 notes 20 and 23).

19/46. Jacobsen (*GGD*, 56 note 8) points out the implied alliteration in *þan hels eþa (h)nakka* 'the heel or neck' and that this could date the phrase to the period prior to the loss of the initial *h* in the latter, i.e. *c.*1100. Schlyter (*CISG* s. v. *hæl*) points out that earlier translations mistakenly take *hels* to mean 'throat', whereas it is the genitive of *hel*.

19/47–49. The six marks of silver that were payable for loss of hand, foot or eye was one quarter of a wergild, in contrast to the one half that was stipulated in *VStL* (I 24 §1, 28 §1, 18). The reduced level has parallels in German regional laws (cf. Brunner 1906–28, II, 823 note 77; Wilda 1960, 762–63; Hasselberg 1953, 305 note 12 and references; Notes to 16/5–8 and 17/19–21).

19/49. The sense 'assault' for the verb *laika*, alongside 'play', is common in other Scandinavian languages, the most infamous example being *Håtunaleken* in 1306, when King Birger was imprisoned by his brothers at the estate in Håtuna (cf. *GGD*, 57 note 1).

19/49–52. Wessén (*SL* IV, 263 note 25) points out that the fine for the loss of two hands, feet or eyes is ambiguous. The issue seems to be whether the fine is twelve marks for the two (i.e. simply twice the fine for one) or twelve marks each, giving the equivalent of a wergild for the loss of both hands, both feet or both eyes in one attack. Wessén thinks that the latter is the more likely, since otherwise there would have been no need to differentiate between this situation and that relating to the loss of one hand, foot or eye.

19/58. Ólafur Halldórsson (1990, 115, 121–22, 130) notes that, in a series of riddles in a sixteenth-century Icelandic manuscript, *uígnyrum*, from *vígnýra* n., means 'testicle' and compares this to *vigniauri* m. 'testicle' in *GL*. He comments that these are the only instances of this word, but that *nýra* is recorded by Ivar Aasen in his *Norsk ordbog* in the sense 'testicle', as is *hvítanýra* in Faeroese, particularly of rams and bulls. There is a single instance in Icelandic of *nýra*, in *Mábilar rímur*, where the sense is obviously 'testicle'.

19/58–61. The fine for the removal of both testicles (i.e. castration) is twelve marks of silver (half a wergild) and it is only if the penis is cut off that the fine rises to ¾ wergild. For the crime of castration *ÄVgL* Sb 4 §6 sets nine marks of silver for the disfigurement and nine for the wound, two wergilds in total (as were payable for a killing), while in *YVgL* Urb 2 §§7, 16 the act is regarded as a despicable act (*niþings værk*) and the fine is fifty-four marks of silver or six wergilds. In *ÖgL* Vb 5, the crime is considered to be the 'most serious' wound (as it is in the laws of Svealand) punishable with a forty-mark fine in coin for the wound and another forty for the disfigurement. This amount is doubled by the addition of forty marks for an unborn son and forty for an unborn daughter, giving a total of 160 marks in coin or four wergilds. The laws of Svealand fall into two groups: *UL* Mb 30 pr and *HL* Mb 15 pr give self-judgement, and failure to pay results in the perpetrator losing both hands and helpers one hand as a retaliatory punishment. *SdmL*, *DL*, *VmL* follow *ÖgL*, with slight variations (see *SL* IV, 263 note 27). The relatively lenient fine stipulated in *GL* might suggest that this provision belonged to an early form of the law.

19/63. The verb *tielga* (here 'split') has led to discussion and two translations: (1) 'cut, score', related to OWN *telgia* (Schlyter (*CIG*, glossary) and Kock (Låle II, 348)) and (2) 'split', related to OWN *tialga* (Noreen 1897, 26; 1904, §231 note). From the context, relating to damage to bones, this latter seems to be preferable. Note that the present translation, which refers to a 'smaller bone', follows all previous editors, but is not explicit in the text.

19/67. The definition of *onytr* 'useless' must be related to the use of sword and sickle as defined at 19/43 (see *SL* IV, 264 note 31).

19/69–70. The right (as well as the obligation) of proof fell to a defendant if there was no visible damage. The clause 'the defendant has the right to substantiate his denial' (*hafi þan vitorþ sum vers*), which occurs three times more, was a standard legal expression (see *GGD*, 58 note 4).

19/72. Swearing an oath on one's own behalf was unusual and an exception to the procedure set out at the start of the chapter (see *SL* IV, 264 note 34). It is the only instance of *ainsyri* 'self-witness' in *GL* although there are a number of occasions on which only one person has to give witness: a priest supporting a woman's claim to have been shriven of infanticide (2/10–11), a man stating that he had witnessed a woman's cry of 'rape' (22/5), a woman confirming that all the laces on her clothing had been restored (23/14–15), someone whose property has been stolen confirming how much had been taken (Addition 8/7–9).

19/73–79. Provisions relating to deafness caused by blows do not occur in Swedish provincial laws, but equivalents are to be found in *VStL* I 15 §§1–4.

19/75. This is the only reference to fowl in *GL*. In contrast to geese, they are mentioned infrequently in provincial laws, although a limit of a cockerel and two hens is set in *DL* Tjb 17.

19/77. A deleted *wi* preceding the phrase *siex manna aiþi* 'six-man oath' appears to be an example of the scribe deciding to substitute the word *siex*, having already written the Roman numeral. In another case (31/4), he has not noticed his error and has not deleted the latter. Pipping (1901a, 95 note 1) argues that the *A*-text possibly originally had Roman numerals throughout for numbers greater than one.

19/80–86 and footnote. Further differences in fines laid down between the *A*- and *B*-texts are in evidence here. The fine for loss of an ear is two marks of silver in all manuscripts of *GL* apart from B 64, and that for damage to an ear without its loss is one mark in the *B*-text and in *daGL*. It is not clear why eyeteeth are singled out for mention, since the fine for them was the same as for other teeth in the same jaw. It is possible that there was a time when they were valued differently. The *B*-text, incidentally, lacks the differentiation found in the A-text (and *tyGL*) with regard to upper and lower teeth. See also Addition 4/3–5.

19/90–91. The concept of a non-verbal insult (*þunki*) occurs several times in *GL*, even if the word itself is not used in every instance. Apart from throwing ale in someone's face, insults included manhandling a person riding or walking on the highway (19/128), making a minor attack on a man's beard or hair (19/100–02), damaging a man's inner clothing (19/110), knocking the clasp of a woman's clothing to the ground or displacing her clothing slightly (23/9–10, 23/15–17), grasping her elbow or knee (23/22, 23/25–26). The fine was eight *örtugar* in each case. Carrying off wood from another man's forest (26/38–46), breaking his fence (26/48–49) or taking his horse in error, leaving your own instead (35/10–12) incurred the same penalty, which gives an insight into the importance that was attached to these non-verbal insults (cf. *SL* IV, 264 note 38). Wennström (1936, 57 notes 66 and 67; 1940, 310–12) compares *þunki* in *GL* with OldSwe *þokki*, which he relates to the OldSwe verb *þykkia* 'think' (see *CISG* s. v. *þokka bot*, *þokki*).

19/91. *Ertaug* was the Gtn equivalent of OldSwe *örtugh* (ModSwe *örtug*). As a weight it was recorded from Viking times as $\frac{1}{24}$ mark or $\frac{1}{3}$ *öre*. The mark, *öre* and *örtug* had the same relationship all over Scandinavia, but the number of pennies (i.e. coin) to an *örtug*, and thus to a mark, was variable over region and time. A fine of eight *örtugar* is common in *GL*, although fines of a half, one, four and five also occur. Eight *örtugar* were equivalent to $\frac{1}{3}$ mark in weight or coin (see *SL* IV, 264 notes 38 and 44). This is confirmed by the fact that the sum is greater than two *öre* (¼ mark, cf. fines for damage to clothing, 19/110) and less than ½ mark (cf. fine for striking off a woman's buckle, 23/9–10). See Appendix C for further details of the monetary system in Gotland.

19/92–94. It is worth noting that admitting to one blow laid one open to an accusation of up to three further blows and gave the initiative to the plaintiff, whereas if one did not admit to an attack, one had the right to present one's defence.

19/97–98. From the context, *lukahagg* is clearly not a blow with the flat of the hand (cf. Note to 19/18), but presumably any blow that did not draw blood, although it might in other cases leave the person disabled (cf. *GGD*, 59 note 6; *SL* IV, 264 note 40).

19/98–99. The words *Pet iru lag guta* 'That is the law of the Gotlanders' must previously have signalled the end of a major section of the law. The *B*-text has the singular of the verb (*ier*), which seems to be more correct grammatically after *þet*.

19/100 and footnote. The *B*-text has a new chapter (20) at this point.

19/100–08 and footnotes. It is possible that the stringent laws against pulling out hair were related to a belief that magic could be wrought using hair (cf. *BorgL* I 16 (*NGL* 1, 350–51)). Hair and nails were considered to have magic properties as they grew visibly, and a bald person was regarded as a possible subject of black magic (cf. de Vries 1957, I, §202 and §239). Note the additional references to pulling hair at 8/11, 8/38 and 41, 11/4, 19/87 and 62/3–5, and the variations in the *B*-text given in Addition 5.

19/101–05. The detailed compensation relating to hair-pulling is reflected only in *VStL* I 15 and not in Swedish provincial laws.

19/105–08. See Note to Addition 5/2–5.

19/109 and footnote. The *B*-text has a new chapter (21) at this point.

The *yfirklepi* 'outer garments' were a cloak or cape, probably the same as the *gangklepi* 'walking-clothes' referred to at 20/108 and 20/113–14.

19/110. Although Pipping (*GLGS, Ordbok*, 46) translates *kurtil* 'kirtle' as 'kjortel, underklädning' (kirtle, underclothing), it more properly referred to a gown worn over a *likvari* 'undergarment', but under any cloak or outer garment, the equivalent of modern 'indoor clothing' (cf. Falk 1919, 145).

Bugge (1877–78, 267) derives *likvari* 'undergarment' from *lik* 'body' and *verja* 'to dress'. The meaning is thus the clothes nearest the body.

19/112. It is not clear whether the author is distinguishing between *serkr* 'vest' and *skyrta* 'shirt', or if this is simply a synonymous alliteration. The two garments seem to have been similar, made of sheep wool, but Falk (1919, 141–45) believes that a *serkr* was possibly sleeveless, although longer than a *skyrta*, which had long sleeves. Pipping's Swedish translations 'linne, lintyg' (vest) and 'skjorta' (shirt) might be anachronistic, but will serve as a distinction.

19/116 and footnote. The *B*-text has a new chapter (22) at this point.

19/120–21. Witnesses were required only to confirm the veracity of the injured man's story, not to give evidence of his injury.

For an account of the system of judges, see Introduction, pp. xxv–xxvi, xxix–xxx.

19/126 and footnote. The *B*-text has a new chapter (23) at this point.

19/132 and footnote. The *B*-text has a new chapter (24) at this point.

19/134–36. Two *öre* is ¼ mark, which is half the fine for extra blows to the free man in the fight.

19/139–41. It is worth noting that minor wounds to slaves, for example a blow with a stone, attracted the same compensation as to a free man.

19/141–42. A slave could neither give nor receive an insult, the latter because of his lack of status and the former because any adverse comment from such a person would presumably have been regarded as unworthy of consideration.

19/142. The paragraph that follows this in the *A*-text has been moved to its proper place in Chapter 20 (Chapter 26 in the *B*-text).

Chapter 20 *Af allum lutum*

The laws of inheritance in Gotland as recorded in *GL* are complex and to some extent contradictory. The most thorough analysis of them is to be found in Holmbäck (1919, 219–41), where previous studies by Pipping (1904), Delin (1909) and others are taken into account. The following notes relate to specific aspects in individual provisions.

20/6. Jacobsen (*GGD*, 63 note 1) suggests that the use of *ar* 'year' instead of *vintr* 'winter' here might indicate that this provision is younger than others in the law.

20/6–7. The phrase *skiaupa ok skalar* 'scrip and scales' might be a fixed expression for the possessions that a younger son took away from the farm. Schlyter (*CIG*, 46), referring to Schildener's German translation 'Pferd und Schaale' (horse and cup) (*G-L*, 211), suggests the noun *sciaut* n. 'draught animal' should be substituted for *skiaupa* f. Säve (*GU*, 14) follows Schlyter. Bugge (1877–78, 269) thinks that the latter is not an error but that the word's sense has been forgotten and that it was a leather bag for keeping one's possessions in, comparable to OWN *skjóða*. The English word *scrip* has the same sense, but probably a different origin. In this particular context, Wessén (*SL* IV, 265 note 2 and references) suggests that the bag could be one in which scale weights were stored. The implication is that when a young man attained his majority, he took charge of weighing out his portion. Although the age of majority appears to have been fifteen here for men, they were not liable to take part in the defence of the province, for which they had been provided with weapons (20/107), until they were twenty years of age (54/2). See also Note to 14/15.

20/8. The verb *selia* is used here to mean 'transfer, make over, entrust, part with' since the context makes it clear that outright sale is not in question.

20/11–12. In the phrase *nequar taki ungan oformaga til sina* 'someone takes the young minor as a ward' Jacobsen (*GGD*, 63) interprets *nequar* as referring to one of the heirs, but this does not seem to be a necessary assumption, and makes the following clause ambiguous (referring either to the guardian or the ward), whereas Wessén (*SL* IV, 266 note 4) argues that it was the minor who retained his full portion. Indeed, it would seem logical that the guardian must have been outside the farm, since his or her action would not otherwise have relieved the situation. Compare this action to that in respect of an illegitimate child by a non-Gotlandic (20/103–05, 20/108–10, 20a/33–35) or a Gotlandic woman (20a/27–28, 20a/31–32), where the obligation seems to be only to raise the child and not to 'take it as one's own'.

20/16. 'Remain in their grandfather's care' (Gtn *sitia i karls skauti*). The literal meaning is 'sit in a man's lap'. The word *karl* is used of the head of a family, in this case the paternal grandfather of the girl or girls. The action of taking a child into one's lap signified adoption or acceptance (especially of an illegitimate child), and the granddaughters would have been treated as daughters of the household, as is clear from inheritance arrangements that immediately follow (cf. *GGD*, 63 note 6, 64 note 1; *SL* IV, 266 notes 5 and 6).

20/19–21. If there were surviving sons (in addition to any who had predeceased their father) then division of the inheritance gave the daughters of each deceased son their father's notional share between them (see *GGD*, 64 note 2).

20/21–23. The property referred to here is evidently the property that the deceased woman possessed in her own right. See Note to 20/71–80.

20/24. All translators and commentators agree that the clause *i hueria quisl sum þet kumbr* means 'to whichever branch [i.e. generation] it has come', that is, 'however many branches [generations] there might be'.

20/24–26. The Gtn *lindagyrt eþa gyrþlu-* 'male or female' has been the subject of considerable debate. It is clear that one of these (feminine or neuter singular) participles refers to the male (line) and the other to the female. The equivalents in OWN were *bauggildismaðr* 'agnatic kinsman' and *nefgildismaðr* 'cognatic kinsman' (cf. *GulL* 37 (*NGL* 1, 22–24)). The English equivalents are 'distaff side' and 'spear side'. Both *lindi* and *gyrþla* have the sense 'belt, girdle', but neither is unambiguously used of female or male dress in medieval sources. Around the beginning of the fourteenth century a type of belt, called in Swedish a *ländbält* or *ländgördel*, was introduced. This fitted lower down (literally around the loins) and was sewn to the garment (see *KL* s. v. *Gördel och gördelmakare*). It is possible that women more commonly used this type, and that the earlier waist-fitting girdle was a male accessory, particularly as it would have been more useful for kilting garments for work. The previous scholarship may be summarised as follows. Those who argue that *lindagyrt* refers to the female (line) and thus translate *tua lindagyrta* as meaning 'two [male descendants] of the female line' are (1) Schlyter (*CISG*, 396–97) and (2) Hadorph (*Gothlandz-Laghen*, 21). Schlyter states that a *linda* was a woman's girdle. He refers to Söderwall (*OSMS* I, 531 s. v. *linde*) and hence to the legend of St George (*MD*, 192 ll. 219–22), a passage about the nuns of St Birgitta (*HBU* V, 42), *Ett fornsvenskt legendarium* (*FL* I–II, 501 ll. 15–19) and to Ihre (1769 s. v. *garland*) who states that *linda* was any belt, especially one worn by a virgin. Schlyter nevertheless acknowledges that Ihre has the opposite interpretation under *Linda* and Hadorph has the reverse translation in the earlier phrase. Those who take *lindagyrt* to refer to the male (line) and thus translate *tua lindagyrta* as meaning 'two [male descendants] of the male line' are (1) Pipping (1904, 7–10); (2) Wessén (*SL* IV, 266–67 note 12) and (3) The Low German translation of *Guta lag* (*tyGL* 21 §2). Pipping argues that the male would be mentioned first and that Hadorph is inconsistent. He also cites Fritzner (1891, 531), who lists instances in which *lindi* is used of male clothing, and Ihre (1769 s. v. *Linda*), who refers to the priest's girdle in *YVgL* Kkb 2. Wessén argues that the grammatical form of *tua lindagyrta* means that it must be male and cites *MLBL*, VIII §8 (*NGL* 2, 271) where *lindi* is used of a male garment. In *tyGL lindagyrt(a)* is translated 'mannes namen' and *gyrþlu(gyrt)* 'vrouwen namen'. Jacobsen (*GGD*, 64–65 note 7), however, retains the ambiguity of the original. She is unconvinced by Pipping's first argument and notes that in *GL* the female is three times referred to before the male. In the present translation Pipping's argument has been accepted with some reluctance, but a certain ambiguity has been retained.

20/25. The word *bloz* (translated 'descendants') means direct heirs of the female in question, i.e. the bloodline. The genitive serves in this case as a nominative (cf. OldSwe *goz*, ModSwe *gods* 'estate; property'). Säve (*GU*, xviii) considers the possibility that *boþs-kyn* or *bloþs-ett* was intended. Relatives not in the direct bloodline were given different designations (cf. Note to 28/13–17).

20/25–29. This provision may be summarised as stating that if there were three male heirs in successive generations, following inheritance from a female, before the direct line ran out, the property in question stayed in the farm where it now resided, following normal inheritance rules, otherwise it reverted to the farm from which it came (cf. *GGD*, 65 note 3; *SL* IV, 267 notes 13–17).

20/30. This provision could refer to property not in the form of land (*lutr* as opposed to *aign*), or it could simply refer to a situation in which an heiress leaves no male heirs, in which case *lutr* refers to all forms of inheritance (cf. *CIG*, 47; *SL* IV, 267 note 18). The latter seems more likely, since this situation is not otherwise provided for.

20/33 and footnote. The *B*-text has a new chapter (26) at this point. 'If there are no sons on the farm' (*Þar sum gangs i garþi*). This and similar expressions are taken by Wessén (*SL* IV, 266 note 6) to refer to the end of the male line at a farm. Holmbäck (1919, 223–27) argues that this expression refers only to lack of surviving sons and that in these circumstances their sons and grandsons were included in the general division of inheritance. Cf., however, Note to 20/71–80.

20/36–37. As Wessén (*SL* IV, 267 note 21) points out, 'their father's maternal inheritance' (*sett faþurmyþrni*) must mean their own (and their brother's) maternal inheritance.

20/38. The word *penningr* is used here to mean 'coin, currency, that which could be counted' as opposed to other property.

The 'paternal inheritance' refers to the father of the daughters (*af feþrni sinu*), that is, the brother of the unmarried aunts.

20/40–45 and footnotes. Wessén (*SL* IV, 265 note 65) gives two circumstantial explanations for this paragraph appearing at the end of Chapter 19/142, footnote), rather than in its proper place here. The more likely, in view of the fact that the *B*-text has this paragraph in the margin, is that the originals for the *A*- and *B*-texts (both assumed to derive from *v* on the stemma on p. xix) already had this paragraph misplaced. The scribe of the former presumably simply copied what he had in front of him, whereas Bilefeld (or the scribe of his immediate original) observed the error. He then either decided to show the error in his original by means of a marginal note, or intended to insert the paragraph at the proper place but subsequently forgot to do so and had to insert it in the margin. The paragraph appears in its proper place in *tyGL* and *daGL*.

20/40–41. From the context, Holmbäck (1919, 223–27) argues, 'the kinsmen . . . fourth generation' (*niþiar . . . a fiarþa mann*) must refer to kin in the male line. He then considers what the last part of this phrase might mean, and comes to the conclusion that the deceased was included in the generation count, although this was not always the case in Swedish provincial laws. This means that the fourth remove from the deceased father was (1) amongst his ascendants his paternal grandfather; (2) amongst his descendants his great grandsons in the male line and (3) amongst collateral kin his brother's sons and father's brothers. These all inherited equally with the deceased's daughters (see following note) but how this division functioned in practice is not known. Diplomas show that during the thirteenth century farms were divided into small, barely supportable, holdings and occasionally it appears that the smaller of these, if sold, returned to the mother farm. The provision in Chapter 28/71 relating to the division of property seems specifically to be limited to liquid assets.

Concerning the form *burnum* 'daughters' in the *B*-text, Schlyter (*CIG*, 247) argues that this variant reading should be ignored, but Valter Jansson (1935, 7–8, 10–13) in a study of a runic inscription from Bro parish in Gotland, offers evidence from other inscriptions that *borna* means 'daughter'. He cites the fact that *tyGL* has *myt den tochteren* 'with the daughters' and the Danish, *daGL*, *medt burne* in support of his suggestion. On this basis Wessén's acceptance (*SL* IV, 267 note 23) that *miþ burnum* means 'with the daughters' has been followed here.

20/43 footnote. 'and the women's portions are discharged' (*ok quinna lutir iru ut rettadir*). Wessén (*SL* IV, 267 note 25) thinks that this clause was original, although it is missing from the *A*-text, since it relates to the immediately following provision. A widow's claim was treated as a debt to the estate, payable before the inheritance was divided (cf. Note to 13/60).

20/43 and footnote. The masculine form *hann* instead of the feminine appears again at 22/20, also corrected by Säve in *GU* (cf. Pipping 1904, 15). The *B*-text continues with the plural here: *En qwindi takin slict yr gardj sum thar i haffdu* 'But women take those things from the farm that they brought to it'. The reference is to the widow of the owner of the farm and to the return of the dowry (*haimfylgi*) she brought to the marriage.

20/44–45. If a dowry claim was not properly laid out in the year immediately following her husband's death, the estate had the right to withhold payment, or at least the right of proof if a case were brought (see *SL* IV, 268 note 27). Iuul (1941, 174–77) suggests that dowry provisions in *GL* represent an earlier situation than those in mainland provincial laws.

20/46–47. The widow of a family where the male line had expired received support for just one year, if she did not remarry. It seems to be tacitly assumed that she was free to do this if she wished, as she would have been in Svealand. In Götaland, she would have had to have agreement from her *giftoman* (the one who received her bride-price). The provisions here seem to be less generous than those laid out at 20/66–70, but they may have been granted in addition to the latter.

20/47–48. Grain and other produce were normally measured by capacity rather than weight in the Middle Ages. A *laupr* was ¼ barrel, roughly equivalent to a bushel (circa thirty-six litres). It has the same derivation as Old English *lēap* 'basket'. The word *laupr* for grain measure was apparently unique to Gotland and it is still current (cf. *GGD*, 105 note 4; *GO* s. v. **löp*[1]; Gustavson 1940–42, 1948, 217; 1936, 300–01). The capacity measure normally in use, equivalent to half a barrel, was variously called a *skäppa* or a *spann*, depending on the part of Sweden (cf. Aakjær 1936, 211; Jansson 1936, 2, 5, 22). Neither is used in *GL*, but *spannamal* and variants are found in Gotlandic dialect.

On the evidence of pollen analysis, rye began to be cultivated in Scandinavia in the early Iron Age, but did not become a significant crop until the Viking Age. It was more resistant to drought and less demanding in terms of soil quality, and its good baking qualities caused it to advance over other types of grain in the sixteenth century. The oldest provincial laws all mention rye, it being the only seed crop referred to in *ÄVgL* (cf. *ÄVgL* Äb 81; *YVgL* Äb 33; *ÖgL* Kkb 2 pr). It also occurs in *UL* Kkb 7 §5, *SdmL* Kkb 5 pr; Bb 13 pr, *VmL* Kkb 6 §4. Rye seems to have been grown as an autumn crop and *MELL* Jb 29 refers to rye in such a context that winter rye must be intended. In southern Sweden rye seems to have been sown after 14th October (about a week later by the

Gregorian calendar), that is, at the start of winter. Rye was also the crop sown on newly cleared land (cf. Note to 48/2–3).

20/50. 'as she has put in' (*han i quam*). The reference is to property that the wife brought to a marriage, not to the wife herself. Pipping (*GLGS*, 31 note 1) expands on Schlyter's translation (*CIG*, 48), considering it to be a misreading. Cf. 'as many as they brought to the farm' (*sum þar þet i garþ flyttu*) at 65/3–4.

20/52. The Gutnish expression for 'all children . . . equally' is *so barn sum barn*, literally 'each child the same as the other; child for child'.

20/53–54. This provision is obscure, but has presumably to be read in conjunction with the provision at 24d/2–7 concerning the protection given to sisters by their brothers before their marriage, and the portion given to them afterwards.

20/54–56. Normally a widow would have a right to her dowry (*haimfylgi*) and bride price (*morgongåva*, *hogsl* in *GL*, see Note to 20/60–61), her bed and best clothes and then that part of the inheritance which fell to her on its division: one third of the liquid assets and land bought during the marriage, up to half the estate. In *VStL* IV 3 §§4–6, for instance, full property sharing rights existed with a man receiving two thirds or a half of the property on the death of his partner and a woman a half or one third depending on the number of offspring. In *GL*, however, there seems to have been no such division and, in the case of a widow left childless, her family reclaimed the dowry. This could represent a much older system of inheritance than was in place on the mainland, perhaps regarding the dowry as an advance on the woman's inheritance (see Amira 1882–95, I, 528–30).

20/60–61. 'Consolation and provision' (*hogsl ok iþ*). The word *hogsl* is used later in the text of a sum of money paid in compensation to an unmarried mother by the father of her child (Chapter 20a). Although no level of payment is mentioned in connection with a widow, full *hogsl* for an unmarried mother was eight marks in coin (two marks of silver). The translator of *tyGL* has related this word to Middle Low German *höger* 'higher', but it might have resulted from a loan word: Middle Low German *hogen* 'gladden, comfort, console' (cf. *CISG*, 279; Amira 1882–95, I, 521–22; *GU*, xxvii; *GLGS*, cxiii; *GLGS*, *Ordbok*, 38 s. v. *hogsl*). This interpretation would suit both situations in which the sum was to be paid: a consolation either for loss of a husband or loss of one's honour.

The word *hogsl* occurs only in *GL* and seems to be equivalent to the *morgongåva* paid by a bridegroom to his bride, according to other provincial laws, on the morning after the wedding (the price for her virginity). This latter also reverted to the woman if she were widowed. Säve (*GU*, xxvii) offers several alternative derivations and relationships for *hogsl*, including one to OWN *hógr* 'friendly, gentle', which he thinks might support a sense equivalent to that of the *morgongåva*.

The word *iþ* means literally 'occupation, industriousness' and it seems likely that this sum was paid in recognition of the work that a widow had contributed to the farm during her years of marriage, although it might have simply been a provision for her new unsupported state (see *SL* IV, 268 note 31). Schlyter (*CISG*, 279 s. v. *hogsl*) suggests that the phrase might be an example of parallelism and that the two sums were not separate. There do, however, seem to have been distinct payments that were applicable. A widow certainly, according to the following provision, received payment for care of her family for the first eight years after her widowhood, if she did not remarry, and if her sons died leaving no heirs during that time. This has led to speculation that the *iþ* might also have varied and been proportional to the length of the marriage (cf. *GLGS*, cxii; *GGD*, 67 note 2; Holmbäck 1919, 221–22).

20/63–64. The presumption is that the widow could, in addition to *hogsl ok iþ*, claim a mark in coin for each year, up to eight, that she remained on the farm supporting her sons or their offspring. It is implied that the sum was taken at the end of the period, rather than year by year and that, even if any sons survived beyond that time or left offspring, she would not have been entitled to further money from the estate, although the wording is ambiguous.

20/66–70. A childless widow received board and lodging (but no payment for care of her family) for as long as she wished, or ½ mark in coin a year up to sixteen years, payable on an annual basis, if she chose not to remain on the farm. The total amount was the same as that for a widow with children and presumably the latter also received her board and lodging if she stayed on the farm. These two provisions seem to be at odds with that at 20/46–49 also relating to childless widows where it is implied that they only received support for a year. It is possible, however, that both were applicable. Previous editors have not commented upon this inconsistency.

20/71 and footnote. The *B*-text has a new chapter (27) at this point.

20/71–80. The first half of this paragraph, together with the provisions at 20/23–25 and 33–59, are taken by Westholm (2007, 72–73) to be evidence of the relatively high status of women in Gotland. She suggests that there might have been farms run and owned by women, giving rise to the Gotlandic farm or estate name *Kvinnogårde*.

20/79. 'And they are both equal in blood relationship'. See Notes to 20/24, 20/25 and 20/25–29.

20/82. The provision that sisters are equal to daughters presumes that the son died before his father in the fire (cf. the provision at 20/14–16), whereas a more modern supposition is that the older person died first, in which case the provisions at 20/33–37 would have applied.

20/87. In the expression *innan staurs* 'within the farmstead', *staur* appears to have been not just a single pole or stake, but a series of poles that marked the boundary of the home farm. The enclosed area had certain rights associated with it, which were important in legal terms, but which were sometimes equally applicable to land lying outside the boundary (cf. 25/38–39, 57/4, 63/2–3).

20/91. The word for land yielding a certain rent was *laigi* and was originally used in connection with the rent to be paid by a tenant farmer. The expression *marka laigi* came later to be used in reference to any area of land that would fetch a mark of silver in annual rent, if tenanted, the equivalent of *markland* in *UL* and elsewhere in mainland provincial laws. This usage seems to have continued into the eighteenth century in Gotland. In *UL* Jb 1 rent is stated to be one twenty-fourth of the freehold value of the land. According to this valuation, a *mark laigi* would thus have been land to the freehold value of twenty-four marks of silver or three of gold (cf. Note to 3/4). One mark of gold in terms of freehold land would thus have been equal to $\frac{1}{3}$ of a *mark laigi* and nine marks of gold, three *markar laigi*. The basis for land taxation was freehold value, but this could also be expressed in acreage, varying from district to district depending on the fertility of the soil (cf. *SL* III, *SdmL*, 95–96; Note to 28/35–39). Land worth one mark of silver was subject to a rent of one *örtug* ($\frac{1}{24}$ mark) and was called an *örtugland*. Lönnroth (1940, 87–101) summarises five different theories relating to the origin of the term *markland* and concludes that it was an assessment unit for land (in relation to inheritance), which eventually became a measure of obligation to taxation. Cf. *CISG* s. v.

laigi; Styffe 1864, 64–66; Jacobsen (*GGD*, 68 note 8); Thulin 1911, 122; Sandström 1927, 41–42; Ambrosiani 1939, 162–63; Wessén (*SL* IV, 269 note 39 and references); Dovring 1947, 357–58.

20/92 and footnote. The *B*-text has a new chapter (28) at this point. The prefix *þy*- used in *GL* to denote illegitimate children was a word for a female servant, female slaves frequently being taken as concubines. The word *þysun* (similarly *þydotir* and *þybarn*) thus originally meant 'son of a slave woman', but here it includes the illegitimate son of a free man and woman (cf. Holmbäck 1919, 228–31). The coming of Christianity brought about a differentiation between children born to married and unmarried parents, particularly after the Synod of Skänninge in 1248. Provincial laws other than *GL* imply that such a child could only inherit from its mother, if at all (cf. *ÄVgL* Äb 8, *YVgL* Äb 11–12; *ÖgL* Äb 4).

20/93. The adjective *aþal* is used in two contexts in *GL*, here meaning 'trueborn' and in Chapter 25 concerning land meaning 'cultivated' as opposed to 'woodland'. In the present chapter there seem to be two senses, both related to 'trueborn': Gotlandic as opposed to non-Gotlandic and legitimate as opposed to illegitimate (20/101).

20/94–96. This provision presupposes that written genealogical tables were common in Gotland, although none survive (cf. *SL* IV, 269 note 43). They did not come into use elsewhere until later in the Middle Ages, although there are genealogical elements on some runic inscriptions, in diplomas and in literature, e.g. *Erikskrönikan* (ll. 202–31). It is worth noting that it was the female line of an illegitimate son that had to be Gotlandic for him to inherit. This presumably excluded both non-Gotlandic women and slaves (cf. Notes to 20/92, 20/93).

20/103–05, 20/108–11. The responsibility taken by a father for the support of his illegitimate children by non-Gotlandic women, as well as Gotlandic, contrasts with certain mainland provincial laws in which they were the responsibility of their mother (cf. *ÄVgL* Äb 8, *YVgL* Äb 11–12; *ÖgL* Äb 4). The laws of Svealand distribute responsibility between the parents (cf. *UL* Äb 23 §2; 24 pr; *HL* Äb 14 §2).

20/107–08. It is possible to detect an alliterative passage behind the list of items to be provided: *fulkvapn ok sengakleþi, faldu ok legvitu ok vengi, ok femtan elnar kleþis til gangkleþa*. Such alliteration would have been an aid to memory.

20/107. The battle weapons (or equipment) for the levy in defence of the province (*fulkvapn*) were distinguished from murder weapons, or weapons used by knights. In *HL* Rb 14 §2, the *folkvapen* are named as sword or axe, iron helmet, shield, *brynia* or *musa* (chain mail helmet or hood), bow with three dozen arrows. These last were also considered (at least potentially) to be murder weapons (cf. *SdmL* Mb 26 §3; *DL* Mb 19; *SL* II, *DL*, 45 notes 61 and 62). Sometimes a spear and club were included, although these are not mentioned in provincial laws and the axe was considered to be the most important weapon of the levy (Grieg 1943b, 124; Hellsten 1943, 186). The shield was originally round and made from lime wood, but this later proved ineffective and was superseded (Grieg 1943a, 69). The word *fulkvapn* occurs also in *SkL* 88 (*CISk* I 87), with respect to breaking and entering, and elsewhere in Danish and Swedish provincial laws. Cf. *GGD*, 69 note 7; *SL* IV, 269 note 48; *SL* IV, 72 note 15 and references.

The top covering of a bed (*falda*) was made of skins, but another skin might have been used under the sleeper to cover the straw (cf. Neogard's collection, *Gautau-Minning*; *SL* IV, 270 note 49).

Mattress fillings were, for example, down, feathers, hair, hay, moss, seaweed, leaves or chaff, according to the social status of the family and what was available. Hay and straw were most common. Säve (*GU*, xxviii) describes beds as having first a straw mattress, then an under sheet ('underkläde'), then a wool or homespun blanket called the 'lägita' or 'legta' and lastly a sheet, but this conflicts with alternative suggestions. According to Bugge (1877–78, 266–67) *legvita* was still current in nineteenth-century Gotland to designate a woollen blanket put on a bed between the under sheet and the top sheet. He thinks that the word derives from elements meaning 'a white blanket for lying on'. The final blanket or bedcovering (*sengaklepi*) was sometimes the sleeper's cloak.

20/108. The *vengi* mentioned may have been a pillow for the bed, or else a *raipvengi* 'saddle cushion'.

From the context, *klepi* in this single instance means not 'garments', but 'cloth'. It was fine woollen material (cf. English '(broad)cloth') in contrast to native homespun (Swedish *vadmal*), of which there is, curiously, no mention in *GL*, although the term appears in *ÖgL* Bb 9 pr and in *MELL* Jb 9.

20/108–14. The assumption that illegitimate daughters remained at home until they were eighteen years of age implies that this was the age of majority for women (as opposed to fifteen for men, 20/6). There is, however, no other support for this in *GL*. Daughters received an extra mark in coin and a cow instead of weapons, which suggests that the latter were worth at least a mark more than a cow.

20/114–16. The rights of illegitimate children had to be honoured in the presence of the parishioners and with their given witness (cf. *SL* IV, 270 note 51).

20/118. The expression 'charged with violation' (*fallas viþr*) is an extension of the usual sense of the Gtn, which is 'be found guilty' (cf. OWN *fallerask* 'prove false', (of a woman) 'fall').

20/120. The compensation (*hogsl*) given here was four marks in coin (one mark of silver), half of the maximum, whereas eight marks in coin (two marks of silver) were payable to a Gotlandic woman (20a/20–21). Cf. *högsl, högen* in *tyGL* (*CIG*, 134, l.24; 136, l.17); Note to 20/60–61.

20/121–22. The difference in penalty applicable to intercourse that was not discovered (a fine, in effect, of one mark of silver) from that in which the couple were *innitakin* 'caught in the act' (mutilation or a fine of three marks of silver) is striking. Both these fines were half of what would have been payable for a wholly Gotlandic woman. The mutilation here and in the next chapter, loss of a hand or foot, was a shaming punishment, but it was not regarded as a mirroring or symbolic punishment, which was only meted out for a specific crime (e.g. loss of the nose for seduction or adultery, hanging for theft) or a retaliatory one, which repeated the result of the crime (e.g. loss of a corresponding limb for a wounding). Burning alive for an arsonist could be considered either symbolic or retaliatory (cf. Brunner 1906–28, II, 767–68; Hasselberg 1953, 235–42; *KL* s. v. *Speglande straff*). This provision is first in a series relating to sexual misconduct and, unusually, mixed relationships are mentioned before wholly Gotlandic ones (see *SL* IV, 270 note 54). As Wessén also points out, it provides a link between the provisions relating to inheritance and those relating to adultery and other sexual misdemeanours. This arrangement is typical of the organic structure of *GL*, with no strict division into sections and with an almost seamless transition from one subject to the next.

20/123–25. It is worth noting that the provisions were the same whether the father of an illegitimate daughter was Gotlandic and her mother non-Gotlandic, or vice versa.

Chapter 20a: <*Af manni innitaknum*>

This new chapter (29) in the *B*-text is not signalled in the *A*-text, although the chapter title appears in the table of contents. The complex provisions relating to sexual misconduct in this and the following chapter reflect a little of the gradually changing attitudes to marital fidelity. In older Germanic laws it was only the husband who was considered to be shamed by the behaviour of his wife, and not vice versa. The Christian view that both parties to a marriage were equally responsible was slowly introduced into Scandinavian law, although equality of treatment is not evident in *GL* or in Swedish provincial laws, and in *GL* no fines to the bishop or other church official are mentioned (cf. Brunner 1906–28, II, 854–55; Wilda 1960, 821–22; Hemmer 1928, 241–42; Hasselberg 1953, 332–33).

20a/4–5. This is the only instance in *GL* in which loss of liberty, as opposed to life, status or money, is mentioned as a punishment. Stocks were used temporarily to hold a wrongdoer until he/she was redeemed by the family. It was only with the development of towns that prisons came into being. Originally, it was the duty of the injured party to keep a wrongdoer at his farm and conduct him to the assembly. As the very act of detention and binding was a serious infringement of personal rights, there were carefully constructed rules surrounding this procedure, and the wrongdoer had to be caught in the act of committing a serious offence (cf. *ÖgL* Db 2 §1; *VmL* Mb 26 §5). On the other hand, if the injured party let such a person escape, they were themselves subject to fines (cf. Hasselberg 1953, 328–29 and notes 5 and 6; Thomson 1972, 89–90; Note to Addition 8/17–20).

20a/5–8. The fine of six marks of silver with which an offender could redeem his hand or foot was ¼ of a man's wergild, but also the sum payable in compensation for loss of a hand or foot (see 19/47–49). This sum was presumably paid to the woman's family (as opposed to the *hogsl* paid to her if she became pregnant).

20a/12–14. The six men were to swear to the truth of the witness statement by the two parishioners, that no word had been heard of the man's involvement in the conception of the child before its birth. They were thus swearing to the truthfulness of the accused man himself (see *SL* IV, 270 note 60).

20a/14–15. The accused man was entitled to obtain a six-man oath if he could obtain two resident parishioners as witnesses. Jacobsen

(*GGD*, 71 note 3) offers the interpretation that the six men were to include the defendant and the two parishioners, but Wessén's translation appears more likely.

20a/17–18. Men of equal birth with the woman would in this instance presumably have been of Gotlandic birth (see *SL* IV, 270 note 62).

20a/18–21. If the man was unmarried as well as the woman, he might be expected to marry her, but if not he had to pay her full compensation (eight marks in coin) as if she were his widow.

20a/22–23. The three marks referred to here are most probably three marks in coin, as silver is not specified (see *SL* IV, 271 note 64). This payment is strikingly low in comparison to the sums payable to Gotlandic or (illegitimate) half-Gotlandic women for a discovered seduction (six or three marks of silver respectively). It is possible that three marks of silver was intended, which would have been equal to the amount payable in respect of an illegitimate half-Gotlandic woman (20/121–22). The sum is, however, the same as that payable by a non-Gotlandic man in similar circumstances, again with no reference to silver or coin (cf. Note to 20a/24–31, 33–36).

20a/23–24. Schlyter's punctuation, with a semicolon after 'discovered *in flagrante delicto*' (*innitakin*), does not seem to be correct. The meaning appears to be that the non-Gotlandic woman must be a resident and not a camp follower or a prostitute. Cf. *GGD*, 71 note 8; *SL* IV, 271 note 65.

20a/24–31 33–36. Compensation rules depended on the status of the woman in the case, and not on that of the man. If the woman were Gotlandic, her 'consolation' was eight marks in coin (two marks of silver), which was one twelfth of her wergild (twenty-four marks of silver). If she were non-Gotlandic, it was three marks in coin, which was just a little less than one twelfth of her wergild of forty marks in coin (see *SL* IV, 271 note 71).

20a/27–28. Since the fine payable in all these cases depended on the status of the woman involved, and a Gotlandic woman is again under consideration here, one can infer from the expression *hogsl atta markar* here that *fult hogsl* (20a/20), compensation payable for undiscovered intercourse resulting in pregnancy, was also eight marks in coin.

20a/32 and footnote. Although the *A*-text has '. . .if she is unmarried' (*en han ogipt ier*), Säve (*GU*, 16) and Pipping (*GLGS*, 34 note 4) prefer the reading of the *B*-text and replace *ogipt* with *ogiptr*, reading *han* in the *A*-text as an error (or an alternative) for *hann* (nominative singular masculine). Both *tyGL* and *daGL* follow the reading of the *A*-text and Schlyter (*CIG*, 54), Jacobsen (*GGD*, 72 note 2) and Wessén (*SL* IV, 271 note 69) consider that there is no need to make a change. The sense is quite clear without any amendment: if the woman was unmarried her father or, if he were dead, her brother was to take charge of the compensation and raise her child, but if she were married, then her husband presumably did so. Since the *B*-text has *han* for the masculine nominative pronoun and *haan* for the feminine nominative pronoun, it seems possible that an error existed in the manuscript Bilefeld was using and that this led to his writing *ogipter* rather than *ogipt*. It is worth noting that in this case the (Gotlandic) woman was not expected to marry the (non-Gotlandic) man.

20a/33 and footnote. The *B*-text reading *ogutnischir* 'non-Gotlandic' is probably correct, although the circumstance of a Gotlandic man having a child with a non-Gotlandic woman is not previously referred to either. Both *tyGL* and *daGL* have this same reading.

Chapter 21: *Gierir mandr hor*

This chapter continues the theme of the end of the previous one, covering provisions relating to cases in which one or more of the parties was married, or in which seduction or violence were involved. It is significant that the chapter title refers specifically to the male partner, and that no punishment is suggested for an erring wife. This is in contrast to some mainland provincial laws. In *ÄVgL* Gb 5 she has to leave home in her everyday clothes and in *YVgL* Gb 5 and 6 she is shamed in her banishment from the house by having her clothes cut if caught in the act, but otherwise must leave in her everyday clothes. The woman also forfeited her *morgongåva* 'bride price' and everything she received at her marriage. Adultery was usually the sole reason for divorce, although there is an exception in *ÖgL* Kkb 27, where incompatibility seems to have been permissible as a reason. In *SdmL* Gb 4 and *VmL* Äb 6 a woman catching her husband in adultery, in her marriage bed, could maim her rival or tear her clothes and in *UL* and *VmL* (Äb 6 §1) she has the right to kill her rival. There is no mention in *GL* of any similar punishments.

The Swedish provincial laws with the sole exception of *GL* have provisions forbidding sexual relations with kin closer than the fifth

degree (cf. *ÄVgL* Gb 8, *YVgL* Kkb 52 and Urb 3, *ÖgL* Kkb 15 pr).
There could be two reasons for this omission: *GL* totally lacks a
section relating to church law, and/or the law was codified during
the period preceding the Lateran Council of 1215, when the fourth
degree limit was imposed, relaxing a previous limit of the sixth
degree. This uncertainty could have led to the exclusion of any
related statutes.

21/2–3. The first provision of this section refers, by a process of
elimination, to payment by a married man committing adultery
with an unmarried woman in addition to her consolation (21/5–7),
or by an unmarried man committing adultery with a married woman
but not caught in the act by her husband. The amount payable was
only nine marks in coin, of which six went to the family of the
woman or her husband.

21/4. Despite Jacobsen's doubts (*GGD*, 72 note 3), it is clear that
yfirhor means 'double adultery' and this is confirmed by the reading in *tyGL*, which is *czwevald obirspil also das sy beide echte
lute synt*. This concept came into being with the introduction of
Christianity and more equal responsibility for faithfulness between
partners (cf. *UL* Äb 6). The existence of married priests is implied
by the phrase *lerdir ella olerdir* in the *B*-text, which all editors
consider should be applied as an emendation to the *A*-text, by
comparison with *tyGL* and *daGL* and with 21/9 (cf. *CIG*, 54; *GLGS*,
34 note 6; *SL* IV, 271 note 2). The wronged party, *malsaigandi*,
was always the husband of the woman in the case. If the woman's
seducer was a married man, rather than a single man, the husband
received double the compensation and the community four times.
Whether different recipients were intended by the use of the word
land as opposed to *þing* is unclear, but cf. 31/10–12. The punishment for discovered adultery was different (see Note to 21/9–12).

21/5–8. The compensation paid by a married man to an unmarried
woman (in addition to that to her family) seems to have been the
same as if an unmarried man fathered a child with an unmarried
woman, that is *hogsl*, presumably dependent upon the status of the
woman (eight marks or three marks). This is the sole instance of
the word *hogsl* used in a circumstance in which no child is involved,
and perhaps compensated for the man's inability to marry his victim. If the situation were reversed, nothing was payable to the
woman, who was considered to be partly culpable in this case, just
to her husband (21/3).

21/9–12. No differentiation between the treatment of a married and an unmarried man is made for discovered adultery with a married woman. Community fines do not seem to have been paid in such cases. The right of a cuckolded husband, who catches his wife in the act of adultery, to kill the male offender occurs in several mainland provincial laws (e.g. *ÖgL* Eb 26, Vb 30). In earlier laws, it was not necessary for the pair to be caught in the act (cf. *ÄVgL* Md 11; *YVgL* Db 22). In the provincial laws of Svealand, but not of Götaland, the woman could also be killed, but suitable proof had to be taken to the assembly (cf. *VmL* Äb 6). Wessén (*SL* IV, 271 note 5) thinks that the option of the wrongdoer redeeming his life for forty marks (the wergild of a non-Gotlander) was borrowed from mainland laws and the sum involved seems to support this suggestion. The clause giving the husband the right to choose between the punishments occurs only in the *A*-text, but this might be presumed to have been the case.

The death sentence is mentioned in *GL* only in connection with five specific types of action: (1) for discovered adultery with a married woman as detailed here; (2) for abducting an unmarried girl without her parent or guardian's consent (21/15–20, 20–22); (3) for rape (22/16–19, 26–28); (4) for theft of property over a certain value, or subsequent theft (38/6–9); (5) for misappropriation or abuse of land of a certain value (63/11–12). The punishment is unconditional only in cases (4) and (5), otherwise the wronged party can choose compensation instead. Loss of one's neck, presumably decapitation, was the punishment for cases (2) and (5), and a shameful death by hanging is specifically mentioned for theft, but not otherwise. Medieval German laws showed a gradual increase in use of the death penalty from about the middle of the thirteenth century, together with a greater variety of means of execution. Swedish provincial laws as well as *VStL* show a similar trend (see Hasselberg 1953, 226–31). *GL* thus exhibits an older pattern of punishment, although a move from direct revenge for crimes of honour is reflected in its provisions (cf. Note to 8/25–26). A number of theories have been proposed concerning the relationship between the death penalty and sacrifice. Mogk (1909, 642–43) concludes that Germanic sacrifice was a cult act, not a punishment, while Amira (1922, 57–64) argues that there was a link between sacrifice and the death penalty, supported by the observation that offences punishable by death were sacrilegious or

shameful in some way. Wennström (1936, 505–07) and Rehfeldt
(1942, 164–66) reject this suggestion and Ström (1942, 277–78)
thinks that superstitions that surrounded the act of killing itself,
even judicial killing, led to the development of rituals that made
such a death appear to be voluntary and self-inflicted. Strömbäck
(1942, 67–69), after a study of new evidence, thinks that there
might have been a connection in some cases between sacrifice and
punishment. Cf. Hemmer 1928, 55–57; 1960, 188–89; Notes to
21/15–20, 22/13–19, 22/26–28, 38/6–9, 63/11–13.

21/12–15. The implication in this and the following provision is
that the agreement of father and close kin was necessary for a
daughter to enter into a lawful marriage. Luring a girl into
betrothal, although not as serious as abduction and forced
marriage, was regarded as a crime. Wessén (*SL* IV, 271 note 6)
thinks that this provision was borrowed from *ÖgL* Gb 6 §1, where
the fine was 13⅓ marks to the *härad* 'hundred'. The word *festa*
in the sense of 'betrothal' is not used elsewhere in *GL*, nor are
there any specific provisions relating to procedures for entering
into marriage. This is in marked contrast to the provincial laws of
the mainland, where there are detailed provisions concerning payments to be made by the various parties. Hildebrand (1879–1953,
I, 90–100) summarises these procedures and implications of marriage for the extended family (dynasty, clan or tribe) in Swedish
provincial laws.

21/15–20. Abduction, without the finesse of seduction, was usually
regarded as a serious crime, not a normal precursor to marriage,
and the punishment was frequently outlawry (cf. *UL*, *VmL*, and *HL*
Äb 1 pr). The penalty imposed in *GL* for abduction of a Gotlandic
woman was either the life or the wergild of the offender (*vereldi
hans*), i.e. twenty-four marks of silver (three marks of gold) if the
man were Gotlandic, otherwise ten marks of silver. The principle
was usually, however, that the wergild of the victim applied, as in
the following clause: if the woman were non-Gotlandic, the sum
was ten marks of silver (her wergild), whatever the status of the
man (cf. Delin 1926, 268 note 1). The sum payable to the general
assembly from each fine was twelve marks, presumably in coin,
although this is not explicit (cf. Delin 1926, 269 note 2). The
abduction of a Gotlandic woman by a Gotlandic man was thus
compensated much more generously than the three other possible
cases. For other instances of compensation or punishment to some

extent depending upon the status of the perpetrator of the crime, see Chapters 22/26–28, 38/6–9, 51/3–4 and 59/6. Whether the general assembly received anything if the family of the woman chose the abductor's life is not recorded. The form of execution was probably beheading, but *GL* does not state this (cf. Notes to 21/9–12, 63/11–13).

21/16–17. The word *ran* '[by] force' generally meant '(open) robbery', less despicable than *þiaufnaþr* meaning '(secret) theft', in Swedish provincial laws, but this meaning does not occur in *GL*. The implication here is the same as in *ÖgL* Äb 8, where *taka kunu rane* means 'force a woman to sexual intercourse', although other forms of violence (*vald*) seem to be included in the crime. Alternatively, one might take this as another example of parallelism (cf. Notes to 13/7–8, 19/33, 25/48 and 50, 60/6).

Chapter 22: <Af quinna skam>

22/1 and footnote. This chapter (31 in the *B*-text) has no rubric in the *A*-text, although it appears in the table of contents. Most editors number it Chapter 22, although Jacobsen (*GGD*, 73) numbers it 21a and subsequent chapters 22 onwards. The content of this and the following chapter should be compared with provisions in *ÖgL* Eb 3 pr; *UL* Kgb 6; *VStL* I 43–47.

22/2–3. The noun *symni* 'forced intercourse' occurs only in *GL*. It is related to the verb *sufa* 'sleep' (cf. *GU*, xxix; *GGD*, 73 note 5). *GL* is the earliest of the Swedish provincial laws to recognise rape as a separate crime before the instigation of *edsöreslag* (cf. *YVgL* Ub 1 §7, which is not found in *ÄVgL* Ub; *SL* IV, 272 note 10; Note to 12/9–10). In mainland provincial laws, the expression *taka kunu mæþ vald* implies not only rape but also the forcible abduction of a woman, particularly one about to be married to another (cf. 21/ 15–17; *ÄVgL* Gb 3; *YVgL* Gb 2). *GulL* 199 (*NGL* 1, 71) specifies an even higher fine for rape (forty marks) or outlawry plus a double wergild to the woman. Westholm (2007, 73–74) notes that a woman does not appear to have been considered legally liable in the case of unlawful intercourse, even if rape was not involved (cf. 21/2–12) and suggests that this is further evidence of the higher status of women in Gotlandic society compared to other Swedish provinces.

22/3–4. It was important that a woman proclaim her attack publicly at the first possible opportunity, if she was to receive compensation. A shout was a common legal device, often associated with counteracting witchcraft (cf. *ÖgL* Eb 3 pr; *UL* Kgb 6; *SdmL* Kgb 6 pr; *VmL* Kgb 3 pr; *HL* Kgb 3 pr; *MELL* Eb 14 pr; *MEStL* Eb 11 pr; *Eriks SjL*1 Text 1 II §20; Holmbäck 1920, 13–14). The use of a shout with legal effect is also evident in Chapter 36/13–14 in connection with an abandoned boat and, as a means of witness, is considered by some researchers to be a feature of early Germanic law. Hammerich (1941, 70–79) postulates, however, that it might have come about as a result of church law in the twelfth and thirteen centuries, referring to Deut. 22 vv. 25–27, although he considers Saxon law a more likely influence (see Westman 1944, 52–56). The notion that a woman who had just been raped would be physically or emotionally able to run after her assailant and name him (22/9) is perhaps an indication of how unusual this law was and how little understanding the lawmakers had of the circumstances involved. That said, it is much more likely that the woman would be able to name her attacker in a close rural community, such as *GL* applied to, than in a town. The idea that the woman might claim to recognise her attacker later (22/21–22), having been unable to do so earlier, is perhaps not so unusual, however.

22/7–12. If there was no witness to her shouting, the victim had to declare her attack before witnesses and name the attacker at the nearest habitation within twenty-four hours. She could then use the inhabitants as witnesses to the truth of her claim (that she had declared the attack). If she delayed, it was advisable to keep silent as the accused then had the right of defence.

22/9, 21. Jacobsen (*GGD*, 74 note 1) remarks that the word *by* 'habitation' occurs only here in *GL* and that it means a farmstead or other inhabited place rather than a town. *Byamaþr* (65/17, Addition 9/1), on the other hand, means 'town-dweller', more specifically an inhabitant of Visby.

22/13–19. The penalty for rape was half of her wergild for a free woman (the amount depending on whether she was Gotlandic or non-Gotlandic) and one-sixth of her wergild for a slave. In each case, this was the same amount as would have been payable for killing a woman within her circle of safety. If the woman was married, the man could be killed (presumably by her husband, although this is not explicit); alternatively he could pay her full wergild. Slave women are excluded from this provision since they could not be lawfully married. The wording seems to imply that the offender could offer to pay compensation in return for his life, whereas in the previous chapter it is the family of the victim who had the choice (cf. Delin 1926, 268 note 1).

22/20 and footnote. This is one of a number of instances in which the use by the *B*-text of the feminine nominative pronoun *haan* assists in reading the *A*-text; others are at 15/7, 18/5, 20/43, 23/21 (cf. Pipping 1904, 15). See also second Note to 20/43.

22/26–28. The phrase 'pays the wergild penalty' (Gtn *miþ vereldi vert hann*, literally 'protects him with a wergild') is ambiguous in that it is not clear whose wergild was involved. Jacobsen (*GGD*, 75 note 2) assumes that it was the woman's wergild, whereas Wessén (*SL* IV, 272 note 9 to Chapter 22) assumes that it was the slave's. If it were the slave's wergild, the amount would be 4½ marks in coin, which would seem to be derisory. Earlier in the chapter (22/13–19) the compensation relates to the status of the woman. One can compare this provision to another in which a slave's master made payment: three *öre* for a theft of up to an *öre*, three times the value plus the property for greater amounts (Addition 8/1–3). In this case the owner was not responsible for more than the value of his slave (Addition 8/30–32). This value seems to have been set at three marks of silver or twelve marks in coin (cf. 16/9–13, 13–17). In Chapters 21/2–8, 38/6–9, 51/3–4 and 59/6, penalties also seem to be related to the status of the wrongdoer. Wessén compares these provisions with those in *ÖgL* Eb 3 pr and *UL* Kgb 6, which represent *edsöreslag* (cf. Note to 12/9–10). Other points of interest are that it is not clear whether a married or an unmarried victim is under consideration and that no mention is made of rape by a slave of a non-Gotlandic woman. This last would appear to be an error of omission.

Chapter 23: *Um quinna gripi*

23/3. A *tuppr* (OWN *toppr* m.) was a pointed linen hood worn by married women and a *huifr* was possibly a headscarf, similar to a wimple, worn underneath this.

23/5–6. In an agreement dated *c*.1199 between the governor of Novgorod and the Germans and Gotlanders trading there (*STFM* I, 106–07), a provision relating to a similar incident set a fine of six old *grivna* for the insult. The value of a *grivna* is not clear, as there were several kinds (as there were of mark) (cf. *MRL*, 24–25; *SL* IV, 272 note 3 to Chapter 23).

23/8–9. The clause excepting slave women from compensation for anything but injury, which applies to the whole chapter, is consistent with the statement in Chapter 19/141–42 that slaves can neither insult nor be insulted.

23/9. The alliterative phrase *nast eþa nestli* refers to the two parts of a clasp that fastened a woman's clothing, the hook and the eye respectively (cf. *GGD*, 75 note 5; *SL* IV, 272 note 5 to Chapter 23). In *Laxdæla saga*, Chapter 75, *nist* f. is taken to be the fastening of Halldórr's gown, whereas *nist* n. was a pin or brooch (cf. *ÍF* V, 219 note 2).

23/11–12. The hook and eye or clasp can hardly be the *hann* 'it' referred to; this must be the cloak to which they are the fastenings.

23/12–14. Reference to the maximum fine must be to the maximum fine in this chapter, that is, two marks in coin. The laces presumably fastened a woman's bodice. The provision that everything must be returned to the woman refers to all the previously mentioned items (see *SL* IV, 272–73 notes 7 and 8).

23/15–30. The provisions in this part of the chapter fall into two sets. The first set relates to manhandling of a generally boorish nature, with fines rising from eight *örtugar* (⅓ mark) to two marks. The second set relates to approaches of a more sexual nature, with fines falling from ½ mark to nothing depending on the intimacy of the area involved, under the assumption that a woman should have registered her protest at the first opportunity, if she was to receive maximum compensation. When a man committed what would today be termed an indecent assault, a woman was held to have agreed to it by implication (see *GGD*, 76 note 3).

23/21. The verb *kera* 'plead [a case]' is common in early Danish law, but has later been replaced both there and in Swedish law by *klaga*, from German *klagen* (cf. *GGD*, 35 note 4).

23/27–28. Bugge (1877–78, 262–63) rejects the translation in *tyGL* and by Schlyter (*CIG*, 58) of *handar mair* as 'en hand längre upp' (a hand further up), and proposes instead that the whole expression means 'videre, længere bort' (further, further away), taking *handar* to be related to OWN *handan*, meaning 'on the other side' and *handar mair* as a comparative (cf. Noreen 1894, 138; *OSMS* I, 463 s. v. *handarmer*; Rydqvist 1850–83, II, 443, 450).

23/28–29. The lack of any compensation for indecent (*ohaiþverþr*) assault, despite the fact that it is called a 'fool's grip', is puzzling. The sequence of fines clearly reflects the notion that a woman should protest at the first opportunity, but in that case one might query why the most invasive assault is described in the way it is.

23/32. The alliterative phrase *frels ok fripvetr* 'free and freeborn' occurs in Swedish provincial laws (e.g. *UL* Rb 9 §4, *SdmL* Rb 9 §4, *VmL* Rb 18 §3). The adjective *frels* and the noun *frelsi* n. 'freedom' derive from *fri hals*, someone who did not have the neck ring that denoted a slave. The person concerned might be a freed slave. On the other hand, *fripvetr* meant 'free-born' (cf. *ÖgL* Äb 24: *fræls ok fripætta*), or 'known to be free' (cf. *GGD*, 76 note 4; *SL* IV, 273 note 10). The expression in *HL* Kkb 2 pr in relation to the tax-free state of a church is *fult och frælst foræ allom wtskyldom* 'fully free from all taxes'. Cf. also Note to 16/23–26.

Chapter 24: *Af bryllaupum*

Only the first section of this chapter in the *A*-text strictly refers to weddings, as can be seen from chapter divisions in the *B*-text and the table of contents in the *A*-text. The remainder of the chapter (the final one in the section covering family law) contains a miscellany of provisions, a number relating to inheritance. It is possible that at least some of these were later additions.

The concept behind the wedding ceremony described was that a bride was taken from her family home to her new home. There is little detail relating to marriage laws and customs in *GL*, but there must have been traditions and accepted forms of ceremony (cf. Spegel, 53). Chapter 21/12–14, 15–17 implies that a woman is only lawfully married if she has the agreement of her father and family, and Chapter 20/15 that a father might arrange a marriage for his son. Only if he had his father's agreement could he have a share in his inheritance to put into the marriage (Chapter 28/69–71). Reading the banns was instituted as a necessary precursor to a lawful marriage in 1215 by Pope Innocent III at the fourth Lateran council and imposed in Sweden on 5/4/1216 (cf. *DS* I, 182–83, note 156; *UL* Kkb 15 §2). Banns and church weddings took time to become established, however, and it was only with Laurentius Petri's church statute of 1571 that church weddings became obligatory for a lawful marriage. In Sweden the church law that replaced the statute in 1686 was instituted as a civil obligation only in 1734, thus the omission of any mention of banns does not provide evidence of an early date for *GL*.

24/2–3. The custom of having a bride accompanied by male members of her family on horseback in a *mågfärd* or *magfärd* 'procession of in-laws' was an enduring one and is noted by Spegel (53), who interprets the word as derived from *makafärd* 'spouse procession', and by Neogard in his collection *Gautau-Minning* (cf. Amira 1882–95, I, 536–39; *GO* s. v. *måg*, *mage*).

24/2. In contradiction to Schlyter (*CIG*, 302), Bugge (1877–78, 272–73) argues that the second element of *vagnikil* 'wagon-rider' is related to the verb *aka* 'travel'. The noun thus refers to 'wagon-travellers' who followed the procession of the dowry. This was done with a certain ceremony, as elsewhere in northern Europe (see *GGD*, 77 note 1). Picture stones from Alskog and Grötlingbo (ninth century) and Levide and Ekeby (eleventh century) show the earliest pictorial evidence of a wagon being used to transport people.

24/3. The pronoun *huar*, used here, as has been pointed out by Säve (*GU*, viii), means 'each of two'. It is rarely confused in older sections of *GL* with *huer*, meaning 'each of three or more', although this confusion occurs in later sections of the text. The implication is thus that only two wagons were permitted, with two travellers on each. The *B*-text, however, has the dative of *huer* and Säve emends to *hwerium* here (cf. Pipping 1904, 5; *SL* IV, 274 note 3).

24/4–5. Weddings originally took place outside the church and were followed by a nuptial mass (*bruþmessa*) in the church. This custom was later forbidden and a church ceremony had to be the centre of the proceedings. Wedding rings, candles, bridal canopies and eventually the bridal crown were all later (re)introductions, although a *pell* 'canopy' is mentioned at 65/12 and was abolished as part of the sumptuary laws.

24/6. Bugge (1877–78, 260) suggests that the second element of *bryttuga* 'chief bridal attendant' relates to a verb meaning to guide or lead. The bride's representative at a wedding was called the *brudefører* in West Norse sources. This person was thus the 'leader of the bride'. The person who usually dressed and decorated a bride for weddings in Gotland was the priest's wife and a bride was only dressed in her bridal clothes when she arrived at the place where she was to be married (see *SL* IV, 274 note 5). No other helpers of the bride are mentioned, nor any formal gifts to the bridal couple. There is also no equivalent of a gift to the sponsor of the bride by the bridegroom, although it occurs in mainland provincial laws (e.g. *ÄVgL* and *YVgL* Gb 2).

24/8–10. Although wedding guests were henceforth forbidden to bring food for the feast, they were invited to bring voluntary gifts for the couple. These gifts are unusual in that they seem to have been given without obligation. The custom of guests bringing an

edible contribution (*föring*) to a feast or party is still current in
Gotland and other parts of Scandinavia (cf. Amira 1882–95, I, 524–
25, 533–34; *GGD*, 77 note 7).

24/13. The host (*drotsieti*) led each of the guests to his seat, and the
ruler of the feast (*gierþamaþr*, cf. John 2 v. 9) organised events and
arrangements (cf. *GGD*, 78 note 1; *SL* IV, 274 note 8). It appears
from *ÄVgL* Gb 9 §1 and *YVgL* Gb 9 §2 that one of the duties of the
latter was to give the speech that finalised the marriage. He was
called the *kunemädre* in Gotlandic dialect (Spegel, 53). The word
gierþamaþr was also used of a spokesman for the witnesses to other
legal proceedings, such as a land purchase and pledging. Later his
function was taken over by the church, just as in the case of land
purchase it was taken over by the civil authorities.

24/17–18. Wessén points out that the high level of fine for breaking
the provisions regarding weddings and the fact that payment was
not to the parish, but to the province, indicate that this was a later
insertion. The drinking of toasts in Sweden was usually associated
with guilds and the practice of drinking a toast to the Virgin Mary
as the final toast of the wedding feast is unique to *GL*, although
toasts to St Catherine are mentioned in other sources (cf. *Stadga*,
150; Amira 1882–95, I, 539; *SL* IV, 274 note 9).

Chapter 24a: <*Af erfisgierþum*>

24a/1 and footnote. This new chapter (34) in the *B*-text is not signalled in the *A*-text.

24a/2–4. The prohibition on funeral feasts might have been to avoid
any suspicion of ancestor worship. A suggested donation of clothing and footwear to the *innansoknafulk*, presumably the poor of
the parish, as an alternative would seem to indicate that this was
not simply another element of the sumptuary laws.

24a/3. Lis Jacobsen (*GGD*, 79 note 1) comments that *kleþi ok skyþi* 'clothing
and footwear' is 'et af de sjældne Exempler paa forsætligt Enderim
i Lovsprog' (one of the rare examples of intentional end rhyme in
legal language). The noun *skyþi* appears only here and Schlyter
suggests it was coined for the sake of a rhyme (see *CISG* s. v. *Skyþi*).

Chapter 24b: <*Af skarlaþi*>

24b/1 and footnote. A new chapter is not signalled in the *A*-text. The
B-text has at this point (the start of Chapter 35) the first nine sentences
of Chapter 65 (the third of the additional chapters in the *A*-text).

24b/2. The coupling of fine woollen cloth and wallcoverings (*skarlaþ ok bladragning*) suggests that both words relate to hangings, and Jacobsen (*GGD*, 79 note 3) assumes that both refer to funeral hangings. OWN *blár* was the colour of mourning, although the word seems to have been used of both 'black' and 'blue'. The latter often referred to fine cloth, since blue was an expensive dye. Falk (1919, 23) suggests that the word is related to Old English *blēo* 'colour; dye', although a connection is usually made with Old English *blæw* (cf. C-V s. v. *blár*). In *Rígsþula*, verse 29, *síðar slæðor, serc bláfán*, the fine shift must be blue (cf. *Edda*, 284). In *GulL* 223 (*NGL* 1, 75), however, *blá-feldr*, listed as legal tender, must be black sheepskin, not blue (cf. Falk 1919, 23–24, 40).

The practice of decorating the walls for a funeral was common in Scandinavia, but such decorations were also used at weddings, when black would have been inappropriate. It is possible, therefore, that the *skarlaþ* cloth in fact referred to hangings in red or some other festive colour used at weddings (cf. *GGD*, 79 note 4; *SL* IV, 274 note 13). The cloth called *skarlaþ* was known from the beginning of the thirteenth century in Scandinavia as a costly imported woollen cloth, which was of various colours: brown, blue, white, although chiefly red. It was a smooth cloth, of a fine and delicate texture, produced by a complex process. That imported from Lincoln was particularly prized, although it was also produced in Germany and the Netherlands. Geirmundr, Kjartan and Bolli Bollason in *Laxdæla saga*, Chapters 29, 40 and 63, each wear a *skarlatskyrtill rauðr* 'a red kirtle of scarlet', and Bolli's cloak in Chapter 77 is a *skarlatskápa rauð* 'red cloak of scarlet', all of which imply that *skarlats-* describes not the colour but the fabric (cf. Falk 1919, 54–55; *ÍF* V, 79, 118, 187, 225). The prohibition of this cloth and other hangings in *GL* might stem from the time of the conflict between the town of Visby and the countryside (1288) and be symptomatic of the economic problems that this tension caused. These provisions appear to be later additions, since the A- and B-texts differ in their disposition of material just here, and the provisions at 65/11–13 are certainly later.

Chapter 24c: <*Af raiþkleþum*>

24c/1 and footnote. This chapter is only indicated in the table of contents of the A-text.

24c/2. Saddles were not used by farmers during the period of *GL*. A thick blanket was used for riding, augmented by cushions for a pack animal. The significance of this provision, which is marked as a new sub-section in the *B*-text, but without a rubric, is unclear. Cutting saddlecloths and cushions into parts (whether more or fewer than four) seems to make little sense and no editor offers any explanation (cf. *GGD*, 79 note 6; *SL* IV, 275 note 16).

Chapter 24d: <*Af gutniskum kunum*>

24d/1 and footnote. This new chapter (36) in the *B*-text is not signalled in the *A*-text.

24d/2–5. This provision clearly relates to a situation in which the father of a woman has died. If her brother or brothers were not willing to arrange a marriage and a dowry for her, they were obliged to commit one-eighth of their land to her. She was to manage the property with advice from her kinsmen and other parishioners. Wessén (*SL* IV, 275 note 18) compares this to provisions in *JLl* I §8 and *ÖgL* Gb 4 and to those in Chapter 20/33–39. In the latter an unmarried sister of deceased brothers, without male heirs, inherited one-eighth of the property once debts were paid and before any further distribution.

Chapter 24e: <*Af ogutnisku fulki*>

24e/1 and footnote. This chapter is only indicated in the table of contents of the *A*-text.

24e/2–3. Since this provision occurs in all extant manuscripts, the redactions lying behind these texts, including the *A*-text, would appear to have a date no earlier than 1260 (cf. Introduction, pp. xx, xxxvi–xxxvii).

Chapter 24f (64): *Af farvegum manz*

24f/1 and footnote. This chapter (37 in the *B*-text) was omitted from its proper place by the scribe of the *A*-text (or possibly by the scribe of his original) and inserted between the last two of the later chapters (63 and 65 in the present translation) (cf. *CIG*, 61 note 56; *GLGS*, 38 note 6). It appears preceding the chapter concerning disputes about woodland in the table of contents in the *B*-text and in *tyGL*, but is absent from *daGL*. All previous editors leave this chapter at the end, whereas Wessén in his translation places it where it belongs. This latter arrangement has been adopted (cf. *SL* IV, 226, 275 note 1).

24f/2–8. A *farvegr* seems to have been a public right of way across privately owned land that was wide enough for wheeled vehicles. The word *ta* means a road or path of any width (see *GGD*, 82 note 9). A fence bordering a road was thus a *tagarþr*. If a landowner had no property bordering a road (*tafastr*), he had the right to cross the land of a neighbour, if that bordered a road (*ypin*), to gain access to that road. As Wessén (*SL* IV, 275 note 4) remarks, this is an interesting provision, in that it seems specifically to exclude general access to a neighbour's property other than in this particular circumstance. This provision runs counter to current Swedish right of access (*allemansrätt*), which applies to most land, provided that damage cannot result and that private land around a house (e.g. the garden) is not encroached upon. The reason behind this stricture in *GL* could be that farming was intensive and that farmers did not wish too much of their land to be lost to unnecessary footpaths of convenience.

24f/4. Schlyter (*CIG*, 91) translates *varst* as 'jord' (ground, land), but Säve (*GU*, xxix–xxx) thinks that the primary sense relates to an enclosed or fenced-in area. This interpretation conflicts, however, with the adjective *ypin* 'open'.

24f/9. The *talaut* was grazing land, outside the farm boundaries, and situated alongside a path or road.

The Gutnish word used for 'path' is related to the Gotlandic dialect word *kväiar*, a narrow path, road or track between two boundary fences, often leading to a single farm or property (cf. *GO* s. v. *kväiar*).

Fifteen paces (about fourteen metres) seems a generous width for a 'narrow path', but presumably this would have been necessary for the movement of sheep, cattle and timber. The provision could also be regarded as an active discouragement from fencing in land bordering a right of way. The width of a similar path between two boundary fences, together with a means of calculating it, is specified in *GulL* 90 (*NGL* 1, 43–44) as about 2.75 metres. In *ÄVgL* Jb 12 it is seven ells, that is, about 3.85 metres. Both of these are narrower than the width specified in *GL*. It is possible, however, that they were not intended for the movement of stock, but merely for access by foot or on horseback.

24f/12. Jacobsen (*GGD*, 112 note 4) interprets *hagi* 'enclosure' as 'indhegnet Græsgang' (enclosed grass path), but points out that etymologically it was any enclosed place.

24f/13. The *lið* 'gap' that had to be made would have been closed by an easily manipulated slip-rail (cf. *SL* IV, 275 note 7).

24f/14. Although the *B*-text reading *lad* could be a straightforward scribal error for *laga* 'lawful', Säve (*GU*, xxxi–xxxii) offers an alternative explanation. He suggests that the writer intended *laþ-farvegr*, a track to or over a *lað* or *laþr*. Säve takes this latter to be related to OWN *láð* n. 'grassland', 'grazing land' or simply 'land'. The meaning of *lað-farvegr* could therefore be 'track through the land'. Since all tracks have to go through some sort of land, a more circumscribed sense, 'track to grazing land' perhaps, would seem to be a more likely alternative. The difference between this provision and the immediately preceding one is subtle and not entirely clear. Both relate to fencing placed across another's right of way and the provision of a gap for access, but in one case an enclosure is mentioned and in the other simply a fence. It is probable, however, that the second provision simply clarifies the responsibilities: the owner of a fence for the provision of a gap, but the owner of a right of way for its security (cf. Note to 25/48).

24f/15–17. The owner/user of a right of way was responsible for ensuring that the gap was properly closed in order to shut out stray animals (cf. *GulL* 83 (*NGL* 1, 41)).

Chapter 25: *Af skoga brigslum*

In general, those with a share in common (*oskiptr*) (wood)land could cut down wood from non-fruit bearing trees irrespective of the size of their holding. Swedish provincial laws have similar provisions in that if someone became dissatisfied with the behaviour of others, they could demand that the land be divided (cf. *YVgL* Fnb 12; *ÖgL* Bb 30 §1; *UL* Bb 14 §12–13; *DL* Bb 43; *VmL* Bb 14 §11).

25/3. The precise sense of *liksvitni* 'evidence of neighbours' is disputed, but it clearly refers to evidence equivalent to the evidence of kin provided in cases involving cultivated land as opposed to woodland (25/12). Schlyter's suggestion that it was the evidence of neighbours seems not unreasonable, but he admits that he does not know what the element *lik-* means here (cf. *CIG*, 276; *GGD*, 80 note 3). The word *ortarvitni* is immediately explained in the text as a 'witness as to work done', but the only deduction that one can make about *liksvitni* is that it involves the testimony of certain persons (cf. *SL* IV, 276 note 1). Hald (1975, 55–56) suggests an original form **liz-*, genitive of **lið* 'evidence from a group of people, neighbours', and that this provides a parallel to the evidence of kin in the following provision.

25/4–7. Three types of forestry crop are mentioned here: *viþr* 'firewood', *troþur* 'fencing wood' and *quistir* 'branches'. These are translated by Wessén as 'ved', 'gärdsle' and 'grenar' and are equivalent to the three types of wood listed at 26/55: 'a man's firewood, fencing wood or timber' (*viþ manz eþa garz virki eþa timbr*).

25/6. Lidén (1892, 94) suggests that OWN *há* could mean 'after grass, grass left over'. If this were the derivation of the first element of *hafall*, the whole could mean 'time of the cutting of the grass left over', i.e. 'haymaking time, autumn', a sense that fits the context.

25/7–8. Wessén (*SL* IV, 276 note 2) observes that *tyGL* offers a translation that is a misunderstanding of this sentence.

25/8–9. The expression 'one of those who owns most' (*an af þaim sum mest a*) could not refer to the parties in the dispute, but must refer to the one amongst the witnesses who was the greatest landowner (Wessén). If this witness did not wish to swear, then his evidence was not valid for either of the disputing parties.

25/10–11. The translation 'either party' for *huargum* (dative singular masculine of *huargi*, 'one or other of two') is derived from Pipping (1904, 6) and from Wessén's 'någondera' (*SL* IV, 276 note 3). Schlyter's translation (*CIG*, 61) 'aldrig' (never) is rejected.

25/14–16. Jacobsen (*GGD*, 81 note 3) interprets *Brigþr þan sum kringum a* 'if one owning neighbouring property disputes this' as referring to a situation in which one of the neighbours was involved in the dispute; he would then not have been permitted to give evidence. She infers from this that the clause cannot refer to disputes about cultivated land, since 'neighbour' witnesses were not required in such cases. It seems simpler to assume that one of the neighbours asked to provide evidence of work on cultivated land disputed that work had been done. The next nearest neighbour would then have been approached for his support.

25/18–25. This entire provision is obscure, but Holmbäck (1920, 18–19 and note 4) offers the following explanation. He first assumes that when there was a dispute of this type, it was between communities or settlements, in relation to common woodland or other uncultivated land, rather than between individual landowners. He considers that the latter would have been such a rare occurrence that it would not have been provided for in *GL*. He further suggests that if, at the point where the two settlements abutted the disputed woodland, their land was of the same type then they would have divided the unclaimed land equally. If one settlement had cultivated land up to the disputed area and the other uncultivated, then the latter took one third of the unclaimed land and the former the remainder, since it would not presumably have exercised all its right to available woodland. Holmbäck also assumes that the provisions for the settlement of disputes in the first section of this chapter also refer to that between residents in different communities.

25/18–20 and footnote. The words *ok skogr ok myr, þa takin aþal iorþ tua luti* 'and woodland . . . two thirds' were evidently omitted by the scribe because consecutive lines in his original began with *oc scogr*. The phrase has been added in the margin, according to Schlyter by a sixteenth-century hand.

25/23. Schlyter (*CIG*, 62) translates *millan stumbla ok starþufur* as 'emellan stubbar och starrtufvor' (between stump and tufts of sedge), which Wessén (*SL* IV, 276 note 5) interprets as meaning 'at the boundary between tree-bearing land and marshland'.

25/24–25. Schlyter (*CIG*, 62) interprets this as meaning that owners of woodland or marshland could not give evidence as neighbours in matters covered by the immediately preceding provisions. The sense, however, is not clear.

25/26. Woodland and marshland described as *oskiptr* was that in shared ownership (cf. 25/41). Swedish provincial laws all contain penalties for cutting wood illegally, often with the power of confiscating equipment (cf. *ÄVgL* Fns 2; *YVgL* Fnb 3–10; *UL* Bb 13–14; *ÖgL* Bb 29, *GL* 26 §9; *SdmL* Bb 15–17; *VmL* 14; *HL* Bb 13; *MELL* Bb 17). For related provisions, see 7/2–9, 26/38–46, 26/55–61, and 63/2–4.

25/27. The sedge called *Cladium mariscus* (Gtn *agr*) was formerly in common use for roofing in Gotland (cf. *HRSH29*, 388 note; *SL* IV, 276 note 7).

25/29. The verb *yrkia* refers to the type of work just described.

25/31. There have been a number of translations of *anbol* (here 'building material'): Schlyter (*CIG*, 62) and Pipping (*GLGS, Ordbok*, 5) have 'körredskap' (driving harness); Jacobsen (*GGD*, 82 note 1) and Wessén (*SL* IV, 276 note 8), have 'virke' (raw material for woodworking, etc.). They cite a Gotlandic dialect *ambul* with widespread usage (cf. GO s. v. *anbol, amble*). Hald (1975, 53–55) argues that *anbol* has the specific sense 'building material', the result of the forestry work, and that this would naturally have been forfeit along with the means of transport (Gtn *faruskiaut*).

25/32. Pipping (*GLGS*, 39 note 6) prefers the plural of the verb 'prove' (*vitin*) in the A-text to the singular (*vitni*) in the B-text, since both parties were witnesses to the act. He refers to instances at 13/57–58, 14/28 and 18/9. The singular seems, however, to be preferable as it agrees with the first half of the sentence.

25/33. The reliance on an eyewitness, sometimes a professional witness or judge, to provide evidence in property disputes or other cases may have originated in Danish law (cf. *Eriks SjL1* Text 1 II §68) and was apparently native to Scandinavia. Further examples are to be found in *HL* Kkb 18, *ÄVgL* Jb 16 and *UL* Bb 17 §4 (cf. Westman 1912a, 208–12; Almquist 1923, 39–40).

25/45–46. See Note to 24f/2–8.

25/46–48. The person responsible for a fence was fined if damage was caused by lack of proper upkeep to it.

25/48 and 50 and footnotes. The extra words *ella hafa* and *ella eygir* appear in the margin in the B-text. They possibly indicate a correction by the scribe, or that the original Bilefeld was using had both words. The scribe of the A-text has dropped the parallelism and used the verb *hafa* in each case (cf. Notes to 13/7–8, 19/33, 60/6).

25/48. The *garþr* originally denoted the fencing put in place to protect crops from grazing cattle, but later came to refer to the fenced-in area itself. When crop rotation was being practised, various different fencing methods were used. Fences were commonly built of verticals and horizontals, but the *halfgierþi*, which marked a shared boundary between fields or pasture, consisted of timber palings (OWN *skíðgarðr*, Swedish *skidgärdesgård*) on top of a low stone wall, called a *vast* in Gotland. The provincial laws have various rules about the construction of lawful boundary fences. *ÖgL* Bb14 gives a detailed description of how strong and high a lawful boundary fence should be and how a gate should open inwards and not outwards. *HL* Bb 5 gives rules similar to those in *GL*. The stated purpose of a fence in all provincial laws apart from *GL*, where the purpose seems to be to protect crops from people and animals, was to divide two villages and there were complex rules about responsibility for its upkeep. Cf.

also *GulL* 80, 82–84 (*NGL* 1, 40–41); *FrostL* XIII 18–22 (*NGL* 1, 245–46).

The adjective *aumbr* 'in a bad state' is cognate with Swedish *öm* 'sore, sensitive, delicate', which, as Jacobsen (*GGD*, 83 note 3) remarks, is only used of sentient beings.

The preceding provisions form a bridge to the following chapter.

Chapter 26: *Af halfgierþi*

Once again the rubric applies only to the first part of the chapter; the remainder contains provisions relating to cutting of wood on someone else's property.

26/3–4. The parishioners were to determine where a fence should be placed, i.e. where the boundary between the two properties in question ran.

26/7–14. The defaulting party had a year to fulfil his obligation of fencing, after which he had to deposit a pledge of ½ mark, as well as paying for any damage, if his animals broke out. This process continued, the deposit being forfeited each fortnight, until the fencing obligation had been fulfilled. The *lutadagr* 'division day' is the equivalent of the *garðskipti* or *gerðing* in *GulL* 82 (*NGL* 1, 40–41).

26/16. The expression *garþr ir granna setir* 'a fence is a mediator between neighbours' is translated by Hadorph (*Gothlandz-Laghen*, 30) as 'laggill hägnat gör godh Gransämia'. The same expression occurs in *GulL* 82 (*NGL* 1, 40–41) and there is a Danish proverb, *Gærde gjør Grander saate* (Mau 1879, I, no. 3342) (cf. *SL* IV, 277 note 6; Pipping 1938, 43).

26/17. There is a new chapter in *tyGL* at this point. This could have been present in the original used by the scribe of *tyGL*, since it follows a proverbial expression, which seems to form a natural break, but there is no similar indication in the other manuscripts of *GL*.

26/21–22. It was the responsibility of a landowner to have a viable fence, once he had been warned (cf. 25/46–48).

26/22–30. These provisions are an extension of that at 26/8–11, with the addition of payment for other damage done by the animal.

26/30–31. A hobble (*hornband*), which tied one horn to a back foot, was still used for bulls in the early twentieth century (see *GGD*, 84 note 3). Cf. the fines for straying animals in Chapters 40–46.

26/33, 26/47–48. Säve (*GU*, xix) argues that the two instances of *banda* (in '[upper] band') come not from *band* (cf. Schlyter, *CIG*,

242), but from *bandi* m., which exists in Gotlandic dialect with the sole meaning 'osier switch, withy'. The dative plural *bandum* (in '[two] bands') occurs at 26/32 (cf. Läffler 1878, 287). The height of the upper tie of a lawful fence was approximately 1.38 metres.

26/34–37. Different, although unspecified, rules clearly applied to fencing for animals that were liable to fly over or crawl under standard fences, or dig holes under them. *Suin* (as here) was the normal word for domesticated pigs, *(sma)gris* being reserved for piglets. Pigs were reared chiefly in richer agricultural areas, but in the medieval period were still relatively small and similar to wild pigs in appearance.

26/38 and footnote. The *B*-text has a new chapter (40) at this point.

26/38–42. The meaning here is that if the wood cut was so much that it could not be carried away by hand, the fine was three marks to the owner and three to the community, but if the thief carried it home the fine was only ⅓ mark. Presumably he had to make full restitution in either case (cf. *SL* IV, 277 notes 14–17). For related provisions, see 7/2–9, 25/26–37, 26/55–61 and 63/2–4.

26/45. The reading of the *A*-text (*oyk vagn*) is taken by Wessén (*SL* IV, 277 note 18) to refer to a wagon drawn by a pair (yoke) of oxen, although his translation is 'ök och vagn' ([yoke of] draught animal[s] and wagon). This latter is the reading of the *B*-text, which seems to be more likely in that it balances the smaller *rus ok kerru* 'horse and cart', or 'pony and trap' that follows. In *CISk* V (5 A 15, 17, 19–20) it is suggested that a *kerra* was half the size of a *vagn* in terms of load capacity, which may also be inferred from *GL* Chapter 6/8–9. In Old Danish laws, *øk* means 'mare', but there is no evidence that this sense was ever current in Gotland (see *GGD*, 85 note 3). Cf. also Notes to 6/8–9 and 48/5.

26/50. Pipping emends *iiii (ertaugar)* to *xiiii*, following Schlyter (*CIG*, 66 note 33) and *daGL*. Wessén (*SL* IV, 277–78 note 20) rejects this and agrees that the fines were cumulative: ½ mark (twelve *örtugar*) for the withy in the first pair of uprights, plus ⅓ mark (eight *örtugar*) for the next pair, plus one-sixth of a mark (four *örtugar*) for the third pair, totalling one mark, almost certainly in coin (cf. Hemmer 1928, 188 and notes; Wennström 1936, 355–61; 1940, 78). Hemmer suggests that even if the lower of the two ties between a pair of supports were also broken, there would have been no additional fine. He comments on the fact that the (additional) fine is reduced with the amount of extra damage. Wennström broadly agrees, but suggests that the fines concerned were in marks of silver (see following note).

26/50–52. The word *lids-meli* or *liss-meli* occurs in Gotlandic dialect with an original sense 'gap the width of a track', from the elements *lid* 'track' and *mela* 'measure' (cf. *GU*, xxviii; *GO* s. v. *led*[1]). It is now used of any gap in a fence of unspecified width, not necessarily for a track, but also of a ride in woodland, particularly one offering a vista (cf. Rietz 1862–1955 s. v. *lid* (3); Wennström 1936, 355–57). The later provision (63/4–6), apparently relating to damage to fences in woodland (as opposed to farmland) wide enough for passage, stipulates a fine of three marks in coin, which was greater than the two marks in coin here, but less than two marks of silver. Wessén (*SL* IV, 278 note 21) thinks that the difference merely records an increase in the fine, but Wennström (1936, 358–59) argues that provisions here, referring to farmland, must have intended marks of silver. His reason is that fences in farming land would surely have been valued more than those in woodland, although he also questions whether Chapter 63 refers only to woodland fencing. The devaluation of the coinage over time should probably also have been taken into consideration and this might restore the balance between the two instances, even if this earlier provision were in coin (cf. Wennström 1940, 299).

26/55. Three types of wood are listed in increasing size. Firewood (*viþr*) was probably lightweight or short in length, fencing timber (*garz virki*) might have been equivalent to paling, although substantial enough to keep out stock, and timber (*timbr*) was probably more substantial wood for buildings, ships, tools and utensils. Although farm buildings in Gotland were not universally wooden as those on the mainland were, *timbr* would have had other uses on the farm and elsewhere. Cf. ModSwe *ved*, *virke* and *timmer* and the three types of forestry work listed at 25/4–6, and for related provisions, see 7/2–9, 25/26–37, 26/38–46, and 63/2–4.

26/57–58. 'if one does not leave one's own behind' (*en hann ekki laifir sett atr*). This clause refers to the offender in the third person, whereas surrounding clauses are in the second person. The implication is that if an offender left his own wood behind, he could have taken another's in error (see *GGD*, 86 note 2). A similar assumption is made relating to horse theft (35/6–12).

26/60–61. Wennström (1936, 220 note 70) considers Schlyter and Jacobsen mistaken and that it was the offender who had responsibility for swearing that full restitution had been made, but cf. 23/14–15, where a woman whose clothing has been disturbed has to declare that everything has been returned to her. The provisions concerning cutting wood in the final paragraph of this chapter seem to be related to those in Chapter 25/26–37.

Chapter 27: Af saupi

27/4–5. Jacobsen (*GGD*, 86 note 5) observes the alliteration in *i engium eþa aign* 'in a meadow or [on another part of] your land' and the fact that the whole chapter is very rhythmical and full of alliterations.

27/5. The expression *gangr ok gata* 'path and track' is probably a synonymous alliteration (or parallelism), although the former is used of a narrower path for animals and the latter for a wider track for wheeled vehicles (see *GGD*, 86 note 6).

27/5–6. The expression *iemgoþr fran sum til* 'as good away as towards' presumably means not that two separate paths had to be made, but perhaps that the path had to be wide enough for two animals or groups of animals to pass.

Chapter 28: Af aignakaupi

28/2. That land could only be sold in time of need was a principle no doubt enforced to prevent the fragmentation of farms (cf. *DL* Bb 1). It seems as if in Gotland ownership of land still mostly lay in the hands of individual farmers, sometimes larger landowners, but not the crown or the church, during the time of *GL*.

28/4–7. The principle of *caveat emptor* seems to have applied to land purchase in thirteenth-century Gotland as now. The main loser in any illegal sale was the potential purchaser, who not only lost the land price, but was also subject to a fine.

28/8–10. The assembly had to agree any land purchase, presumably with the support of witnesses in cases of dispute. There are no surviving deeds of transfer of land from Gotland, from which one may infer that they were not customary (see *SL* IV, 278 note 2).

28/9. The masculine noun *afraþr* 'kinsman's portion' was a payment made to the nearest kin of the seller of a piece of land if that kinsman were not the purchaser. This recognised his right of preemption in the purchase and amounted to an eighth of the purchase price, according to *tyGL* (cf. *CIG*, 146; *SL* IV, 278 note 3). This right is only mentioned in *GL* and *afraþ* n. means 'annual rent' in mainland provincial laws (see *CISG* s. v. *afraþ*). If a kinsman did not take up his right within a year, thus approving the sale and confirming that he could not or did not wish to purchase the land, the payment lapsed and the sale was validated by default. Various exceptions are listed at 28/33–35 and 28/35–39. Arrangements for placing land in surety for a loan were the same as for an outright sale. There are further details of these arrangements in Chapter 63.

28/13–17. Three (or possibly four) different types of blood relationship were recognised: *skyldir menn* 'closely related kin', *quislarmenn* 'relations from another family branch' and *etarmenn* (more distant family members, those who 'belonged'). The terms *frendi* and *niþi* were used of (male) kinsmen in general, with the context, or an adjective, determining how closely related they were. At 25/16–17, for instance, it seems that *niþiar* refers to more distant relatives, whereas at 28/31 more closely related kin are intended. In Gotland, as on the mainland, the concept of land as a birthright to be kept within the family prevailed (cf. *ÄVgL* Jb 3; *YVgL* Jb 5 and 6; *ÖgL* Jb 3; *UL* Jb 1, 2 §4). The *frendar* seem particularly to have been involved in approving marriages (e.g. 21/14, 24/14) and other legal arrangements, such as ransoming captured family members (e.g. 28/48–49, 56–57). A woman passed from one family to another on her marriage, as did the property she took with her. Any stock, for example, could be rebranded (see 46/3). The provisions in the present chapter should be compared with those in Chapters 20/86–89 and 63/9–13. Although it is specifically stated that land may not be sold outside the family, it seems that *in extremis* such a sale was legal, but resulted in the seller losing his rights of citizenship (cf. *DL* (and *VmL*) Bb1; *HL* Jb 1; *SL* IV, 278–79 notes 5 and 6).

28/22–23. As Wessén (*SL* IV, 279 note 7) states, lack of any relevant kin meant that only a twelve-mark fine to the assembly was applied.

28/32–33. The phrase *þa iru quindismenn nerari þan utanmenn* 'then the female members are nearer than outsiders' suggests that land sales could be made outside the family (cf. Note to 28/13–17). The word *utanmaþr* is, however, unique to *GL* and similar words in mainland provincial laws refer to people outside the province (*utlænzker man*) or outside the village (*ut byamæn*), who might still have been members of the family (cf. *VgL* III 87, 117).

28/33–39. The apparent contradiction between the two juxtaposed provisions is explained by the fact that in the first case, land was exchanged value for value, for the convenience of the owners, and no sale occurred that reduced the value of the estate (see *SL* IV, 279 note 11).

28/35–39. The first provision exempting a sale from *afraþr* covers a situation in which the whole family sells the estate and the second that in which land must be sold to pay wergild. The fourth exemption allows land to be sold to pay compensation for theft. The third provision, relating to dowry in the form of land specifies land yielding a maximum of one mark in rent (see Notes to 3/4, 20/91). Wessén assumes that the freehold value of a *mark laigi* of land was calculated to be twenty-four marks of silver or three of gold (cf. *SL* IV, 273 note 1, 281 note 2 to Chapter 32). Since three marks of gold was the wergild for a Gotlander, Wessén's assumption is reasonable in this context and that of 20/91. A comparison should, however, be made with the provision in Chapter 65, which specifies a maximum of two marks of gold for the value of a dowry, although what form it may take is not specified. Wessén (*SL* IV, 279 note 12) states this to be equivalent of two *mark laigi*, but it should, of course, be ²/₃ *mark laigi* (cf. Note to 65/9–11). Schlyter (*CIG*, 273) observes that in one Gotlandic source from 1527 it appears that a *mark laigi* was equivalent to twelve marks (presumably of silver) in land value, that is, 1½ marks in gold (cf. Note to 32/6). It is obvious from these differing opinions that the rental value of a plot of land with a certain freehold value varied considerably with time and it is not possible to determine an exact equivalence.

28/37–38. According to *ÄVgL* Jb 1, *haimfylgi* to a daughter was one of five lawful ways of passing property from one person to another. The others were: inheritance, *hemgæf* to a son on his marriage, purchase and by gift. According to *MELL* Jb 1, the five ways were: inheritance, exchange, purchase, gift, and mortgage (provided the mortgage was of long standing). This second list is enshrined in the law of 1734 and is still current in Sweden.

28/38. The *malaþing* 'betrothal meeting' was a meeting at which a mutual promise of marriage was confirmed, and a dowry agreed, with a ceremonial feast and exchange of gifts. The word is related to OWN *málþing* 'interview', but it seems here to have had judicial importance (cf. Amira 1882–95, I, 80, 266, 278). A dowry could be up to one third or even half of the inheritance of the sons, and was probably no less than one-eighth of the total value of the farm, which a daughter would have received if unmarried (24d/3–6) (cf. Amira 1882–95, I, 528–30). It included stock (65/2–4) as well as household goods, jewellery, precious metals and land (cf. *SL* IV, 273 note 1).

28/44 and footnote. The *B*-text has a new chapter (43) at this point. No differentiation was normally made between combatant and non-combatant hostages. Non-combatants were often sold as slaves in the medieval period, although combatants could be executed. The idea of a hostage as the property of the victor is confirmed by the fact that he or she could be released by payment of a ransom as described here.

28/45. Jacobsen (*GGD*, 89 note 2) suggests that the use of *eþa* instead of *ok* in the synonymous expression *iorþ eþa aign* 'land or property' is remarkable, since both mean property in the form of land, as opposed to money or movables. There are, however, further examples of *eþa* where *ok* would seem more natural.

28/47–48. The maximum sum that a third party could redeem another's son for unchallenged was the same as the value of a slave (cf. *ÖgL* Gb14 §1; Note to 28/44). A limit was presumably set because, in addition to the money to pay the ransom, the third party received a third of that sum for himself, making a maximum of four marks in all. It seems that this was a courtesy payment and that if the overall sum, including his third, exceeded three marks of silver the relations could contest it.

28/54–57. What appears to be some sort of international agreement is not referred to elsewhere (cf. *SL* IV, 279 note 16).

28/63–80. The remainder of this chapter contains provisions relating to inheritance and more properly belongs in Chapter 20. There is a link, however, between the first of these provisions and the immediately preceding ones, which has clearly influenced the existing sequence. Wessén (*SL* IV, 280 note 25) gives a more detailed explanation of the provisions, which expands upon his translation. Cf. also Kock 1926, 12–31.

28/65–67. Cf. provisions in *SkL* 85–86 (*CISk* I 84–85) and *SkL Add* II (*CISk* Add B 5).

28/68 and footnote. The *B*-text has a new chapter (44) at this point.

28/69–70. The implication here seems to be that the marriage of a son, as well as that of a daughter, had to be with the agreement of the family (cf. Note to 21/12–15). The *B*-text has the parallelism 'counsel and consent' here.

28/71. Division of property on a per capita basis is considered by some to represent an older custom than that exhibited in mainland provincial laws (cf. Iuul 1941, 113–15, 122–24).

28/74–75. Schlyter (*CIG*, 71), and Pipping (*GLGS*, 46) take their emendation (Gtn *raiþi to raþi*) from the *B*-text to give the reading 'have the authority' (*raþi*). Kock (1904, 72–73), however, does not think that the *A*-text reading *raiþi* need be changed. He believes that it comes from a verb *raiþa* (cf. OldSwe *reþa*), meaning 'prepare himself'. This would give the clause *raiþi sielfr firi sir fara huert hann vil* the sense 'prepare himself to travel where he wishes'. Kock observes that this makes as good sense as 'have the authority to go where he wishes'.

28/75–80. The remainder of this chapter appears in the margin in the *B*-text, and is not found in *tyGL*. There do not seem to be any mainland provincial laws that contain the provision set out here. Both *ÖgL* and *UL* Äb 8 pr, however, exhibit a reduced right of sons to demand a division of property (cf. Holmbäck 1919, 64–65; *SL* IV, 280 note 25). On a son's right to inheritance in advance, see Kock (1926, 12–13). The rights of daughters to dowry are covered in Chapter 24.

28/77. Schlyter (*CIG*, 71) and Pipping (*GLGS*, *Ordbok*, 61) translate *oraþamaþr* 'unreasonable person' as 'en obetänksam människa' (an inconsiderate person). Wessén (*SL* IV, 279 note 24) suggests that the word, as well as meaning a father who makes an unfair division of property, could also mean someone who was foolish (perhaps suffering from dementia) or a bad householder. Jacobsen (*GGD*, 90 note 5) translates it as 'urimelig', which could have either sense. Kock (1926, 16) thinks that the passage means that if a father was considered to be asking too high a rent (for the farm that the son inhabits), a property division should occur at once (cf. *ÖgL* Gb 19).

28/77–80. For non-Gotlanders, rules were more stringent in that, even if they were married, sons could not force a division of the estate except in the case of their father being 'unreasonable', in whatever sense. In both this and the previous provision, the verb *skynias* 'prove to be' suggests that outside evidence was required, possibly from relations or parishioners (cf. *GGD*, 90 note 6).

Chapter 29: *Af gieldum*

29/2–3. A person could become indebted up to the extent of his personal share in his inheritance. His fellow heirs were not liable for any of his debt (cf. *GGD*, 91 note 1).

29/3–4. Payment for a deceased person's debts could not exceed his liquid assets (cf. *UL* Äb 25 pr; *GGD*, 91 note 2; Note to 5/7–9).

Chapter 30: *Af veþium*

30/2–4. Jacobsen (*GGD*, 91 note 6) infers that the one who had taken the surety (*veþ*) kept what he had taken, but was to pay back to the debtor the difference between the value of the surety and the (outstanding) debt (cf. *UL* Kmb 7). Cf. the provision in 63/9–11 and the accompanying note.

30/3. The *stefn* was a summons in a civil case. It is assumed that judgement took place under the leadership and on the advice of one or two legal experts, who obtained unanimous agreement from the rest of the assembly. Later this responsibility passed to special judges. The cases considered were originally only those that affected society in general, while others were decided between the respective families. If agreement was not reached, or was not honoured, a wronged party could resort to 'self counsel' (independent judgement).

30/4–5. Other examples of parishioners (or assembly members) making a valuation occur in respect of stray animals (40/4, 41/5, 45a/4) and concerning land valuation (32/8). For the alternative meaning of Gtn *virþa* 'seize in payment of a debt, claim [something] from [someone]', see Notes to 10/5, 63/9–11, Addition 9/5–6.

Chapter 31: *Af þingum*

31/4 and footnote. Pipping (1901a, 95 note 1) thinks that the scribe has here inserted *þria* and then in error also copied *iii* from his original (cf. Note to 19/77).

31/8–9. A similar restriction concerning the duration of the assembly occurs in *ÖgL* Rb 12 pr. Cf. also *UL* Rb 5 §3.

31/10–11. A three-mark fine (in coin) to the (local) community (*mogi*) is referred to in Chapters 12/7, 19/131, 25/28–29, 40, 42, 26/40, 31/7, 35/4–5, 9 and, by implication, 36/17. In these instances a similar sum was paid to the complainant. Wessén (*SL* IV, 281 note 4) assumes that the sixth assembly was referred to in these cases,

but cites further instances of fines at that level where the riding
(*priþiungr*) assembly might be intended: see 2/17, 4/14–15, 11/5,
21/2, 37/26, 48/8, 52/4 and 61/4.

31/11–12. A six-mark fine is mentioned in respect of unpaid wergild
(see 13/62–63) and unspecified fines to the *priþiungr* for lost animals (see 41/4, 42/3, 42/5, 45a/3).

31/12. Fines of twelve marks to the general assembly (*land*) are
mentioned a number of times, but despite the limit laid down here,
fines of forty marks are stipulated on a number of occasions (cf.
Appendix D (ii)). The forty-mark fine may well have originated
later than the present chapter, under influence from the mainland.

Jacobsen (*GGD*, 92 note 2) assumes that the limits simply apply
to the listed misdemeanours committed at the assembly. This is a
possible explanation, although it seems rather narrow.

31/12–14. Further provisions concerning legal procedures are given
in Chapter 8/18–21 and Chapter 32.

Chapter 32: *Af fearkrafi*

32/2–20. These provisions do not specify which party had the right
of proof.

32/6. The phrase *mark gulz* refers to land worth a mark of gold
freehold. Chapters 47/10, 53/3–4 and, presumably, 65/10 refer to
the same method of land valuation, whereas Chapters 20/91, 28/37
and 63/11–12 refer to land valued in terms of the rent that it will
yield (*mark laigi*).

32/12–13 and footnote. The phrase 'forward to the third' (*fram til
priþiu*) relates to an assumed 'another period of a fortnight' (**half
manaþ frest aþra*), which is missing from both the A-text and the
B-text. The phrase in angled brackets is supplied from *tyGL*, by
comparison with the following provision, which refers to disputes
relating to land worth less than a mark of gold. The implications
of these provisions seem to be that if a defendant did not appear
after six or three weeks (depending on the value of the property in
dispute) a plaintiff either took his oath in his absence (if he had
the right of proof) or possibly won his case by default (if the defendant
had the right of proof) (cf. *SL* IV, 282 note 5 to Chapter 32). Wessén
assumes that in each case a defendant could move the oath-taking
twice from the original four or two weeks. It seems more likely,
however, that he could move it once, to give himself half as much
time again (making a total of six weeks or three weeks), provided

that he did this within the first fortnight or week respectively. He would be 'moving it by a fortnight (or a week) to the third fortnight (or week)' from the date of the summons. This interpretation is adopted by both Schlyter and Jacobsen.

32/15. Wessén interprets the phrase *vi manna stemnu* 'a six-man summons' as meaning that one summoned the defendant to take a six-man oath.

Chapter 32a: *Af manna kaupi*

32a/1 and footnote. See Addition 7.

Chapter 33: *Kaupir þu uxa*

33/3–4. Concerning oxen 'breaking out', see 26/27–30.

Chapter 33a: *<Af kauptri ko>*

33a/1 and footnote. In the table of contents in the *A*-text, but not the *B*-text, a separate chapter *Af kauptri ko* 'Concerning a purchased cow' is recorded, although there is no equivalent indication in the text. There is a new chapter in *tyGL*.

33a/4. If a milking cow was dry, this was regarded as a sign of witchcraft. Witches were supposedly able to steal milk from the cow of a stranger (cf. Heurgren 1925, 297–98; *SL* IV, 283 note 3 to Chapter 33). In *GulL* 57 (*NGL* 1, 29) it is specified that a slave may be returned to the vendor if he sucks cows. Also in *GulL* 44 (*NGL* 1, 25) one hidden fault listed in a cow is that it suckles itself. This could be regarded as the same problem, expressed differently, in that one assumes she was then lacking in milk for her owner. *DL* Bb 31 pr is alone in setting a value on the quarters of a cow's udder: one *öre* for one quarter, two *öre* for two and the option of returning the cow for faults in three quarters.

Chapter 34: *Kaupir þu hest*

34/4. The form of blindness termed *starblindr* 'moonblind' usually refers to cataracts (Swedish *gråstarr*), although the word can be used figuratively to mean 'purblind'. Cataracts in horses can occur as a result of periodic ophthalmia, which is a well-documented equine disease, probably viral in origin. It was first recorded in the fourth century and called 'moon-blindness' because symptoms appear at roughly regular intervals, with periods of remission. The effects are progressively more severe and the horse eventually becomes totally blind in the affected eye. In view of the fact that the periods of remission could last for several months at a time, the three days allowed for detecting the problem seem less than generous (cf. Hayes 1968, 167–68). *FrostL* X 48 (*NGL* 1, 228) lists the following faults related to horses: deafness, blindness, being disabled ('broken down'), permanent lameness, shying or stubbornness. A purchaser had five days within which to return the horse. *HL* Kmb 3 refers to lameness or *noko annær laster* 'any other disablement'.

Chapter 35: *Af hesti*

The chapter titles in the tables of contents in the *A*-text and in the *B*-text are more specific: *Af hestatekt* 'Concerning the taking of horses' and *Ridir tu annan mans hest* 'If you ride another man's horse' respectively.

35/6–12. Presumably if one left one's own horse behind, one could simply have made a mistake. There was still, however, a fine attached to this action (35/10–12). Compare this to taking wood from another person (26/57–58), where there does not seem to have been a fine if an equal amount were left.

35/11. Jacobsen (*GGD*, 96 note 2) assumes that, in the phrase *kum hanum hailum haim atr*, the pronoun *hanum* refers to the owner of the horse ('bring [it] back unharmed to him'), but *kuma* in the sense 'bring' takes the dative, so *hanum* in all probability refers to the horse.

Chapter 36: *Af skipa gezlu*

36/2–3. The generic term for any vessel, 'ship', in which one put to sea was *skip*, but there were many terms to designate the size and type of vessel. The general term for a merchant ship of a smaller type (thirteen ribs and three benches as it states here) was *kaupskip* (see Hjärne 1929, 103). Trade between Gotland and the Baltic countries had begun by the end of the Viking Age, but during the eleventh century trade with Russia was of increasing importance and this continued into the twelfth century. With the rise of the Hanseatic League the focus changed and trade was more directed to the south and west. Gotland had few natural resources but farmers dealt in weapons, ships, horses and provisions, all referred to in a papal letter of 1229 (*DS* I, 255–56, note 253, 16/2/1229). This trade was also recognised in 1285 by Magnus Ladulås. The merchant vessels were principally sail-driven, although they would have had a few oar-benches fore and aft (three in the case of the *kaupskip* described here). They were wide-beamed, deep-keeled and seaworthy, as opposed to the narrower, faster and more tender ships for the levy (cf. *KL* s. v. *Skibstyper*).

36/4. A cargo vessel was a *byrþingr*, a term covering ships of various sizes, from those used for coastal traffic to larger cargo ships, eventually succeeded by the *kogge*. Jacobsen (*GGD*, 96 note 3) remarks that forms of the word *byrþingr* are still used in the Baltic of cargo vessels and that in *Eriks SjL1* Text 1 III §58 the word is used of a small ship for freight, larger than a *baat*. In *MLBL*, VI §17 (*NGL* 2, 250–52) a *byrþingr* is stated to be smaller than a *knarr* and it seems generally to have been a small, broad-beamed coastal vessel. In *tyGL* it is glossed as a cargo boat. The word *birþakiʀ* on inscription G 351 from Visby is interpreted by Snædal (2002, 87–88) as *byrþing* (cf. Brøgger and Sheteling 1950, 284–85; *AEW* s. v. *byrþing*; *KL* s. v. *Handelssjöfart*).

36/5–6. The expression *hus þet sum þiauþ sufa i* 'a house in which people sleep', describing the building to which a *byrþing* had to be tied, refers in all probability to the sort of seasonal fishing hut (e.g. the *fiskiahus* mentioned in *HL*) found along the coastline in all Scandinavian countries (see Erixon 1955, 132–33).

36/6–7. This, the only reference to a housewife in *GL*, implies that she was more likely to have the keys than her husband. In *UL* Äb 3 pr there is reference to a wife having the right *til lasæ ok nyklæ* 'to lock and key' as a symbol of her control over the care and protection of the house. This right was claimed for her by her own family, before the marriage act itself and brought with it great responsibility, as much of the wealth of a household would be in the silver and jewels to which she had access.

36/11, 14, 16. The relative sizes of the two types of vessel referred to, a 'small vessel' (*myndrikkia*, 36/11) and a 'boat' (*batr*, 36/14, 16), are obscure. It may be that no distinction is intended. Both were certainly small coastal vessels, probably driven by oar or paddle only. Säve challenges Schlyter's translation of *myndrikkia* (based on the text of *tyGL*) as 'mindre skuta', a small sailing vessel or ferry for cargo. He suggests that a *myndrikkia* might originally have been a small vessel propelled with a single oar by a backward-facing boat-man. He further suggests a derivation from OldSwe *mynda* 'row backwards' and that the second element meant either 'drive forward' or 'rock to and fro' (describing the mode of propulsion of the vessel). Säve agrees it is logical to assume that the vessel was slightly larger than a boat (*batr*), and not just a punt (flat-bottomed boat), since the sequence of vessels mentioned appears to go from the larger to the smaller. The way in which the provision is phrased, however, is ambiguous: a *batr* could have been valued more highly than a *myndrikkia*. The former should not be left on the shore without supervision, or anyone could claim it, whereas the latter could be left if the owner were within shouting distance, otherwise it could again be taken with impunity. Furthermore, if a *batr* were taken from a landing place or mooring, the theft was treated in the same way as that of a horse, whilst no penalty seems to be attached to the taking of a *myndrikkia* if accepted procedures were followed. Cf. *GU*, xxvii–xxix; *GO* s. v. *mynn-vricka*; *KL* s. v. *Myndrik*. Another word for a small boat was *fluti* (cf. Addition 8/42).

If a vessel was found *varþalaus* 'unattended' it could be treated as a wreck to all intents and purposes in certain cases, and the finder could claim a higher proportion of the value (cf. *BjR* 19 pr).

36/13–14. On the use of a shout as a legal instrument, see Note to 22/3–4.

36/15–17. This provision seems to contradict the previous one, unless one assumes that a 'landing place' was always under watch, or was deemed to be so, or that *at staþum* specifically means 'tied up at a mooring', i.e. that the boat was obviously owned by someone who intended to return to it.

For further responsibilities with regard to ships and boats, see Addition 8/39–50.

Chapter 37: *Af ranzsakan*

37/6–7. Tracing property by means of house-searches has ancient origins (see Westman 1912a, 223–24). The reason for the insistence on the searchers being loosely girded and without coats was to avoid the possibility of evidence being planted. A similar stipulation is made in *MLBL*, VIII §8 (*NGL* 2, 271): *þeir skulu ganga in linda lausir* 'they should go in ungirded' (cf. *ÄVgL* Tjb 5 §1; *UL* Mb 47 §1). Jacobsen (*GGD*, 97 note 4) suggests that the *kapa* referred to (in 'coatless') might have been a hooded cloak. This implies that the searchers were to be easily recognised, as well as unable to conceal evidence (cf. Hammerich 1959, 196–99; Wennström 1936, 148–64). The provisions relating to house-searches varied considerably between different Swedish provincial laws and in *MEStL* Tjb 2 §1 anyone wishing to search without official permission had to lay down a deposit of forty marks.

37/7–9. The removal of immunity, effectively *haimafriþr* (cf. Note to 12/2), from the dwelling of a person who refused a house-search was a serious matter. The doors could be broken down without redress, irrespective of whether stolen goods were found (cf. *ÄVgL* Tjb 5 pr, 6; *YVgL* Tjb 30, 34; *ÖgL* Vb 32 §4).

37/12–13. According to Wessén (*SL* IV, 283 note 5 to Chapter 37) *þa al laiþznum fylgia* 'the warrant for ownership must be traced' is a standard Scandinavian legal expression. The meaning is that proof of ownership must be traced from the previous owner to the person now in possession of the goods. Wessén (*SL* IV, 233) inserts the explanatory word 'fångesman' (assignor) in his translation of this passage. This person was the one who had granted the right in property (of whatever type) to the assignee (in this case the person under suspicion).

37/14. 'The person to whom he first referred' (*þar sum hann fyrsti til skiautr*). Wessén (*SL* IV, 283 note 6 to Chapter 37) and Jacobsen (*GGD*, 97) call the person to whom the accused refers the 'hemulsman' (Swedish) or 'hjemmelsmand' (Danish). This was the person who had a legal obligation to defend a buyer's right to goods against a challenge and to defend a buyer's innocence if he consequently lost ownership; in many circumstances this would have been the previous owner or keeper. It is not clear from Wessén's notes if he intends this person to be the same as the assignor referred to in his note 5, but Jacobsen (*GGD*, 97 note 6) assumes only one person is involved. The circumlocutions of the text make this passage rather obscure, but a translation assuming a single third party, the assignor, from whom the accused person claims he received the property, makes perfect sense.

37/22–24. It appears from the context that the goods planted by the miscreant were assumed to be his own, which he was intending to accuse his neighbour of having stolen, rather than goods he himself had taken and was trying to dispose of.

37/24–26. The wergild to be paid would be three marks of gold for a Gotlander, or ten marks of silver for a non-Gotlander.

37/26. The emended words, 'But if', derive from Pipping (*GLGS*, xxxvi note 4) who prefers the *B*-text reading *þar til, en* '. . . in addition . . . If' to the *A*-text reading *þar til et* 'until, unless'. Schlyter (*CIG*, 78) and Säve (*GU*, 25) accept the *A*-text reading. Wessén (*SL* IV, 233 and 284 note 11 to Chapter 37) follows these two but acknowledges Pipping's alternative interpretation, which is perhaps to be preferred; it would be unusual to mention a fine relating only to a non-Gotlander before that to a Gotlander. The twelve marks to the general assembly were according to Pipping in addition to the three marks payable to the (presumably) local assembly, rather than instead of them (see also Jacobsen *GGD*, 98).

Chapter 38: *Af þiaufa ret*

Theft (*þiaufnaþr*) was secret theft of movables, as opposed to open robbery. Although it is sometimes assumed that in pre-Christian times this crime was regarded as a particularly serious offence against the community at large, alongside murder and rape, and had to be atoned for to the gods with the life of the perpetrator, there is little evidence of this in the provincial laws. Admittedly, the worst crimes were punishable by death, but the limit varied between the provinces: *ÄVgL* Md 8 sets the limit at two *öre*, *GL* at one mark of silver, the remainder of the laws at ½ mark (two marks in coin). *GL*, *SdmL*, *UL* and *HL* are the only provincial laws that rely purely on monetary value to judge the severity of a theft, indicating the generalised use of coinage in these areas (cf. Hemmer 1928, 159–64; Wennström 1936, 58–65; Hasselberg 1953, 341–47).

38/3–4. The word *snattanbot* in the sense 'fine for petty larceny' does not occur widely in medieval Scandinavian law (cf. Wennström 1936, 17).

38/5–6. 'And [be] marked and be committed to pay wergild' (*ok merkia ok til vereldis dyma*). The thief was to be branded (which was normally done on the cheek), or possibly had his ears cut off, as a visible punishment. Whether *merkia* always signified one or other punishment is a matter for conjecture (cf. Brunner 1906–28, II, 788; Hemmer 1928, 62 note 9; Carlsson 1934, 102; Wilda 1960, 514–15). A thief also had to pay a fine of either three marks of gold or ten of silver. Schlyter's note (*CIG*, 79 note c) is ambiguous on how this was determined: 'D. ä. till lika stor bot, som hade skolat erläggas om han hade blifvit dräpen' (That is, to a fine as great as would have been paid if he had been killed). The use of the passive gives no indication of the principal of *han* 'he'. Jacobsen (*GGD*, 98 note 8) assumes that the sum was determined by whether the person robbed was a Gotlander or not. On the other hand, Wessén (*SL* IV, 284 note 2) assumes that the sum depended on whether the thief was a Gotlander or a non-Gotlander. In view of the fact that the immediately previous mention of wergild related specifically to the status of the wronged person, Jacobsen's interpretation seems the more likely, although some payments for abduction, rape, fire damage and damage to fruit trees depended on the status of the person inflicting the injury (see Chapters 21/2–8, 22/26–28, 51/3–4 and 59/6). Hasselberg (1953, 231) assumes that if a thief could not pay the wergild, he lost his life, but there is no direct evidence of this.

38/6–9. Wennström (1936, 76) points out that *GL* is the only Swedish-related provincial law to follow the Germanic laws in stipulating hanging for a subsequent theft of whatever value. Hanging, as opposed to beheading, was a shameful death and even female thieves were not hanged (cf. *ÖgL* Vb 35). Hanging is the only means of execution specified in *GL*, but there are examples from mainland provincial laws of other forms, for example stoning on a beach (cf. *DL* Tjb 2 pr; *KL* s. v. *Dödsstraff*; Notes to 21/9–12, 63/11–13). A summary of non-monetary punishments appears in Appendix D (i).

38/8–9 and footnote. The *B*-text omits this final provision but has further provisions relating mostly to theft by slaves, presumably omitted from the *A*-text for the same reason that provisions regarding the purchase of slaves were omitted. These are given in Addition 8.

38/9. Schlyter in his glossary (*CIG*, 310) suggests that *þau* 'nevertheless' be emended to *þa* 'then'. Pipping (*GLGS*, 50 note 7) rejects this and refers to Kock (1895, 126) for corroboration. The meaning is that a thief who took a mark of silver or more was to hang, even if this were his first offence.

Chapter 39: *Af oqueþinsorþum*

The fines for verbal insults in *VStL* I 53 pr are double those for the most serious bodily injury, whereas here in *GL* they are equivalent to those of a more minor wound. The punishment was more severe in Iceland: lesser outlawry and a fine of six marks of silver, irrespective of the social standing of the person insulted (cf. *Grágás* II §237 (*LEI* 2, 195)). In Norwegian laws, the fine for a similar offence was three marks for a landowning farmer, and on a sliding scale for other social classes (cf. *GulL* 98, 178, 196 (*NGL* 1, 46–47, 66, 70)).

39/2. The insult *morþingi* 'murderer' refers to a killer who does not admit his or her killing and attempts to hide the crime, or perhaps accuse another. Here it is equated with the shameful epithets thief (*þiaufr*) and highway robber (*rauferi*), which were punishable by death if serious enough, or second offences. The word is not used elsewhere in *GL*, where *bani* is the usual word for a killer.

39/2–3. The term *ran* has been translated elsewhere as 'open robbery', and was not originally considered as shameful as secret theft. It usually (but not always) involved a greater or lesser degree of violence, and provincial laws differed in the weight they gave to the two elements of the crime. Over the period covered by the provincial laws, the punishment became more severe and in the national laws *rån* was treated as an *edsöresbrott*, a crime against the king's peace (cf. Introduction, p. xxxviii; Note to 12/9–10). It seems that in *GL* it was regarded as equal in severity to secret theft.

39/3. The word *kasnavargr* 'murdering arsonist' is also found in Swedish provincial laws (cf. *ÖgL* Eb 31 pr; Wennström 1936, 270–74, 301). The table of contents of *VmL* (*CIS* V, 80) has *kaxnawargh*, which prompts Säve (*GU*, xxxi) to speculate whether the first element of the word had its origins in a form *kâx* 'landing place, place for boats', which he takes to be Estonian. If this were the case, he suggests, *kasnavargr* could originally have meant 'burner of boats', *vargr* being the perpetrator of a violent action, criminal or outlaw. The connection seems tenuous, however, and Schlyter (*CISG*, 340–41) offers a number of alternatives for the origin of the element *kasna-* amongst which are Latin *casa* 'house', OldSwe *kasa* 'to pile up' and Swedish dialect *kase* 'bed warmer'. Wessén (*SL* I, *ÖgL* 51 note 50) offers the explanation that *kase* meant 'hög av ris, ved, stubbar o.d. att brännas, bål (vårdkase)' (pile of brushwood, firewood, stubble or similar for burning, pyre (beacon)), but gives no source for this information. No punishment for the crime itself is given in *GL*, or in *SdmL* 34, where it is also listed as a punishable insult. In Norway, however, actual murderous arson was considered to be an *úbótamál*, that is, an injury not able to be reconciled by fine, and the perpetrator was called a *brennuvargr* (cf. *GulL* 98, 178 (*NGL* 1, 46–47, 66)).

39/4. Jacobsen (*GGD*, 102 note 2) rightly points out that *hordombr* 'adultery' and *fordeþskepr* 'witchcraft' are abstract nouns and do not refer to the person committing these acts, as do all the remaining nouns. Säve speculates whether the *B*-text reading *fordenschep'r* reflects an older *fornskapr*, comparing it with *fyrnska* 'old customs, superstition' at 4/3. The word used in *Guta saga* (*GLGS*, 64 line 13) to describe Avair Strabain is *fielkunnugr* 'skilled in many things', and this word and its equivalents were also used, frequently with a positive connotation, to indicate 'skilled in magic arts', especially in OWN sources. The word *fordeþskepr* and its equivalents were more often used negatively in the sense 'witchcraft, black arts'. In the Christian law provisions, all forms of witchcraft, white or black, were forbidden although sometimes the punishment for the two was different. Both Norwegian and Swedish provincial laws vary in the severity of the punishment to be meted out to witches, including the death penalty. The stricter attitude stems from the southern tradition of Christianity and church law. The more moderate punishments laid down are closer to those of the Irish church. *GL* refers only to *fordeþskepr* as an insult against women, and not to the crime itself.

Insulting a woman by calling her an adulteress implies that this was considered to be disgraceful behaviour, but as noted earlier (Note to Chapter 21) *GL* prescribes no punishment of the woman for it. On the other hand, accusing a man of such an act does not seem to have been considered an insult, although his life might be forfeit (21/10).

39/8. Jacobsen (*GGD*, 102 note 4) observes that the prefix *o-* in *osinum*, literally 'at a bad time, untimely', is not the usual negation, but pejorative, as in Swedish *otyg* 'witchcraft, nuisance' (cf. Note to Chapter 17). It (*osinum*) seems to be the dative of a noun meaning 'a bad time'. Insults offered when the speaker was drunk would be treated leniently if they were duly retracted and compensated for.

39/9–12. Once summoned to the church, a person accused of slander must either defend himself or offer restitution, both accompanied by a three-man oath, sworn by parishioners. Public apology is demanded for insults in *GulL* 196 (*NGL* 1, 70) and *VStL* I 53 pr, but is not mentioned in Swedish provincial laws, although shaming punishments are laid down for other crimes. The involvement of a parish in the legal process is also incorporated in Chapter 30, relating to surety.

39/13. The expression *sokn all* means 'all the parishioners' in the same way that *land alt* means 'the general assembly'.

39/15–16. The more public insult incurred a much higher penalty. Wessén (*SL* IV, 285 notes 4 and 5) compares the fines and procedures in these provisions (the *siex manna aiþi* 'six-man oath') with those for breaking the assembly peace (Chapter 11) and to accusations against women (Chapter 2). Cf. *CISk* IV 21–22 for insults in general.

Chapter 40: *Af smafilepi*

In the table of contents, and in the *B*-text, it is made clear that this chapter refers specifically to unbranded (*omerkt*) small livestock. The word *omerkt* in the *B*-text has, however, been added later and may not have been in the manuscript from which Bilefeld made his copy. By elimination, only immature stock is covered by this provision since adult pigs, sheep, goats, cattle and horses are specifically named in later, and different, provisions. Otherwise, sheep, goats and other small livestock were normally included in the concept of *smafilepi*, OldSwe *söper*.

40/3. The assembly intended here must be the sixth assembly, since the riding assembly is mentioned specifically in later chapters where relevant.

40/4, 41/6, 42/4, 43/3 and 43/4 and footnotes. Bugge (1877–78, 265–66) gives an account of possible forms: *-lausn* and *-launs*, concluding that the latter is an appropriate correction for all instances of *-laun* in the manuscripts of *GL*. He notes that *lausn* rather than *launs* is used in *Guta saga* (*GLGS*, 67 line 18), but takes this to be an example of linguistic differences between the two texts. He considers the form *laun* to be incorrect, the sense not being a reward to the finder, but a fee to secure the release of the animal. Pipping (*GLGS*, 53 note 8) follows this correction, but notes that *daGL* offers two different translations: *lön* for the first and third occurrences and *lösen* for the last (cf. Läffler 1878, 287–89; *GLGS*, xlii note 4). Although *daGL* recognises a difference, the translation appears to be inconsistent. Wessén (*SL* IV, 285 note 3 to Chapter 40) implies that the *pinglaun* (of one *örtug* per visit) was compensation for taking an animal to the assembly if it were unclaimed, and that this was different from the *heptalauns*, paid by the owner of a stray animal to redeem it (see Chapter 43). Wessén does not, however, maintain this distinction; he translates *ping(s)laun* as 'tinglösen' and *(hepta)launs* as 'lösen'. A translation *lön* 'reward' appears to be more appropriate for the former, in the same way that a *fundarlaun* (Addition 8/34) is the compensation or reward paid to a person who returns a slave and the goods he has stolen. Incidentally, Pipping has not suggested a change to the latter. It is entirely possible that two different words, *(ping)laun* or *(pings)laun*, related to OWN *laun* n. pl., Swedish *lön* 'payment, reward', and *(hepta)launs*, related to OWN *lausn* f. pl., Swedish *lösen* 'fee, ransom', are involved, and have become confused. This assumption has been followed in the present translation.

40/4–5. In neither this chapter nor in the following one is it stated what happened to the animal(s) in question if unclaimed. Presumably the finder kept the animal(s), paying to the parishioners the difference between their valuation and the *þinglaun* 'assembly payment' due to him.

Chapter 41: *Af suinum*

41/4. Specific mention of the riding assembly in relation to the third presentation of the beasts in this and the next chapter suggests that the sixth assembly is intended elsewhere in this section.

41/6–7 and footnotes. The clause and word in angled brackets are supplied from the *B*-text.

Chapter 42: *Af bolambum*

The eventual fate of stray sheep is even more ambiguous in this chapter, nor is it clear what was paid by an owner to a finder, although this can perhaps be assumed to have been an *örtug*, as in Chapter 43. No mention is made of valuation, only of the ownership of any lambs carried by the ewes. These went to the finder, presumably regardless of whether the sheep itself were claimed. The word *bolamb* refers to a tame sheep as opposed to the *utegångsfår* of Gotland, which lived out all year round. These retained several primitive characteristics, such as the mane and genetically inherited extra horns (encouraged by selective breeding) on the tups or rams. Selective breeding was made possible by the fact that the ewes were frequently kept indoors. It is reasonable to suppose that a *bolamb* was such a housed ewe or possibly a castrated ram, reared for meat.

Chapter 43: *Af fastum veþuri okliptum*

The use of the participle *(o)klipt* '(un)shorn' in 43/1, 43/2, 44/1 and 44/2 is to some extent ambiguous in the *B*-text since *kliptr* can itself have the meaning 'gelded'. (See relevant footnotes.) The *A*-text, however, refers in both Chapters 43 and 44 to ungelded (*fastr*) rams: unshorn (*okliptr*) and shorn (*kliptr*) respectively, and this reading seems preferable.

43/3 and footnote. The word *heptalauns* (literally 'tethering ransom') clearly means a fee paid by a legal owner to redeem his animal, as opposed to a payment (in effect for expenses) to the finder simply for bringing an (unclaimed) creature to the assembly (cf. Note to 40/4, 41/6, 42/4, 43/3 and 43/4; *GGD*, 103 note 4). Various forms of restraint were employed to prevent straying and it is possible that a fine was imposed because the animal had been inadequately tethered. Schlyter (*CIG*, iv) takes *heptalauns* as an example of the degradation of the language in that the genitive form has been used instead of the accusative following the preposition *firi*. Säve (*GU*, xvii) takes it for a scribal error, whereas Pipping (*GLGS*, 53 note 8), following Bugge, accepts the manuscript reading (cf. Läffler 1878, 287).

43/4 and footnote. The form *launs* instead of *laun* in this instance has been taken by earlier commentators (Bugge and Läffler referred to above) to support the argument that the latter was incorrect in all cases. Säve (*GU*), on the other hand, following the *B*-text, uses the form *laun* throughout. The differentiation suggested in the preceding Notes is preferred.

Chapter 44: *Af fastum veþuri kliptum*

Whilst an unshorn ram seems to have been treated similarly to a *bolamb*, a shorn ram was not, because of the season of the year.

44/2–3. The feast of Saints Simon and Jude is October 28th, so the case imagined is one of a breeding ram being loose over the winter period.

44/3–4. The clause 'up to the time that it is usual to release them' must qualify the phrase 'after the feast of St Simon and St Jude' and not the intervening clause in *GL*, 'it has rendered itself forfeit by wandering'. The normal time for the release of the ram with the ewes was in the early spring, possibly on Lady Day, the 25th March (cf. Note to 57/2–3).

44/6–9. In this case it appears that the animal was not taken to the assembly and valued. The finder neither received expenses nor paid anything to the parishioners. His reward was simply the ram itself, unless his owner redeemed him (for an unspecified fee).

Chapter 45: *Af gaitum ok bukkum*

Goats do not seem to have been widely kept in Sweden, but they were important elsewhere in Scandinavia. They were clearly not highly

valued in Gotland since the price for redeeming a goat was half that
of a horse or cow and much less than for a sheep, but in Norway and
Denmark they were kept as milk-yielding animals, giving profitable
cheese, and for their meat and skins.

45/3–4. 'Then they shall be redeemed: a nanny for six pence for each
assembly' (*so skal atr loysa gait firi siex penninga a hueriu þingi*).
This provision implies that an owner redeeming his goats paid
according to how many assemblies the finder had attended. The
previous reference to payments by an owner (Chapter 43) does not
mention multiple assembly visits, so it is not possible to infer that
this was the rule in all cases. The finder, however, received expenses
for each assembly visit, so it seems to be a logical conclusion.

45/3–4. The *penningr* 'penny' was the lowest unit of currency in
Scandinavia up to the end of the thirteenth century. It is referred to
only here and in Chapters 47, 49 and 56a. The number of pennies per
örtug and thus per *öre* and mark varied from area to area, although
no records exist earlier than the end of the thirteenth century (cf.
GGD, 25 note 1; Jansson 1936, 65; *KL* s. v. *Ørtug*). Contemporary
sources state that the Gotlandic system was taken over by Riga (cf.
the letters of the Bishop of Riga *HRSH29*, 1–14) with an *örtug*
divided into twelve pennies. The same system is recorded for Öland,
although later the sixteen-penny standard current in Götaland was
in use (cf. *DS* I, 456, no. 549 (6/4/1271); *DS* I, 591–93, no. 736
(29/12/1281)). In Svealand, from around 1300 there was a unification
of the system: a mark was eight *öre*, each of three *örtugar*, each of
eight pennies, giving 192 pennies to a mark (in coin), i.e. half as
many as in Götaland. Norway adopted the same system at about
this time. Although the consensus amongst scholars appears to be
that there were eight pennies to an *örtug* in Gotland during the
period of *GL*, other rates have also been proposed and the relationship between the fees for a nanny-goat and a billy-goat might
suggest a rate of twelve pennies to an *örtug* (see Appendix C).

Chapter 45a: <*Af nautum ok russum*>

45a/1 and footnote. The chapter title occurs in the table of contents,
but not in the *A*-text, although a new chapter occurs in both the *B*-
text (63) and *tyGL*.

45a/7–8. '. . . not travel to Visby with them' (*. . . fari ai til Visbyar
miþ*). This is the only reference to Visby in *GL*. It is not clear

what the implications are of this provision. It might be that there was a horse fair at Visby and that the finder of a horse or pony was not to take it there for recognition or possible sale, but to the assembly. It could also mean that, whilst they might use the horse on their farm, they were not permitted to use it for travelling longer distances until they had presented it three times at an assembly.

45a/10–11 and footnote. A *motstukkr* was one of the posts at the centre of the assembly, possibly marking an area with legal significance. Four *tingstockar* are mentioned in several medieval sources from Skåne (e.g. *CISk* IV 21) (cf. *CISk* IV, 408 note 8; *SL* IV, 200 note 22). Stray cattle and ponies were to be tied up within sight of these, but a distance away so that they were not confused with animals belonging to the people attending the assembly. It is possible that the assembly was in a natural hollow and that by having the animals a distance away the men holding them could see the posts over the heads of others at the assembly, or alternatively that potential claimants could see the beasts (cf. *GGD*, 105 note 1; *SL* IV, 286 note 2 to Chapter 45a).

Table iii in Appendix D summarises the provisions in chapters 40–45a.

Chapter 46: *Af merki*

46/2–4. The crime referred to here is that of altering an existing earmark on a sheep, or other creature, to one for a different owner. Such earmarks have been used until relatively recently to distinguish sheep grazing on common land and are still used on the reindeer herds of the Sami. Altering a mark was equal to theft in some provincial laws (cf. *VmL* Mb 26). Obviously, if an animal had been purchased or received in dowry, a change was quite lawful.

Chapter 47: *Af akrum*

47/6. Jacobsen (*GGD*, 105 note 2) remarks that a *landboi* 'tenant' was someone who leased or rented land, as opposed to owning it freehold. The word *land* was not generally used to describe property (Ruthström 2002, 128) and the original form seems to have been *lanbo*, meaning someone living on leased property (related to the word for 'loan'). This changed as a result of folk etymology to *landboi*, a word that occurs only here in *GL*. The common OWN equivalent *laigulenningr* occurs at 3/18 (cf. *SkL* 238–39 (*CISk* I 225)). Tenancy conditions were fixed and for a limited period, with an initial payment and often an annual rent. Jacobsen also points out that the only other word for farmer in *GL* is *bondi*. This is in contrast to the several words used for different classes of landowner in Danish and mainland Swedish laws.

47/7. The standard area measure for arable land in Gotland appears to have been *laupsland*, the land upon which a bushel (about 36 litres) of seed corn (barley) could be sown. One equivalent, recorded in early fourteenth-century Norway, was ¹/₃ *markebol* (cf. Steinnes 1936, 142; Note to 20/47–48).

47/8. Haymaking generally ran from the first weekday after St Peter's day (29th June) and could continue until St Michael's day (29th September). After this, cattle could graze on the meadows, just as they could graze on arable fields after the harvest (cf. *UL* Bb 10; *DL* Bb 8).

47/9–10. Unlike other instances of *lass* 'load', the reference here is to a specific volume. The standard conversion for a ship's cargo was that a *lass* or *läst* was twelve *skeppund* and the same relationship appears to have been current with the *lispund*. This does not, however, give an absolute volume, since the capacity of a *pund* varied from time to time and place to place (cf. Note to 6/8).

47/10. The expression *at markum* refers to the calculated value of the land according to the same principles as those in Chapter 32. Wessén (*SL* IV, 286 note 4 to Chapter 47) uses the word *marktal*, equivalent to Gtn *markatal* (cf. Note to 53/3–5). The word refers to weighed marks, despite the element *-tal*.

Chapter 48: *Af rofnakrum*

48/2–3. Turnips were introduced to Scandinavia at an unknown date, but by the Middle Ages they were a significant crop and numerous statutes related to their cultivation occur in the provincial laws, except for *VgLL* and *SkL*, the very earliest laws. *UL*, *SdmL*, *DL*, *VmL* have several less categorical statutes mentioning the cultivation of turnips. *UL* Kkb 7 §5 names turnips as one of the crops on which tithe was to be paid and this occurs also in some Norwegian laws. In *ÖgL* Bb 28 §5 there is a description of crop rotation on clearings: turnips (for a year), then rye (for two years), the land to be left fallow after three harvests.

48/3–4. Those 'who have no arable land, but have a house' (*sepalaust fulk sum hus hafr*) were crofters who perhaps only kept livestock (see Chapter 56a). It is not clear from the wording whether the land for the turnips was part of the holding, or extra land provided by the landlord, but he was clearly expected to provide the means of cultivation. The provision given here for care of the poor in a parish seems to be unique to *GL*.

48/5. This is the only case where *oykr* refers to ploughing in particular, as opposed to draught in general. Yoked oxen did this work in southern Sweden, whereas in the north of the country a horse and chest harness was used. Cf. Notes to 6/8–9 and 26/45.

Chapter 49: *Af hafreki*

For all the provisions in this chapter, it must be assumed that (as was the case in respect of stray animals) the remainder of the find was returned to the owner of the property, or to the parish or assembly if no owner was determined. The sliding scale of payments to a finder of jetsam, flotsam and lagan reflects the risk involved in recovering the goods, and the likelihood of determining the original owner. Similar provisions are to be found in Swedish provincial laws and in *VStL* (cf. *UL* Mb 54 pr; *VStL* III iii 13; Hasselberg 1953, 117–18).

49/6. The expression *yr lanzsyn* 'out of sight of land' is rendered in *tyGL* as *us der kennunge*, the same expression as is used in *VStL* III iii 8 to indicate that a sea voyage has properly started.

Chapter 50: *Af eldi*

50/3. The word *skurstain* 'hearth' appears in Gotlandic dialect as *kurstain* or *kustain* and is a loan word from Middle Low German *scorsten*. It meant originally the whole of the covered hearth and chimney (but now only the latter). This former sense was current in Danish as late as the early nineteenth century and according to Lis Jacobsen (*GGD*, 106 note 6) survived in Danish dialects a century later. The form of fireplace with a covered chimney arrived in Scandinavia in the Middle Ages and this reference in *GL* is one of the earliest (see *SL* IV, 287 note 1 to Chapter 50).

In *MELL* Bb 28, if fire broke loose from a *stova* 'dwelling', *stekara hus* 'kitchen' or *kölno hus* 'malt kiln', the farmer was not liable.

Chapter 51: *Af bierueldi*

51/2. It was previously common to take burning material from one place to another to kindle further fires or ovens, because of the difficulty of starting a fire (see *GGD*, 107 note 1). One might even have to borrow fire from a neighbour, carrying it from one farm to another. Similar provisions occur in *UL* Bb 24 §1, *DL* Bb 45 §4, *VmL* Bb 24 §1, *SdmL* Kkb 2 pr and *SdmL* Bb 18 §7 (cf. *SL* IV, 287 note 1 to Chapter 51).

51/3–4. For further occasions on which compensation to some extent depended upon the status of the perpetrator of a crime, see Chapters 21/2–8, 22/26–28, 38/6–9 and 59/6.

Since the wergild of a minor was the same as that of an adult (cf. 18/16), the compensation payable by the responsible adult was the same. This is the reverse of the situation at 14/25, relating to killings and 59/6 relating to damage to fruit trees, where compensation is halved if a minor commits the crime.

Chapter 52: *Af broagierþ*

52/1. The verb *bro* 'make a bridge' or 'surface a road' survives in Gotlandic dialect (cf. *GO* s. v. *bro*[1]). Here *bro* is a noun meaning a filling of stones, branches or other material placed annually across a track to make marshy and otherwise inaccessible places passable.

52/2. The routes concerned were recognised summer roads, as opposed to simple cleared tracks in the forest, and their upkeep was a communal responsibility. Only in later times was the whole track surfaced (cf. *GGD*, 107 note 3; *SL* IV, 287 note 1 to Chapter 52). Most mainland provincial laws (e.g. *ÖgL* Bb 4 and 5) contain statutes concerning roads, road building and road repair (*broagierþ*) (cf. Yrwing 1940, 104). One important purpose of these constructions was to provide routes to the parish churches, mills and other necessary destinations. *ÄVgL* Jb 12 and *YVgL* Jb 26 mention *markvägar* and *kyrkovägar*, but also (Fnb 32) *quærnæuægher* and *allmannævægher*, which foreshadow the more detailed statutes of the national law. In Uppland alone seventy-five runic inscriptions commemorate *bro* builders.

52/4. The three-mark fine extracted for default was presumably paid to the sixth assembly.

Chapter 53: *Af skuti*

As Jacobsen (*GGD*, 107 note 4) comments, the taxes referred to in this chapter are those funds gathered together from contributions made during time of need. The word survives in the Swedish *förskott* 'advance', *sammanskott* 'collection' and *tillskott* 'contribution', each relating to a contribution in some form (see *SL* IV, 287 note 1 to Chapter 53). The annual tax (*skattr*) to the Swedish crown and the levy tax (laiþingslami) are described in Guta saga, but are not referred to in GL (cf. GS, xxxiii–xxxvi, xlviii, 32 note to 6/12, 59 note to 14/5).

53/3–5. Despite the fact that the words markatal and tald mark were used elsewhere in Scandinavia to mean marks counted (i.e. in coin, rather than weighed), it seems that the Gotlandic tax based on markatal was calculated on the gold or silver value of property and liquid assets, rather than on the penningr value. This would have had the effect of taking into account any devaluation of the currency in respect of liquid assets. Wessén (SL IV, 287 note 2 to Chapter 53) simply refers to the value of the land in marks (as described in Chapter 32) and liquid assets, but by implication intends weighed value, e.g. ounces (oyrar) of gold, silver and other goods that could legally be used as currency. The phrase ai af garrum gersemum 'not of manufactured valuables' specifically excludes such items, but covers manufactured household chattels of gold and silver. Gradually, (lös)öre came to apply to all movables (see Ruthström 2002, 141–42, 180). Later sumptuary laws (Chapter 65) forbade the purchase of gold and silver items, presumably since this would constitute tax avoidance, as they were non-taxable assets (cf. Notes to 2/35, Addition 9/5–6).

53/4–5. The word gørsomme in the sense 'valuables' was still found in Danish dialect when Lis Jacobsen produced her translation in 1910 (GGD, 108 note 1).

Chapter 54: Af varþi

Provisions relating to the watch are to be found in UL Kgb 12, SdmL Kgb 12 and HL Kgb 9. Farmers in coastal areas carried a particular responsibility. The duty of the watch was to light beacons to summon troops in case of an attack. Those sitting watch paid their own expenses, and any fines due if they failed in their duty. The level of the fine is not given in GL, but in UL it is forty marks. In SdmL and HL the fine varies depending on the nature of the failure in duty. The Danish translation (daGL) records an increasing level of responsibility with the increase in the age of the person from eighteen to twenty-two years. Another aspect of defence was the laiþingr, referred to in Guta saga (GLGS, 68).

54/2–4. Although Pipping (GLGS, Ordbok) defines the varþpenningar as 'en årlig skatt, som erlades af alla vapenföra män' (an annual tax, paid by all men capable of bearing arms), comparison with mainland provincial laws suggests that it refers to fines payable for not keeping proper watch.

54/3. The *skyldir* 'expenses' were usually communal taxes, but it seems more likely that expenses incurred in keeping watch are intended here.

Chapter 55: *Af husum ok husþiauþum*

55/1. The *husþiauþ* 'household servants' were people working in the (farm)house itself, perhaps specifically as opposed to those doing outside farm work, referred to in the following chapter.

55/4. Wessén (*SL* IV, 288 note 2 to Chapter 55) observes that the scribe of manuscript B 65 (*tyGL*) has here mistaken *(hus)þiauþ* for *þiaufr* 'thief' and inserted a new chapter heading, *Van husdyben* 'Concerning house thieves'. This provision probably refers to permanent members of a household, rather than seasonal workers, but the reason for it is obscure. Since those who did not grow their own crops could be pressed into service by any farm for harvesting, it might have been regarded as unethical to subsume people into one's household, thus making them unavailable for this work.

Chapter 56: *Af byrslufulki*

56/4. The payment for a day's hire is set out in the following provision, Chapter 56a. The *byrslufulk* 'harvesters' were hired seasonal workers who received daily wages.

Chapter 56a: *<Af seþalausu fulki>*

56a/1 and footnote. This new chapter (75) in the *B*-text (and in *tyGL*) is not signalled in the *A*-text, although the chapter title appears in the table of contents.

56a/2. The *seþalaust fulk* (with no arable land) were crofters, as described in the notes to Chapter 48.

56a/3–5. Payment was according to the area worked and the grain harvested and did not include provisions. The barley and rye would have been for flour and food and the oats possibly to feed horses and perhaps make porridge and soup (see *KL* s. v. *Havre*; *Korn*; *Råg*).

Chapter 57: *Af ikornum*

57/2–3. Only the winter pelts (*gråverk*) of squirrels were valued as currency, so the close season coincides with the period when they were in their summer coats (*routhskyn*). The open season was usually from 13th October (28th October in Gotland, 1st November in Uppland) to 14th April (25th March in Västmanland and in Gotland, 2nd February in Södermanland). Forty skins were equivalent in value to one timber. Sources from 1235 mention rights granted to four Gotlandic fur traders to trade toll-free in England for three years, and payments to Gotlandic merchants for these skins are recorded in 1237, 1242, 1244, 1248 and 1250 (cf. *HansUB* I, 270, 283, 322, 359, 333, 395).

Chapter 58: *Af herum*

58/2–3. Once again the close season for hare trapping was the summer half year. Although a gin is referred to, the usual method for catching hare in the winter was in a snow-pit, loosely covered with brushwood (see *KL* s. v. *Harar*; *Jakt*). *GL* is the only provincial law that specifies a close season for catching hares, although hares are mentioned in *ÄVgL* Fnb 7 §1, *YVgL* Utb 15 and *ÖgL* Bb 36 §5 in relation to who owned a hare that had been caught.

Chapter 59: *Af skafli*

59/1. The word *ska(f)vel* is used in Gotlandic dialect for fruit from trees, e.g. apples (cf. *GO* s. v. *skavel*). Schlyter (*CISG*, 550) and Jacobsen (*GGD*, 109 note 4) think that edible fruit in general might be meant in this instance. The word *skafl* occurs in *UL* in the table of contents against Chapter 49 of Mb and in *HL* in the chapter heading of Mb 32 referring to one who steals any edible crop (e.g. turnips, peas). In *UL* Bb 14 §6 and other provincial laws there are fines for felling another person's fruit trees, with varying levels of fine depending on whether a tree was in fruit or not. The fine in *GL* for picking fruit before September 8th appears to apply even to the owner of the trees in question, or it might refer to trees on commonly owned land. The date might suggest the type of fruit that was cultivated in Gotland (possibly apples), or the time when the fruit concerned was ripe. Cf. *KL* s. v. *Frugttræer*.

59/6. Further instances of variable penalties depending on the person committing an offence are to be found in Chapters 21/2–8, 22/26–28, 38/6–9 and 51/3–4.

Chapter 60: *Af messufalli*

60/5–6. A feast of nine lessons in the Catholic Church was one on which nine lessons (Bible or other readings) were included in the service of Matins. These services were reserved for the more important minor feast days, others having fewer readings.

60/6. Schlyter (*CIG*, 379; *CISG*, 415) takes *eþa hafas* 'or held' as a scribal correction for *lesas* 'read', rather than a parallelism, but cf. Notes to 13/7–8, 19/33, 21/16–17, 25/48 and 50.

60/7. The fine for omitting to say mass on a Sunday or major feast day was twice that for a Friday or lesser feast day.

Chapter 61: *Af dufli*

61/4 and footnote. The sixth assembly is presumably intended here as elsewhere. Dicing is forbidden in *MEStL*, which has a separate *Dobblara balker*, and in *MLLL* VIII 28 (*NGL* 2, 165), but there is no equivalent in any of the mainland provincial laws. Wessén (*MEStLNT*, 292) assumes, therefore, that the phenomenon was one encountered in towns rather than in the countryside. For the *B*-text version, see Addition 9.

61/5–10. The second half of this chapter forms the closing section of the *B*-text (following Chapter 83). Neither there nor in the *A*-text is there a separate chapter heading, nor is the section listed in the table of contents of either text as an independent chapter. It is this paragraph that seems to suggest that *GL*, as it has been preserved in the two Gutnish manuscripts, was either a living statute book or a justice book, rather than merely a scholarly work.

61/6–10. Wessén compares this passage to the final words of the preface to *VStL*: *unde queme en niye recht dat in dem boke nicht were, dat scolde man richten also id recht, unde scriuen dat in beyde böke* 'and if there comes a new law, which was not in this book, then one should judge what the law should be, and write it in both books'. He also makes the not unreasonable assumption that additions following this paragraph in the *A*-text have been made in just the manner described. In the *B*-text, following the chapter on gambling and preceding these closing words, there are chapters covering purchases on credit (absent as a separate chapter from the *A*-text) and misuse of woodland (the first half of Chapter 63 in the *A*-text). The remainder of the additions in the *A*-text have been absorbed (in appropriate places) into the body of the *B*-text and the chapter on tracks and paths appears in its proper place.

61/7–9. Wessén (*SL* IV, 288 note 2 to Chapter 61a) points out that legislation would have taken place at the general assembly.

Chapter 62: *Hitta ier þet sum nylast var takit um loyski*

62/1 and footnote. Cf. Chapter 19/104–07, where the fines are half of those stated here. The content of this chapter appears in Chapter 20 of the *B*-text (cf. Addition 5).

Chapter 63: *Um skoga*

The title of this chapter covers only the first provision. The remainder of the chapter contains a miscellany of provisions.

63/2–4, 4–6. Cf. provisions in Chapter 26/38–40 and 50–52, and for related provisions see 7/2–9, 25/26–37 and 26/55–61. The older provision relating to tearing down a neighbour's fence limits the fine to two marks, rather than the three stated here. On the implications of the difference, see Note to 26/50–52.

63/7. A *glugga* was an opening, not large enough for passage with a vehicle and possibly no larger than a window, but perhaps large enough for a person on foot to crawl through.

63/9–11. It seems that a pledge was originally a sale with right to purchase back within three years (as in the *B*-text of *GL*, Addition 9/3–7). This gradually changed to a much shorter period and Chapter 30/2–5 suggests that change: the pledge-holder is instructed to call the pledge-giver to the church or assembly to redeem the pledge on a certain date. If he did not, the pledge should be valued by the parishioners or men of the assembly, although the creditor would still obviously receive payment.

Wessén (*SL* IV, 289 note 4 to Addition A) suggests that the Gtn verb *virþa* here means 'to sell' rather than 'to value'. The translation offered in the present translation, 'to take in payment (of a debt)', is intended to cover both senses. Cf. Notes to 10/5, 30/4–5 and Addition 9/5–6.

63/11–13. Further examples of loss of status or money as a result of a misdemeanour in relation to land occur in Chapter 25/26–29 and Chapter 28 (e.g. lines 22–23). The penalty here seems particularly harsh (hanging or beheading) but the crime was one of theft of land or misappropriation of it in some other way, and in particular a breach of trust, since the miscreant was presumably a steward of the land in question. Although later editors translate *firigiera* as 'föröda' (lay waste, devastate), Schlyter translates it as 'förskingra', which is particularly associated with a breach of contract or duty in respect of the misappropriation of property. This latter, translated as 'misappropriation', seems to be preferable, although the former is also a recognised crime in current law, involving the poisoning of land or animals. On the means of execution, see also Notes to 21/9–12, 38/6–9.

63/12. The expression *at þranglausu* 'without coercion' implies that there might be cases in which such an action was permissible. Schlyter assumes that this meant that a sale was forced by straitened circumstances (Swedish *trångmål*). There is, however, a Swedish legal concept of *tvång* 'coercion' and this might be intended.

Both *kirkiurum* and *kirkiustedr* (in the *B*-text) refer to an allocated pew. Most preserved early medieval church pews in Sweden are from Gotland. The designation of pews to particular people is not recorded before the end of the fifteenth century on the mainland (see *KL* s. v. *Kirkestole*).

63/14–17. Cf. the provisions in the first section of Chapter 24 (i.e. lines 14–17), where the number of toasts is unlimited. The *B*-text has this material only in Chapter 33 (Chapter 24 in the *A*-text).

63/15. There is no record of the size of *en half skal* 'half bowl' nor of whether this measure covered the entire quantity of drink offered or that offered to each guest.

63/16. The exact level of a double fine (*tuibyt*) is not clear. This is the only occasion on which such a fine is specifically referred to and no previous editor has suggested an amount. On various instances of *twibote* in *VStL* and other contemporary laws, including *Bjärkörätten*, see Hasselberg 1953, 62–65, 168–72. These, however, refer mainly to acts of violence in church or market, or in a bathhouse or latrine. Wennström (1931, 45–46, 77–80) suggests that the three-mark fine evolved as double an older twelve-*öre* fine (cf. Björling 1893, 104 note 3; Hemmer 1928, 71; Wilda 1960, 345). It is possible, therefore, that a three-mark fine is intended here.

Chapter 65: *Af quinna ret*

65/2–4. Cf. the provisions concerning widows in Chapter 20/43–45. Even if a widow had brought more than ten oxen with her, she could not take more away. She could, however, take as many horses and sheep as she had brought, presumably even if the actual animals were no longer alive.

65/3. The word *band* 'pair' here must mean the same as *oykr* elsewhere, i.e. yoke joining a pair of oxen, and hence, by transference, the actual pair of animals.

65/5. The word *tassal is unknown elsewhere, but must have the sense 'buckle, clasp'. Schlyter (CISG s. v. tassal) relates it to English tassel. According to CODEE, this comes from Old French tas(s)el. It is first recorded in English in the thirteenth century in the sense 'clasp, fibula' and only from the fourteenth century as 'pendant ornament with a fringe attached'. Schlyter, in the light of the fact that gilding is in question, seems correct in assigning the earlier of these meanings and rejecting Ihre's translation (1769 s. v. tassal), which follows the later sense. Schlyter also refers to FrostL IX 9 (NGL 1, 210, 211; 282) where gullað appears alongside assala. He suggests that the latter must mean the same as tassala. Säve (GU, xxix), citing the same reference, suggests further alternatives, including snöre 'laces'.

65/6. The word gullaþ 'golden headdress' describes a circlet for the head, such as was worn both by men and women. Bolli Bollason in Laxdœla saga, Chapter 63, has knýtt gullhlaði um hǫfuð honum (cf. Falk 1919, 114–15; ÍF V, 187). Wessén's translation, 'guldbräm' (gold edging), assumes that the adjective slungin 'plaited' applies to this word as well as silkisband, and that fringes with gold thread woven into them are intended (see SL IV, 240). This description seems more likely to apply only to silfrband referred to below.

65/7. Jacobsen (GGD, 113 note 3) translates slungin silkisband as 'Snørelidser' (laces). These were presumably laces to fasten a woman's bodice, and plaited silk would have been the strongest, most durable material available, and therefore valuable. Cf. the reference in Chapter 23/13–14 to the fact that the laces had to be returned to their owner if they were pulled out. They are in this case called snoþir, but they were probably the same item.

65/9–11. In relation to the value of a haimfylgi 'dowry', see Chapters 20/54–56, 28/37–38 and Notes, also Notes to 3/4, 20/91, 28/35–39. Wessén's assumption in his note to Chapter 24 (SL IV, 273 note 1) is that the amount of the dowry in this later provision relates to property in movables only.

65/11. The bladragning 'wall covering of blue cloth' referred to in this instance was no doubt of the same quality and value as that referred to in Chapter 24b, but would hardly have been black for a wedding, which is the subject here. It is possible that the cloth was scarlet, since this is referred to in the following sentence, or it might have been blue, which was another expensive dye (cf. Note to 24b/2).

65/12. The word *pell* 'canopy' derives from Latin *pallium* 'cover; mantle', not *pellis* 'hide, skin'. In OWN, *pell* was any type of expensive cloth, originally specifically satin from China or India, used as a bed-cover or to cover a bier (see Falk 1919, 67–69, 73). It could also be material used for clothing. In *Laxdœla saga*, Chapter 77, it is said that Bolli Bollason *vildi engi klæði bera nema skarlatsklæði ok pellsklæði* 'would wear no clothes that were not of scarlet and satin' (*ÍF* V, 225). Here the sense is either a festive altar covering, or a canopy held over the bridal couple at a particular point in a wedding ceremony. This is still done in some Eastern Orthodox churches.

65/12–13 and 15. Linen was one of the currencies in which tithes or fines could be paid (cf. *UL* Kkb 6 §5; *ÖgL* Vb 6 §1). The prohibition against expensive gifts was presumably intended to prevent the impoverishment of farms through marriage, and possibly to reduce any chance of dispute when wives were widowed.

65/16. The silver bands (*silfrband*) referred to were most probably decorative ribbons or bindings that had silver thread woven into them (cf. Note to 65/7). Silver wire had been used in the costliest materials from the time of the Vikings, as witnessed by the Gokstad find, and silver was used in a variety of ways to decorate fabrics. Towards the end of the Middle Ages, new techniques developed, and were imported from Italy and elsewhere.

The underskirt decoration (*kurtilbonaþr*) was any decoration on the kirtle or gown.

65/17–19. The normal method of purchase in the medieval period was in currency (coin or otherwise). The word *burgan* 'buying on credit, related to OWN *borga* 'borrow', had various senses apart from the one here 'purchase against a promissory note'. It could also mean 'hostage' or 'bail', as well as a promise of service rather than money. One could avoid arrest for debt by raising a surety (*borgen*) with a *borghans maþer* (OWN *borganarmaðr*) (cf. *SdmL* Kmb 9 pr; *VmL* Rb 12 §2). No interest appears to have been payable, although this was not forbidden by the church. The prohibition against borrowing from the people of Visby was probably a later addition, motivated by the conflict between them and the farming population outside the town (see Introduction, pp. xii–xiii, xxxvii; Addition 9/2–7). The twelve-mark fine might apply to an infringement of any of the provisions in this chapter, since no other fines are prescribed.

Addition 1: *Aff prestom och prestbarnom*

Addition 1/2–3. The phrase *han taki i verra* 'he marries beneath him' is possibly corrupt, as Jacobsen (*GGD*, 33 note 4) suggests. The meaning is, however, that a priest by marrying a woman who was not free lost his right to the status of a Gotlander.

Addition 1/8–10 and footnote. As indicated in the Note to 5/7–9, this sentence, which is also on the *A*-text, is out of context. The *han* 'he' who is assumed to have died is the wrongdoer, the lay son of a priest (*prestson olerþr*) referred to at the end of the previous paragraph (*SL* IV, 249 note 10).

Addition 1/14. The fact that it is stated that a claimant (in this case against a priest rather than a lay person) can accept compensation without shame makes it clear that immediate acceptance of compensation was regarded as less honourable than taking revenge. Even after the abolition of blood vengeance, protracted negotiations were considered to be desirable before compensation was accepted (see *SL* IV, 249 notes 12 and 14).

Addition 1/19–20. Pipping explains the whole phrase *Tha en han hempn at eyger so budit* 'If he should take revenge when it has been offered' by assuming it to be a mechanical translation from a statute in medieval Latin: *Si vindicatum habet, (damno) sic præbito*, . . . He considers it very likely that a provision relating to priests would first have been formulated in Latin. Wessén (*SL* IV, 250 note 19), on the other hand, thinks that the text is corrupt. Schlyter (*CIG*, 105 note 9) and Säve (*GU*, 36) suggest the emendation *hempnar, þa so ier budit* 'takes revenge, when [compensation] is offered'.

Addition 1/21. The priest was to be compensated for with his full wergild, despite the fact that the killing was blood vengeance.

Addition 1/25. A *taki* 'surety man' was a receiver of a promise (cf. OWN *taka* 'bail' and *tykr* 'forfeit', 6/29). The nearest equivalent to a *taki* as referred to in *GL* would be a Swedish *löftesman*, who went bail for the person concerned to the effect that he would bring witnesses to his innocence. In mainland provincial laws a *taki* is mentioned where a case concerns goods claimed by the plaintiff. He had responsibility for the fulfilment of any oath taken and had to live in the same hundred and be accepted by the parties involved. A farmer could not refuse to take on this responsibility (cf. *ÄVgL* Tjb 8–12; *YVgL* Tjb 39–44; *ÖgL* Rb 6–8).

Addition 1/35–36. It is not quite clear what procedure was intended by *raþin þeir fyrir fe* 'be responsible for the payment'. Schlyter

(*CIG*, 106) offers the translation 'råde de om godset', but then adds as a note 'D. ä. folket tage boten'. The first could mean that assembly members 'discuss the level of compensation' or 'take custody of the compensation', but the note implies that assembly members received the fine itself. How the money was then distributed is not stated. Cf. the provision at Addition 1/18–19 (see *SL* IV, 250 notes 17 and 24).

Addition 1/39–41. This is the sole instance in *GL* in which direct speech and the first person singular are used. The first person plural is used in the introductory section, (1/3–9) but not otherwise. This passage is similar in style to some of the oldest Swedish provincial laws, so it seems reasonable to assume that it formed part of the earliest edition of *GL*.

Addition 2: *Aff osoydom*

Addition 2/1. Swedish *nöt* is used of beef cattle, both on the hoof and at table. The word *rus* (cf. OWN *hross* m.) is used here in the *B*-text where *hestr* occurs earlier in the chapter, and in the *A*-text. Whilst it is possible that no significance can be attached to this difference, *rus* is used only of draught animals and *hestr* is used in only two cases out of eleven (6/9 and 10/5) in a context that precludes reference to a riding horse. The modern Gotlandic pony, the *skogsruss*, is descended from animals native to Gotland since the Stone Age. They are small, tough animals that perform well in harness, but are not of traditional riding type. As late as the fifteenth century, horses from Gotland were exported to the Teutonic Order. They, like the horses from Öland, were particularly tough and hardy, since they came from herds that lived out all year.

Addition 2/6. The expression *than sakir wird* 'than the case is worth' has led to a number of translations, several involving amendments to the text. Schlyter (*CIG*, 107) offers the reading *warder* for the manuscript's *wird* and translates 'som varder saker' (who keeps the thing [the animal in question]). Säve (*GU*, xxiv) considers this change too radical and takes *sakir* to be genitive and *wird* to be a noun meaning 'värde' (worth, value). He translates 'än sakens värde' (than the value of the thing), but further expresses doubts as to the meaning of *sak* that this interpretation imposes, and thinks that the context could alternatively carry the usual sense of *sak* '(legal) case'. Wadstein (1894–95, 14–15) suggests a reading *sak ir* for *sakir*, with no further changes necessary, and translates 'än saken uppskattas till' (than the case is valued at). This requires minimum change and retains the usual sense of *sak*. Pipping (1901a, 23 note 5) offers palaeographic support for this and it has been followed in the present translation. The seemingly overriding provision that no one was to be liable for more than the value of the creature involved cannot have applied in the case of carelessness, otherwise this latter provision would make no sense.

Addition 2/7–8. Jacobsen (*GGD*, 52 note 4) observes that the sentence *Þa en minni lastir . . . halfu minna* 'If the damage . . . half as much' is far from clear. It appears to mean that if damage was less than the creature was worth, the owner was liable to half of the actual value of the animal. This might, of course, be less than the value of the case, and can thus hardly apply to cases involving carelessness, which were to be doubly penalised. The structure of the sentence makes it possible that Bilefeld has made a scribal error and omitted a clause.

Addition 2/10–14. The latter part of this paragraph gives an alternative version of fines payable for injuries by dogs to that laid out in the *A*-text.

Addition 3: *Aff sara farom*

These provisions offer a slightly different reading from the equivalent ones in the *A*-text (19/62–66). The following differences are apparent in the level of fines.

Addition 3/1–2. Damage to bones in a hand or foot are valued at two marks in coin instead of one. The provision in the *A*-text relating to more bones being broken but a full recovery being made does not appear in the *B*-text. There is however, evidence of a scribal amendment to the latter at this point, and it is possible that Bilefeld derived this clause from a third manuscript (see Pipping 1901a, 27 note 1).

Addition 3/2. Each rib is valued at two marks in coin, as in the *A*-text, but there is no limit set on the number of ribs to be counted for compensation.

Addition 3/3. The compensation for disability is two marks of silver as in the *A*-text. The provision is here inserted in the margin, according to Pipping from a lost manuscript other than that of 1470, as touched on in the Introduction, pp. xviii–xx.

Addition 3/4–5. The provision relating to visible wounds does not occur in this form in the *A*-text.

Addition 4: *Aff sara farom*

These provisions offer a slightly different reading from the equivalent ones in the *A*-text (19/81–86). The following differences are apparent in the level of fines.

Addition 4/1. The fine for a damaged ear is two marks in coin in the *A*-text, rather than a mark of silver, i.e. half as much.

Addition 4/1–2. Fines relating to shinbones and forearms do not appear in the *A*-text. They appear in the margin of the *B*-text, which lends support to Pipping's theory that Bilefeld had a third manuscript to hand when he was writing AM 54 4to (see Introduction, pp. xviii–xx).

Addition 4/3–5. Fines for teeth in the *A*-text are two marks in coin for each of the two central upper teeth, one mark in coin for each of the eye teeth and one mark for each of the other teeth in the upper jaw. Teeth in the lower jaw were valued at half of this throughout. The *B*-text does not differentiate between the upper and lower jaw and the fines are twice as much as the *A*-text specifies for the upper jaw.

Addition 5: *Aff loyski*

Addition 5/2–5. These provisions offer a slightly different reading from the equivalent ones in the *A*-text (19/104–08, 100 respectively), but they correspond exactly with Chapter 62, a later addition in the *A*-text. Specifically, the fine for pulling out hair more than the flat of a hand can cover, or all the hair, is doubled in both cases. The remaining provisions are repeated unchanged. For the different treatment of these additions in the two manuscripts, see Introduction, pp. xv, xvi, xx and *SL* IV, 264 note 47.

Addition 6: *Aff wagnikla ferdir*

Addition 6/1–4. These provisions correspond exactly to those at the end of the *A*-text addition, Chapter 63/14–17.

Addition 7: *Af manna kaupi*

This chapter, although listed in the table of contents in the *A*-text, following Chapter 32, does not appear in that text. Addition 7 is taken from the *B*-text, where it appears in the position expected in the *A*-text. The chapter appears in *tyGL* and *daGL*. Schlyter (*CIG*, viii–ix) thinks that the reason for the omission of this chapter, and sections of the chapter on theft, can be found in an assumption that slavery was no longer current when the A-text manuscript was written. He considers that slavery was dying out even when *GL* originated, since the period of slavery was limited (2/37–38). Jacobsen (*GGD*, 93 note 4) observes that the word *þrel* 'slave', although used elsewhere in *GL*, does not appear in this chapter. She also remarks that the chapter was most probably present in the manuscript from which the scribe of the A-text made his copy. For an analysis of the provisions relating to slaves in *GL*, see Nevéus (1974, 54–67).

Addition 7/2. Säve (*GU*, xx) does not interpret *mandr* as 'slave', but simply as a 'man belonging to another'. The translation 'slave' in this particular context does, however, make the meaning clearer.

Addition 7/8–10. Wessén (*SL* IV, 282 note 5 to Chapter 32a) remarks that in Gotland it appeared to be the one who followed usual legal process who had (the right) to substantiate his claim, rather than the one who deviated from it.

Addition 7/15. The symptoms of epilepsy or falling sickness (*brutfall*) were described in accounts of miracles as early as 1134 and appear in detail on the gravestone of Abbot Vilhelm in Æbelholt from *c*.1205. One description mentions frothing at the mouth, clenching of the teeth and the following coma, lasting several hours. The patient was cured by drinking from the holy well at Haraldsted (see *KL* s. v. *Ligfald*). In *GulL* 57 (*NGL* 1, 29) and *FrostL* V §41 (*NGL* 1, 182) epilepsy was, as in *GL*, considered to be a fault in a slave for which the seller was responsible for a month. The OWN word for the condition is *stiarva* or *stjarfa*.

Jacobsen (*GGD*, 94 note 5), unlike other editors, is clear about the implications of *bedroyta*, describing it as bed-wetting, whether deliberate or through negligence, which would indeed have rotted the straw in a bed. In *GulL* 57 (*NGL* 1, 29) a slave can be returned if he is incontinent in any way, not just in his bed.

Addition 7/16. The phrase *ny ok niþan*, referring to the waxing and waning of the moon, was used in a number of contexts to denote a month, although *manaþr* is more usual (cf. *GulL* 56, 57 (*NGL* 1, 29); *ÄVgL* Tjb 19; *YVgL* Tjb 54). The two Swedish instances also are in connection with the detection of faults in a bought slave.

Addition 7/17. The nature of the illness represented by the phrase *beyni verkir*, literally 'he hurts in the bone or leg', is not clear. Wessén suggests that it was *benröta* 'caries', or something similar. Arthritis is another possibility. The parallel passage in *GulL* 57 (*NGL* 1, 29) specifies *oc við stinga* 'a stitch in the side'.

Addition7/18. The word *brigsl* 'ownership claim' has a number of meanings, but here it clearly means a dispute relating to ownership. The vendor was deemed responsible in perpetuity for the legal ownership of a slave he was selling in *ÄVgL* Tjb 19 and in *GulL* 57 (*NGL* 1, 29–31) (cf. *SL* IV, 282 note 9).

Addition 7/23. The expression *mid mala*, translated here as 'under conditions', seems to imply that the sale was temporary, for a limited period of time; the agreement was effectively a lease. It is not clear whether this provision relates specifically to the immediately preceding one or not, but presumably the argument presented by the vendor was that the purchaser had to return the slave after a stipulated period. Whether the slave was his to sell or not was thus irrelevant, since he would expect eventually to be able to return him or her to the legal owner. Right appeared always to have been on the side of the person who believed that the transaction was a straightforward purchase, and they had the right of proof (cf. Note to Addition 7/8–10).

Addition 8: *Aff tiaufa rethi*

The contents of this addition occur also in *tyGL*. The provisions refer to theft by slaves, which accounts for their omission from the *A*-text.

Addition 8/1–3 and 3–5. Wessén (*SL* IV, 284 note 4) observes that the implication in each of these cases seems to be that if the owner of the slave (rather than the victim) detected his theft and returned the goods, he had nothing further to pay.

Addition 8/6. A *þrigildi* 'triple fine' is referred to only in the *B*-text and not in mainland provincial laws.

Addition 8/8. The noun *þiaufnaþr* is here a synonym for *þypti* (Addition 8/2) 'stolen goods'. The noun can also mean the abstract concept of 'theft' itself. At Addition 8/28, either meaning would make sense.

Addition 8/11. The translation 'bar nor bolt' (*hun ella hell*) reflects the alliteration of the original Gutnish, but previous scholarship has led to a number of translations. (1) *hun* 'takås' (roof ridge) and *hell* 'tröskel . . . sten' (threshold stone) (Schlyter (*CISG* s. v. *hun*, *hell*); *GO* s. v. *hun*); (2) *hun* 'bom' (bar) and *hell* 'hängsle' (padlock) (Wadstein 1890–92, 228–29); (3) *hell* 'tränagel varpå dörren vrider sig' (wooden pintle on which the door rotates) (Lidén 1892, 89–90); (4) *hun* 'dørrskodde' (door shutter), related to OldDan *hund,* and *hell* 'tværbjælke' (cross-timber) related to OWN *hæll* and Danish dialect *hæl* in *tøjre-hæl* 'mooring peg' (Jacobsen *GGD,* 99 note 4); (5) *hun ella hell,* 'hun och häl' (lock mechanism and bolt) (Wessén *SL* IV, 284 notes 6, comparing to *VmL* Kkb 5 pr and *SL* II, *VmL,* 23–24 note 12). A concrete translation is preferred to an abstract interpretation of Schlyter's translation: 'if the house is undamaged from top to bottom'. The inference drawn from the fact that no part of the door lock was damaged was that no break-in had taken place. Either the owner had failed to secure his property, or his own household people were involved.

Addition 8/12. The use of torture to extract a confession where the goods concerned were not under lock and key seems to be exceptionally harsh, but is another example of betrayal of trust being regarded as particularly reprehensible. The assumption is that at least some of the stolen items were found (cf. Addition 8/15) and that there was reason to suspect the slave. Although instances of torture in Scandinavian medieval laws are uncertain, it formed part of Roman law, and there is a suggestion of it in *VStL* I 41 (cf. Munktell 1939, 103–05; Hasselberg 1953, 67 note 1).

The concept of *viþrlag, væþ* or *witæ* 'compensation, deposit' occurred across the Scandinavian laws. It meant either a forfeit (*pant*) or a deposit in relation to a legal case, so that one could charge a slave on suspicion. Both parties placed deposits with a *taka* either at the beginning of a case, or at the end of a case after judgement had been passed, in which case the judges and the person who had lost the case laid down money with the *taka.* The result of the appeal determined if the appellant or the judges received the deposited money (cf. *KL* s. v. *Veddemål*). In the first instance, the accuser forfeited the money if the case was not proved. The *viþrlag* referred to here is the six-*öre* deposit demanded under other circumstances.

Addition 8/13–14. Jacobsen (*GGD,* 99 note 7) takes *bainheilom* 'whole in bone' to refer to the slave's joints, rather than his bones in general.

It is not certain what is meant by *brustheilom* 'whole in ... breathing', but it was clearly part of a stock phrase that has an exact parallel in that used of horses: sound in wind and limb. In other words, the slave had to be in a state in which he could resume his duties.

Addition 8/15. In reference to the meaning of *agripr* 'material evidence', Wessén (*SL* IV, 284 note 9) questions that offered by Schlyter and Pipping: 'tjufgods, hvarmed någon blifvit befunnen' (stolen goods with which someone has been discovered). He thinks that this might be a possible translation here, but not at Addition 8/22. He suggests a translation meaning in general 'items left behind by or taken from a suspected thief, which are to be used as evidence'. For the meaning of OldSwe *agriper* or *agreper*, see *DL* Kkb 9 §3; *SL* II, *DL*, 17 note 57.

Addition 8/17–18. 'Bring him back uninjured and pay a fine of six *öre*'. There is an apparent corruption in the *B*-text at this point. The suggested interpretation by Pipping (*GLGS*, *Ordbok*, 45) does not entirely solve the problem as an auxiliary verb appears to be missing and the subject of *byti* 'pay a fine' cannot be the slave. If the sense of *kuma* is 'to bring', with the dative object (the slave) understood (as in the parallel passage at Addition 8/13–14), the verb should be in the third person singular subjunctive (as is *byti*). This interpretation has been used in the translation.

Addition 8/17–20 and footnote. 'Bring him back uninjured and pay six *öre* for the wristbands . . . six *öre*' (*Kumi ok hailum atr ok byti vi oyra fyri baugband . . . vi oyra*). Schlyter (*CIG*, 110 note 24), Jacobsen (*GGD*, 100 note 3) and Wessén (*SL* IV, 284 note 10) recognise that the scribe has omitted a line of text. Wessén reconstructs the missing text from *tyGL* and this reconstruction has been incorporated in the present translation in angled brackets. The fine for unlawful imprisonment is low here in comparison to that in Swedish mainland provincial laws and in *VStL*, where it was forty marks, i.e. the equivalent of a wergild. Even a slave's wergild of 4½ marks in coin was considerably higher than the six *öre* offered here (cf. Hasselberg 1953, 326–29 and note 6).

Addition 8/18. There appears to be no description of wristbands (*baugband*), and they may have been no more damaging than a pair of handcuffs with which a thief was restrained for presentation before the assembly (see Wennström 1936, 131). This in itself was considered to be a severe infringement of a person's rights and so could not be done on mere suspicion (or at least not without payment of a deposit). It is, however, possible that *baugband* were an instrument of torture or punishment, which would explain why an accuser had to pay for inflicting them upon the slave, even if a confession were extracted. Thieves were sometimes bound with their hands behind their backs, which was considered extremely insulting, or with their hands in front of them, which was less so (cf. *KL* s. v. *Fängelse*). Although Åke Ohlmarks (1976, 613) glosses *baugband* as a strap around the elbows (which, if fastened behind the back, would have been particularly uncomfortable), *baugliþr* 'wrist' seems to be a more likely connection than **albugi* 'elbow'. A combination *tjuva-band* 'thief band' is listed as occurring in Gotlandic dialect, but no meaning or instances cited (cf. *GO* s. v. *band*). On the other hand, a *båg-band* is defined as a tie to fasten an animal in a barn, while *baug* is found in Gotlandic dialect in senses relating to the training and restraint of oxen and horses (cf. *GO* s. v. *båge*, **bög*).

Addition 8/20–21. 'In need someone forced says things he has not done' (*I nauþ segir naupugir, þet han ey valdir*). The implication here is that one could not take a confession extracted under torture as proof of guilt if there were no material evidence to support it (see *SL* IV, 284 note 11 to Chapter 38).

Addition 8/21–28. Further to notes on *agripr* at Addition 8/15, Wessén (*SL* IV, 284 note 12) argues that a person who had had his property stolen could clearly not bring the latter when he was conducting a house-search. What must be referred to here is further material evidence against the slave in question: enough to instigate a search of his master's farm. If the farm owner refused a search, but one was nonetheless conducted and stolen goods were found, he was liable to a triple fine. There is thus no question of the stolen property having been brought to the scene by the accusers. Receipt of stolen goods (as here by the master of a slave) was treated in some mainland provincial laws as equal with theft itself (cf. *ÄVgL* Tjb 4; *YVgL* Tjb 29; *ÖgL* Vb 32 §5). The laws of Svealand, however, seem to differentiate between the two (cf. *SdmL* Tjb 10 §1; *VmL* Mb 31; 26 §9; *HL* Mb 31 §4). See also Notes to 37/7–9, 37/12–13 and 37/22–24.

Addition 8/28–30. If treble the value of the stolen property exceeded the value of the slave, then the master was not expected to pay this amount, but to relinquish the slave instead.

Addition 8/30–32. This sentence reinforces the meaning of the preceding one. The verb *firistiela* means 'forfeit as a result of theft'. Cf. the use of the verb *firibiera* (37/24).

Addition 8/34–35. One-eighth of the value appears to have been a usual reward for finding stolen property (cf. 49/2–3). No specific mention is made of a portion of the value of the goods themselves being paid, but it is possible that *fundarlaun* 'reward' is also intended to cover this. The *alag* 'fine' referred to was presumably the three-fold fine that the owner of a slave had to pay to a victim of theft, since no other fine is mentioned. Elsewhere in OWN *álög* usually refers to an extra payment made if a deal settled by a handshake is not honoured.

Addition 8/36. The expression *mulslaghu* (or *muslaghu*) *maþær* 'fugitive' appears also in *ÖgL* Bb 34 §1 in relation to an escaped slave and the suggestion by Ihre is that the first element derives from a verb *musla* meaning 'hide, abscond'. Schlyter, however, thinks a simpler derivation from *mus* 'mouse' and *liggia* 'lie' is more likely. Such men were fugitives and had to lie low as far as they were able to avoid detection, 'as quiet as a mouse' (cf. *CISG*, xiii and s. v. *muslaghu maþer*). Once the slave was on the run, his master's responsibility for his actions in regard to his survival ceased and no compensation was paid for any theft of food that he might commit.

Addition 8/41. 'on land' (*a landi*). This means in Gotland, that is, before he had escaped overseas.

Addition 8/43–44. Provisions relating to the lawful securing of vessels of various types are contained in Chapter 36. It is notable that the owner of an unprotected ship was responsible to a slave's owner for his safety, even if the slave were a thief (Addition 8/48–50).

Addition 8/44–45. The clause specifying that a slave's owner had to redeem (i.e. pay recompense for) any goods stolen by the slave while he was on the run appears to contradict the clause at Addition 8/37–39, but this latter refers presumably only to food.

Addition 8/51. 'in the absence of material evidence' (*agripslaus*). This is translated by Pipping (*GLGS, Ordbok*, 2) as meaning 'one on whom no stolen goods have been found'. Wessén, on the other hand, takes the view that this has the broader sense of the Swedish *utan avtäkt*. This means strictly 'in the absence of the right by a property owner to confiscate tools, weapons or stolen goods held by a thief', but 'in the absence of material evidence' is probably a preferable translation (see *SL* IV, 285 note 22).

Addition 8/51–56. Jacobsen (*GGD*, 101 and note 9) assumes that 'a man' (*naquar maðir*) in Addition 8/51 refers to a slave and supports this theory by pointing out that this final paragraph is also missing from the *A*-text. On the other hand, Wessén (*SL* IV, 285 note 24) considers that this paragraph is clearly a continuation of provisions in Chapter 38 relating to free men and that it was

inadvertently omitted when the A-text was constructed. Since no mention of assemblies occurs otherwise in the section on theft by slaves, Wessén's interpretation seems preferable.
Addition 8/56. The action to be taken in the case of material evidence being available was to be the same as if there were none. Schlyter, in line with his interpretation of *agripr*, and with different punctuation, translates this passage thus: 'De skola vitna det som de höra, om han är skyldig eller oskyldig, så ock om han är funnen med tjufgods' (They should bear witness of what they hear, if he is guilty or innocent, even if he is discovered with stolen goods). See Note to Addition 8/15.

Addition 9: *Af burgan viþr byamen*

Addition 9/2–3 and footnote. These two provisions coincide with those in the addition to the A-text, Chapter 65/17–18. No fine is laid down here, although the fine implied in the A-text is twelve marks to the general assembly.
Addition 9/3. The verb *betala* 'pay for' is a loan word from Low German; in the A-text, *gielda* is always used.
Addition 9/5–6. This provision relates to the one in the addition to the A-text (63/9–11), but expands upon it. Cf. the use of the verb *virþa* in these passages, where it means 'take in (or make) payment (of a debt)' to those at e.g. 30/4–5 and 40/4, where it seems to mean 'place a value on'. (Cf. Notes to 10/5, 30/4–5 and 63/9–11). As the provision here is a later one, it is possible that the meaning of *virþa* changed over time. The whole expression carries the implication that liquid assets (*oyrar*) and real estate were not interchangeable in respect of debt payment, except by agreement (cf. Notes to 2/35, 53/3–5).

2

Þer byriar lagh sior i oc fer...
ɢo at fyrftu coᴍᴍ̄axxᴍᴍ
...tta ir fyrft upp hafr tla C.21.
ɢurıg oru þer wir ftatu
...nætta haipui oc i actaen
...uı Oc troa allır aaıu ɢup altıvat
ðauða · Oc hauu par bifıa
per hauu uıtıu os ar oc fᴍp figr oc
hauſu oc þer er vrr magu haıða
criftındouıı oru Oc tro varı retu oc
laudı oru bygdu Oc vir magu buerıy
ðaɢ þer fyfla r allıuı ɢarum gup
Oc vılıa oruıu fiuı gup fiı ðyrp 1
Oc or fei meft part ar beþı tıl tıfs oc
ftalar Af barnuım coxxᴍᴍᴍ
...er ıer uu þı neft at barıu huerr C. 2
...fcal ala tu fyr vevbr a laudı oru
Oc ecu ir catta vıta fill huerıuı
euıd feuɢ fıua þaıu hauı barufaru

Copenhagen, Den Arnamagnæanske Samling, MS AM 54 4to, 41r
(reproduced by permission of Den Arnamagnæanske Samling)

APPENDIX A: COMPARISON OF MANUSCRIPTS

(i) *Manuscript content comparison*

Manuscript Content	B64	AM 54 4to	B65	AM 55 4to
Oldest statutes	Chapters 1–47	Chapters 1–65	Chapters 1–59	Chapters 1–67
Later statutes	Chapters 48–61	Chapters 66–80	Chapters 60–75	Chapters 68–80
Priests' children	No (Chapter 5)	Yes (Chapter 4)	No (Chapter 5)	No (Chapter 5)
Rights of betrothed women	–	–	–	Yes (Chapter 13)
Extra clauses relating to unruly animals	No (Chapter 17)	Yes (Chapter 17)	No (Chapter 17)	No (Chapter 18)
Clause concerning bruising	Yes (Chapter 19)	Yes (Chapter 19)	No (Chapter 19)	No (Chapter 21)
Clause concerning partial disability	Yes (Chapter 19)	Yes (Chapter 19)	Yes (Chapter 19)	No (Chapter 21)
Clause concerning hidden disability	No (Chapter 19)	No (Chapter 19)	Yes (Chapter 19)	No (Chapter 21)
Clause concerning ale throwing	Yes (Chapter 19)	Yes (Chapter 19)	No (Chapter 19)	Yes (Chapter 21)
Clause concerning slaves fighting	Yes (Chapter 19)	Yes (Chapter 19)	Yes (Chapter 20)	No (Chapter 22)
Clause concerning inheritance of childless man	Yes (misplaced in chapter 19)	Yes (Chapter 25)	Yes (Chapter 21)	Yes (Chapter 23)
Statutes concerning seduction	Yes (misplaced in Chapter 20)	Yes (Chapter 29)	Yes (Chapter 23)	Yes (Chapter 24)
Clause concerning displacing a woman's coif	Yes (Chapter 23)	Yes (Chapter 29)	No (Chapter 26)	Yes (Chapter 27)

Concerning travellers' pathways	Yes (Chapter 64, misplaced from after 24)	Yes (Chapter 37)	Yes (Chapter 31)	–
Purchase of slaves	No (although in Contents)	Yes (Chapter 49)	Yes (Chapter 43)	Yes (Chapter 43)
Care of ships	Yes (Chapter 36)	Yes (Chapter 53)	Yes (Chapter 47)	–
Statutes relating to theft by slaves	No (Chapter 38)	Yes (Chapter 55)	Yes (Chapter 50)	No (Chapter 49)
Gilded items	cf. Chapter 24	cf. Chapter 35	cf. Chapter 28	Chapters 51, 30, 81
The sale of ale	–	–	–	Yes (Chapter 52)
Watch duty	cf. Chapter 54	cf. Chapter 72	cf. Chapter 63	Chapters 53, 71
Cutting down specific trees	–	–	–	Yes (Chapter 54)
Cutting down trees in someone's enclosure	–	–	–	Yes (Chapter 55)
Taking timber	cf. Chapter 26	cf. Chapter 40	cf. Chapter 36	Chapters 56, 35
Cutting down a slip rail	–	–	–	Yes (Chapter 57)
Cutting down doors	–	–	–	Yes (Chapter 58)
Cutting down posts or supports	–	–	–	Yes (Chapter 59)
Concerning taxes	Yes (Chapter 53)	Yes (Chapter 71)	Yes (Chapter 62)	–
Epilogue	Yes (Chapter 61)	Yes (after Chapter 82)	Yes (after Chapter 75)	Yes (Chapter 75)
Concerning hair pulling	Yes (Chapter 62)	Yes (Chapter 20)	–	Yes (Chapter 82)
Concerning woodland	Yes (Chapter 63)	Yes (Chapter 82)	–	Yes (Chapter 83)
Clause limiting toasts at weddings	Yes (misplaced in Chapter 63)	Yes (Chapter 33)	No (Chapter 27)	No (Chapter 28)
Concerning women's inheritance	Yes (Chapter 65)	Yes (Chapter 35)	–	Yes (Chapter 81)
Forbidding credit	Yes (first clause ends Chapter 65)	Yes (Chapter 81)	–	Yes (first clause ends Chapter 81)

Where a clause does not appear in a certain manuscript, the chapter containing the related clauses, if any, is shown; otherwise a dash appears in the table.

(ii) *Chapter sequence comparison of the fourteen later statutes*

Manuscript Chapter	B64	AM 54 4to	B65	AM 55 4to
Concerning turnip fields	48	66	60	77
Concerning shipwrecks	49	67	74	68
Concerning fire	50	68	72	69
Concerning carried fire	51	69	73	70
Concerning road repair	52	70	61	79
Concerning taxes	53	71	53	–
Concerning the watch	54	72	63	71
Concerning houses, etc.	55	73	64; 65	78
Concerning harvesters	56	74; 75	66; 67	76
Concerning squirrels	57	76	68	72
Concerning hares	58	77	69	73
Concerning tree fruits	59	78	70	74
Concerning failure to read mass	60	79	75	75
Concerning gambling	61	80	71	80

APPENDIX B: CHRONOLOGY OF HISTORICAL EVENTS

Outline of Gotland's history and related mainland Swedish events

1164 Swedish archbishopric, under that of Lund, founded in Uppsala
Cistercian monastery of Beata Maria de Gutnalia founded at Roma

1195 Henry of Livonia leads a crusade against Kurland including Gotlanders

1203 Name *Wysbu* appears in the Chronicle of Henry of Livonia

Andreas Suneson, Archbishop of Lund, visits Gotland

Battle of Lena. Sverker defeated and Erik Knutsson assumes Swedish throne

Letter from Pope Innocent III concerning the rural deans in Gotland

1216 Johan Sverkersson king of Sweden

1217 Gotland's tithe distribution law confirmed by Pope Honorius III

1221 Letter from Andreas Suneson and Bishops Karl and Bengt concerning the relationship between Gotland and the See of Linköping

1222 Erik Eriksson king of Sweden

1225 The name Visby appears in a letter from Bengt, Bishop of Linköping

Records relating to Riga mention *ius Gutorum* as applying there

1230 Gotland's tithe law again confirmed by Pope Gregory IX

1248 Birger Magnusson appointed Jarl
Papal legate Vilhelm of Sabina declares priestly celibacy at Synod of Skänninge

1249 Erik Eriksson dies; Birger Jarl governs Sweden

1250 Valdemar Birgersson crowned; Birger Jarl regent

1253 Tithe arrangements again confirmed by Pope Innocent IV

1255 German and English merchants start to take over Gotlandic trade

1260 Law of inheritance makes two daughters equal to a son in Sweden

1266 Birger Jarl dies; Valdemar Birgersson rules in his own right

1275 Magnus Birgersson (Ladulås) king; position of *jarl* replaced by *sveahertig*

1285 Annual *laiþingslami* tax declared; Gotland effectively under Swedish rule

1288   King Magnus intervenes in civil war between Visby and the farmers
Visby stadslag put in place

1290   Magnus Birgersson dies

1298   Birger Magnusson king of Sweden

1310   Sweden partitioned; Birger Magnusson assigned Gotland

1313   Taxes in Gotland increased
Battle of Röcklingebacke; Birger defeated in his attempt to annex Gotland

1318   Birger flees to Gotland, then Denmark

1319   Magnus Eriksson king, but with a minority government

1320   Taxes in Gotland reduced to previous levels

1322   Visby's privileges confirmed

1332   Magnus Eriksson king in his own right

1335   Slavery abolished under the Statute of Skara

1347   *Magnus Erikssons landslag* replaces mainland provincial laws

1350   Black Death in Visby

1361   Valdemar IV Atterdag of Denmark invades and conquers Gotland

1398   The Teutonic Order seizes power in Gotland from the Vitalian Brotherhood

1408   The Teutonic Order returns Gotland to Erik of Pommern

1645   Gotland finally returned to Swedish rule at the peace of Brömsebro

APPENDIX C: MONETARY SYSTEM

Units of Value

Denomination	Standard	Equivalent	Reference
Mark (weight)	gold	8 silver marks	e.g. Chapter 15/3
Mark (weight)	silver	4 marks in coin	e.g. Chapter 13/62
Mark (counted, Gutnish *mark penninga*)	coin		e.g. Chapter 15/5–6
Half mark	usually coin, once silver		e.g. Chapter 19/3, 28
Öre (Gutnish *oyrir*)	usually coin	$\frac{1}{8}$ mark	e.g. Chapter 2/35
Örtug (Gutnish *ertaug*)	usually coin	$\frac{1}{3}$ öre (i.e. $\frac{1}{24}$ mark)	e.g. Chapter 19/91
Penny (Gutnish **penningr*)	coin	8, 10, 12 or 16 to the *örtug*	e.g. Chapter 45/3

For the relationship between the mark of gold and that of silver, see Wessén (*SL* IV, 259 note 1). There is little doubt that his conclusion is correct. The exact relationship between the silver mark (a unit of weight, also divided into 24 *örtugar*) and the coined mark (a counted unit) is far from unambiguous and interpretation is not assisted by the following circumstances: (1) the definitions *silfr* and *penningr* are often omitted; (2) the manuscripts of *GL* occasionally give different fines for the same offences (Wennström 1940, 74–75). Jacobsen (*GGD*, 25 note 1) suggests that the silver mark was 'mere end det dobbelte af en Mark Penge' (more than double a mark in coin), whereas Wessén (*SL* IV, 245 note 4) equates a silver mark to four marks in coin and there is certainly internal evidence (19/80–81) to suggest this. It seems to be generally the case that, if a qualification is omitted, a mark in coin is intended (cf. *SL* IV, 245 note 4), but this assumption must naturally be made with circumspection and there is certainly one instance in which this is not the case (see Appendix D (ii) note 2). Lilienberg (1908, 12) states that Birger Jarl introduced a standard in mainland Sweden of two marks in coin to one of silver as shown in *ÖgL*, whereas in the time of Magnus Ladulås the relationship was three to one. By 1303 there were four marks in coin to one of silver and, by 1311, five.

The number of pennies to the *örtug* in Gotland has been given variously as:

8	Schlyter (*CIG*, 287), Pipping (*GCGS, Ordbok*, 62), Jacobsen (*GGD*, 25 note1)
12	Hildebrand 1879–1953, I, 893, 941; Jansson 1936, 65; N. L. Rasmusson in *KL* s.v. *Penning*
16, later 8	Hauberg 1891, 9–10
'probably' 8	Thordeman 1936, 17
8 or 10	Wennström 1940, 15
10	Lilienberg 1908, 11, referring to the period 1013–22; Hasselberg 1953, 204 n. 1, referring to the time of *VStL*

Jansson (1936, 12) states that a weighed *örtug* was 7–9 grams with an *öre* being 24–27 grams. He also holds (1936, 65) that there were twelve pennies to the *örtug* in Denmark, Gotland, and Öland and in the rest of the Baltic. Jacobsen (*GGD*, 25 note 1) states, however, that the number of pennies to the *örtug* was ten in Denmark as in Norway, and this is confirmed in Andreas Suneson's translation of *Skånelagen* (e.g. *SkLAS* 119; *CISk* II 65). Suggestions that there were twelve pennies to the *örtug* in Jylland during the medieval period are unsubstantiated. In Svealand there were eight pennies to the *örtug*, in Götaland (particularly Västergötland) initially 16 (although later 8). It was thus possible that the *penning* coin was originally considerably smaller in size in some areas, and a mark was respectively 288 (Gotland, Öland and possibly Jylland), 240 (Denmark), 192 (Svealand) and 384 (Västergötland) pennies. Rasmusson in *KL* states that there were four, not three *örtugar* of twelve *penningar* to the *öre* in Gotland, but this is not supported elsewhere. The standard of Svealand gradually took over in Sweden after 1300.

APPENDIX D: TABLE OF PENALTIES EXACTED

(i) *Non-monetary penalties*

Chapter and line	Crime	Penalty
2/37	If a female slave commits infanticide	Six extra years of bondage (plus a fine paid by her master)
6/10	Carting more than permitted on the Sabbath	Confiscation of the load until redeemed
6/37–38	If work is done on the Sabbath by a slave man or woman	Three extra years of bondage (plus a fine paid by the master)
7/5	Damaging or stealing monastic property	Excommunication
8/15–18	Killing or wounding during Church Festivals	Withholding of church offices (excommunication) until fines are paid
13/60	Refusing to offer compensation for a killing within the specified time	Outlawry (and see below for additional fines)
16/9–11	Killing of a Gotlandic or non-Gotlandic man by a slave	Master to bring slave bound to the farm of the dead man within forty nights
19/133–134	A slave fighting a free man	Two blows to the slave equate to one and matters are considered even
20/87–89	Selling the family farm illegally	Loss of inheritance shared with siblings and reduction of weregild to that of a non-Gotlander
20/122	Adultery of any man with the illegitimate daughter of a Gotlandic man with a non-Gotlandic woman (or vice versa) when taken in *flagrante delicto*	Loss of a hand or foot (or payment of three marks in silver as stated below)
20a/4	Adultery with an unmarried Gotlandic woman when taken in *flagrante delicto*	Placing in the stocks for three nights, followed by loss of a hand or foot (or payment of six marks in silver by his family)
21/10	Adultery with a married woman	Life (or 40 marks as chosen by the wronged husband)
21/18	Carrying off a woman without her family's consent	Life (literally 'neck') (or his wergild if she is Gotlandic or ten silver marks otherwise)
22/17–18	Rape of a married woman, whether Gotlandic or not	Life (or the wergild set on the woman)
22/28	Rape of a Gotlandic woman by a slave	Life (unless the woman prefers to be paid her wergild by the slave's master)

25/30–31	Working in another man's woodland or marsh	Confiscation of the result of his work and his draught animal
38/5	Stealing more than two *öre* and up to a mark in silver	Presentationn before the assembly and branding (as well as a wergild fine)
38/6–9	Recidivist theft, or theft of a mark in silver or more	Hanging [considered a shameful execution]
63/11–13	Misappropriating land worth three marks in rent, without cause	Life (literally 'neck') for the man and loss of her church pew for his wife

The non-monetary punishments could be summarised as:
1. Hanging
2. Other unspecified method of execution.
3. Outlawry
4. Excommunication
5. Loss of inheritance and status
6. Loss of a hand or foot
7. Branding or other disfigurement
8. Placement in the stocks
9. Temporary withdrawal of church offices
10. Increase of period of bondage
11. Confiscation of goods involved in offence

(ii) *Monetary penalties*

Chapter and line	Crime	To whom paid (if not clearly the victim or his heirs)	Fine (in coin unless stated otherwise)
2/9	Infanticide by a free woman	Parishioners, returnable if she is found innocent	Three marks
2/18–19	as above	(Local or hundred) assembly members, if the case goes further, and the dean	Three marks to each
2/20–21	as above	General assembly	Twelve marks
2/22–23	Sheltering a child killer	Unspecified	Three marks
2/35	If a slave commits infanticide		Six *öre* (paid by the master, and see above)
3/19	Failure to pay tithe on time, or before moving parish	Parishioners, church, priest	Three marks
4/8	Heathen practices	Parishioners	Three marks
4/14–15	as above	(Local) assembly	Three marks

4/16	as above	General assembly	Twelve marks
6/10	Overburdening an animal or transporting forbidden goods on the Sabbath	Half to the informant and half to the priest and parishioners	Six *öre* to redeem the load and six *öre* in fine
6/33	Working on the Sabbath by free men or women	Half to the informant and half to the parish, priest and church	Six *öre* and the loss of the work done
6/36	Working on the Sabbath by slave men or women	Unspecified	Three *öre* in fine to be paid by the master (and see above)
7/5	Damage to or theft from monastic property		A fine twice that payable to a farmer (and excommunication as noted above)
7/8	Damage to or theft from monastic property	General assembly (if it comes that far)	Three marks (above the fine to the cloister)
8/8	Killing during Church festivals	Parishioners, church, priest	Three marks
8/8–9	Wounding during Church festivals	Parishioners, church, priest	Twelve *öre* (three if done by a slave)
8/10	Striking with a blunt instrument during Church festivals	Parishioners, church, priest	Six *öre*
8/10–12	Scuffling or punching in anger during Church festivals	Parishioners, church, priest	Three *öre*
8/25–26	Killing in a church	General assembly	40 marks (Ten marks in silver)
8/26 footnote	Killing in a churchyard [and it might be assumed wounding in a church]	General assembly	Twelve marks (of which three go to the dean)
8/32	Killing a criminal in sanctuary in one of the three sanctuary churches, churchyards or rectory grounds	General assembly	40 marks
8/36–37	Bruising in church or wounding in a church-yard	Parishioners, church, priest	Six marks
8/37–40	Scuffling in a church or bruising in a churchyard	Parishioners, church, priest	Three marks
8/40–42	Scuffling or punching in a churchyard	Parishioners, church, priest	Twelve *öre*
8/42–44	Reconsecration after the above	Church	Three marks
9/9–11	Killing during the universal sanctity	General assembly	As much wergild as the man is worth (as well as the normal payment to the heirs)

9/11–12	Wounding or attacking during the universal sanctity	Unspecified (presumably the general assembly)	Three marks
9/14–16	Destroying property during the universal sanctity	Unspecified (presumably the general assembly)	Three marks
10/4–7	Taking a man's horse or ox as surety during the spring sanctity	Unspecified	Three marks
11/4–6	Taking someone by the hair, or punching them during the assembly	Unspecified	Three marks (in addition to fines for the crime)
11/7–8	Striking someone with a blunt weapon or causing a wound at the assembly	Unspecified	Three marks
11/8–9	Killing or maiming a man, except in revenge, at the assembly	Unspecified	Six marks
12/3–5	Killing or maiming a man at his home	General assembly and the victim or his heirs	Twelve marks to each (in addition to wergild in the case of death)
12/5–7	Striking someone in their home with a blunt weapon or causing a wound	The community and the victim	Three marks to each (in addition to the normal fine)
13/61–65	Refusing to offer compensation for a killing within the specified time, or not keeping to his circle of truce	General assembly and the claimant	Six marks in silver to each
14/25	Killing by a minor		Twelve marks in silver (i.e. half a wergild)
14/32–33	Killing a pregnant woman		Twelve marks in silver for the child and full wergild for the woman
15/2–3; 7–9	Killing a Gotlander or the child of a Gotlandic man	His or her heirs	Three marks in gold (i.e. 24 marks in silver, 96 marks in coin)
15/4; 15/11–12	Killing a non-Gotlander or the child of a non-Gotlandic man	His or her heirs	Ten marks in silver (i.e. 40 marks in coin, as in Sweden)
15/5–6	Killing a slave	[His master, presumably]	Four and a half marks[1]

[1] This does not seem to be the same as the *value* of the slave, which appears to be three marks in silver.

16/2–3	Killing a Gotlander in his circle of truce		Twelve marks in silver (half a wergild)
16/3–4	Killing a non-Gotlander in his circle of truce		Five marks in silver (half a wergild)
16/4	Killing a slave in his circle of truce	[Presumably the victim's master]	Six öre (a sixth of a slave's wergild)
16/6–7	Maiming a non-Gotlander's hand or foot		Ten marks in coin ($^1/_4$ wergild)
16/7–8	Other maiming		[$^1/_4$ wergild, presumably]
16/11	Killing of a Gotlandic man by a slave		Nine marks in silver (plus the slave, valued at three marks in silver)
16/12–13	Killing of a Gotlandic man by a slave who then escapes		Twelve marks in silver (i.e. half the wergild for a Gotlander from the slave's master)
16/13–14	Killing of a non-Gotlandic man by a slave		Two marks in silver (plus the slave)
16/15–17	Killing of a non-Gotlandic man by a slave who then escapes		Five marks in silver (i.e. half the wergild for a non-Gotlander)
16/18–19	In both the above cases, if the master does not get an oath to deny his own involvement		Full wergild for the dead man (24 or ten marks in silver)
16/20–22	Killing of one slave by another	[Presumably the victim's master]	Four and a half marks in lieu of the slave himself[1]
17/2–4	Killing of a man by an uncastrated ox of five years old or more		Tweve marks [in silver], i.e. half his wergild[2]
17/14–16	Killing of a Gotlander by an ox, horse, three-year-old or older boar or dog		Tweve marks in silver
17/17–19	Killing of a non-Gotlander in the same circumstances	.	One third of his wergild, i.e. $13^1/_3$ marks in coin ($3^1/_3$ marks in silver)[3]
17/24–25	Wounding, etc. by animals		One third of the normal fine

[2] This is one of the few instances in which 'silver' is not stated explicitly, but is clearly intended.

[3] This is quite specifically at odds with the practice for a Gotlander, where half the wergild is offered.

17/26–27	Dog bites		Two *öre* per bite, up to four
18/2–3	Striking a woman so that she miscarries		Half a wergild
18/14–16	Killing a properly supervised child under three by accident at a gathering		Full wergild
19/2–4	Causing a wound one or more nail-breadths deep		Half a mark for each nail-breadth in length and depth [*c*.one inch] up to eight
19/5–6	Causing a wound less than a nail-breadth deep, but needing treatment		A quarter of a mark for each nail-breadth in length
19/13–15	Causing a body wound		One mark in silver
19/15–16	Stabbing with a knife		Two marks in silver
19/16–17	Throwing stones or other missiles		Three marks
19/17–20	Causing a visible wound that does not bleed		Half a mark for each blow up to four
19/21–23	Causing a wound through the nose or lips that heals		Two marks and then extra for the scar
19/24–25	As above, when it does not heal		Maximum price for a wound (i.e. two marks in silver)
19/25	As above two entries, for an ear		One mark (and extra for the scar if applicable) or one mark in silver if it does not heal
19/25–30	Causing a scar on the face between hat and beard		Half a mark in silver or a mark in silver if the scar is very noticeable
19/30–32	Splitting the scalp		One mark (in coin) or two if the skull is visible
19/32–34	Cracking the skull		One mark in silver, or two if the membrane is visible
19/35–36	Each sizeable fragment of bone chipped off		One mark
19/36–38	Each larger bone		Two marks for each up to four bones
19/38–40, 40–42	Each finger lost or badly damaged		Four marks (in coin)
19/40, 42–44	Loss of a thumb, or damage to the hand so that it is partly disabled		Two marks in silver (i.e. twice as much)

19/44–47	Loss of mobility or breaking the heel or neck	Two marks in silver
19/47	Each toe lost	Two marks
19/47–49	Loss of hand, foot or eye	Six marks in silver for each (of these *different* things)
19/49–52	Loss of both hands or both feet or both eyes in a survived attack	Twelve marks in silver for each (of these *different pairs* of things, disagreeing with *SL* IV, 263, note 25)
19/52–54	Loss of the nose	Twelve marks in silver
19/54–56	Loss of the tongue	Twelve marks in silver
19/56–68	Loss of a testicle, resulting in infertility	Six marks in silver
19/58–59	Loss of both testicles	Twelve marks in silver
19/59–61	Loss of the penis	Eighteen marks in silver
19/62	Each broken rib	Two marks for each up to four
19/62–64	Smaller bones in hand or foot	One mark
19/64–65	Larger bones in hand or foot	One mark in silver, or two if disability results
19/70–72	An invisible injury resulting in minor disability	One mark
19/73–76, 78–79	Injury resulting in deafness	Twelve marks in silver, or six if it is partial
19/80–81	Loss of an ear	One mark in silver; two marks in coin if the ear is retained damaged[4]
19/81–86	Loss of teeth	Two marks for each upper front tooth, one for every other upper jaw tooth; lower teeth at half this rate
19/87–89	Hair-pulling	Two *öre* (¼ mark) if done with one hand, otherwise half a mark
19/89–90, 91–92	Shaking, pushing, kicking or punching someone	Two *öre*
19/90–91	Throwing ale in someone's eye	Eight *örtugar* (⅓ mark), for the insult

[4] A silver mark is thus more than two marks in coin, probably twice as much.

19/95–97	Striking someone with a staff		Half a mark per blow up to two marks unless disfigurement results
19/101–105	Creating a bald patch the size of a finger, two fingers, two fingers and a thumb, hand		Eight *örtugar*, half a mark, a mark, two marks[5]
19/105–107	Pulling out all a man's hair		One mark in silver[4]
19/107–108	Removing a man's scalp		One mark in silver
19/109–113	Damage to outer clothing, kirtle, undergarments		One *öre*, two *öre*, eight *örtugar*, plus repair to the clothing
19/126–128	Blocking someone's way, or turning them aside		Eight *örtugar* (for the insult)
19/128–131	Violently forcing a man to abandon his route	The victim and the community	Three marks to each
19/134–136	A slave getting more than two blows for one from a free man	[The slave's master, presumably]	Two *öre* per blow, up to four blows
19/136–137	A free man getting more than one blow for two from a slave		Half a mark per blow, up to four blows
19/137–139	Any non-injuring attack on a slave		Half the free man's compensation
19/139–141	Any injury to a slave		The same as for a free man up to three marks
20/118–121, 123–125	Seduction by any man of the illegitimate daughter of a Gotlandic man with a non-Gotlandic woman (or vice versa)		*Hogsl* of four marks
20/121–122, 123–125	Any man taken in the act of seduction of the illegitimate daughter of a Gotlandic man with a non-Gotlandic woman (or vice versa)		Three marks in silver (to avert the loss of a hand or foot)

[5] Eight *örtugar* must thus be less than half a mark and more than a quarter of a mark. This shows that there were most likely three *örtugar* to the *öre* (⅛ mark) in Gotland as elsewhere.

20a/5–8; 24–26	Any man taken in the act of seduction of a single Gotlandic woman		Six marks in silver (to avert the loss of a hand or foot)
20a/18– 21	If a Gotlandic man loses a paternity case, when he was not taken *in flagrante delicto*		Maintaining the mother and child, or full *hogsl*, if she is Gotlandic
20a/21– 24; 35– 36	Any man taken in the act of seduction of a non-Gotlandic woman in her home		Three marks
20a/26– 28	If a non-Gotlandic man is not taken *in flagrante delicto* with a Gotlandic woman, but has a child with her		Eight marks in *hogsl* (and brings up the child), if he acknowledges it
20a/28– 32	If a non-Gotlandic man loses a paternity case, when he was not taken *in flagrante delicto*		Full *hogsl*, if she is Gotlandic, the child being maintained by her father or brother if she is unmarried
20a/33– 35	If a non-Gotlandic man has a child with a non-Gotlandic woman		Three marks in *hogsl* (and he is to bring up the child)
21/2–3	Adultery (presumably by an unmarried man)	The wronged party (presumably the husband) and the (local) assembly	Six marks and three marks respectively
21/3–5	Double adultery	The wronged party and the general assembly	Twelve marks to each
21/5–8	Adultery by a married man with an unmarried woman, but not vice versa	The unmarried woman	*Hogsl*
21/9–12	Adultery by any man taken *in flagrante delicto* with a married woman		40 marks (or execution, as decided by the cuckolded husband)
21/12– 15	Luring a woman to marriage without her family's agreement	Father or guardian and the general assembly	40 marks, of which twelve went to the assembly
21/15– 20; 20– 23	Taking a woman by force without her family's agreement	Father or guardian and the general assembly	Man's wergild (or ten marks in silver if she was non-Gotlandic), of which twelve (in coin) went to the assembly (otherwise his neck)

22/13–15	Rape of a woman: Gotlandic, non-Gotlandic or slave		Twelve marks, five marks or six *öre* respectively (cf. the *banduvereldi*)
22/16–19	Rape of a married free woman		Her wergild value (in return for his life)
22/26–28	Rape by a slave of a Gotlandic woman		Her (or his) wergild (from his master) only if the woman allows this instead of the slave's life
23/2–6	(Half) uncovering a woman's head (of a free woman only)		(One) two marks
23/9–12	Striking off a clasp or buckle or both, or knocking them to the ground		Eight *örtugar* or ½ mark or one mark
23/12–13	Pulling off a woman's lacing		½ mark for each up to the maximum [probably two marks] and the return of them
23/15–17	Pushing a woman so that her clothes are displaced		Eight *örtugar*
23/17–20	If clothing is displaced to mid-calf, knee, loins		½ mark, one mark, two marks
23/20–21; 22–24	Grasping a woman by the wrist, elbows, shoulders, breast		½ mark, eight *örtugar*, five *örtugar*, one *öre*; half this if the woman is not Gotlandic
23/24–25; 25–27	Grasping a woman by the ankle, lower leg, thigh		½ mark, eight *örtugar*, five *örtugar*; half this if the woman is not Gotlandic, but freeborn
23/27–30	Grasping her higher up		No fine, as the woman is held responsible by this time
24/17–18	Providing more than the stipulated ale at a wedding	The general assembly	Twelve marks
24/19–20	Gate-crashing a wedding or other feast		Three *öre*
25/26–29	Giving leave for another to cut wood or reeds in unallocated wood or marsh	The wronged party and the community	Three marks to each

25/33–37	Refusing to allow a search for property taken from another's wood or other property		Unspecified fine
25/38–40	Damaging another person's property	The wronged party and the community	Three marks to each
25/40–42	Enclosing unallocated land	The wronged party and the community	Three marks to each
26/8–14	Not having a stock-proof fence, resulting in animals breaking through		½ mark (towards the fencing), exacted again each fortnight if the fence is not made good
26/25–27	Animal breaking through a legally constructed fence		The damage caused (due from the animal's owner)
26/27–29	Ox breaking through a fence of any sort		The damage caused (due from the ox's owner)
26/29–30	Ox jumping over a fence, but only if it is legally constructed		The damage caused (due from the ox's owner)
26/38–40; 41–42	Cutting wood on another's property	The wronged party and the community	Three marks to each and an extra eight örtugar if he takes it home and full restitution
26/47–48; 48–49; 49–50	Breaking a man's fence at the top tie, then a second section or a third		½ mark plus eight örtugar plus four örtugar (i.e. one mark in all)
26/50–52	Breaking open a whole fence section		Two marks (and the mending of the fence)
26/55–56; 56–58	Stealing firewood, fencing or timber		Six öre (three marks if he has driven it to the road) plus full restitution
28/4–7	Purchasing land unlawfully	The wronged parties and the general assembly	Twelve marks to each. The purchaser also lost the price of the land
28/22–23	Selling outside the family or parish	The general assembly	Twelve marks
28/47–49	Maximum ransom for a farmer's son, etc.		Three marks in silver, whoever is paying the ransom
28/66–68	Brothers possessing undivided property and a killing occurring		The appropriate fine (by the brother who does the killing)
31/4–5	Any magistrate (raþmaþr) not attending the assemby by midday	The hundred (local) assembly	Three öre

31/5–7	If all the magistrates are absent	The first person bringing an action and the community	Three marks to each
31/9–10	Continuing cases after sunset		The highest fine that the assembly concerned can command: three, six or twelve marks
35/2–5; 6–9	Horse theft	The wronged party and the community	Three marks to each
35/10–12	Taking the wrong horse by mistake		Eight *örtugar*
36/15–17	Taking a boat from its moorings and using it	The wronged party and the community	Three marks to each (by implication)
37/22–26; 26–28	Planting stolen goods on another	The wronged party and the (local) assembly respectively	The person's wergild and three marks (or twelve marks to the general assemby for a Gotlander)
38/2–4	Theft of two *öre* or less		Six *öre* for petty theft
38/4–6	Theft of up to a mark in silver		Wergild (plus branding as detailed above)
39/10–12	Specific insults at church level		Three *öre*
39/12–16	Specific insults repeated at a higher level		Three marks
46/2–4	Altering a brand on an animal neither bought nor inherited		Three marks
48/5–6	Not planting turnips	The parish	Three *öre*
48/6–8	A parish not enforcing turnip-planting	The assembly	Three marks (from the parish)
50/4–5	Causing damage to other farms from your fire	The affected farms (to be divided between them)	Three marks (maximum)
51/2–4	Causing damage with fire carried into a man's farm (to light his fire)		Half the wergild of the perpetrator or responsible adult
52/3–4	A parish not maintaining roads	The (local) assembly	Three marks (from the parish)
55/2–4	Building a house without permission	The parish	Three marks (and demolish the house)
55/4–5	Employing indoor workers without parish permission (presumably during harvest)	Unspecified	Three *öre*

56/2–5	Harvest workers taking unauthorised leave	The farmer	One *örtug* per day and an extra day's work
56a/6–7	Crofters refusing to work at harvest time	The farmer	Three *öre*
57/2–4; 58/2–4	Hunting squirrels or trapping hares between the Annunciation and the Feast of Simon and Jude	[Presumably the parish]	Three marks
59/4–5	Harvesting fruit too early	Parishioners, with half to the informant	Three *öre* (1½ for minors)
60/2–4; 4–7	Failure to say mass on Sunday or feast day; on Fridays or days when the litany is said	The dean and the parish	Three marks to each; twelve *öre* to each
61/2–3	Gambling	The parish	Three *öre*
61/3–4	A parish not prosecuting a gambler	The (local) assembly	Three marks
62/3–5	Revised punishment for pulling out hair to the size of a palm or completely		One mark in silver and two marks in silver respectively
63/2–4	Cutting wood in another's woodland		Three marks plus restitution
63/4–6	Breaking down another's fence to pass through		Three marks
63/6–8	Trespassing or tearing a gap in another's fence		Three *öre*
63/16–17	Providing too many drinks at a wedding	The general assembly	A double fine and twelve marks
65/18–19	Buying on credit from town-dwellers	The general assembly	Twelve marks
Addition 1/8–10	Cases in general		No fine is to be greater than the perpetrator can afford
Addition 1/19–21	If a priest inherits a defence in a murder case and the complainant does not wish to accept compensation	The complainant and the general assembly respectively	Full wergild; 40 marks

Addition 1/27–28	If two brothers, one ordained and the other not, inherit a case and need to compensate		Each their own personal portion
Addition 2/1–3	Personal injury caused by cattle, horses or pigs		The value of the animal at the most
Addition 2/5–6; 7–8	Injury caused by an animal declared at church and to the parish to be a rogue animal		Twice the normal fine for the injury, but half as much if the injury is normally fined at less than the animal's value
Addition 2/9–10	Dog causing damage		Up to half wergild
Addition 2/10–11	Dog bites		Two öre per bite up to four
Addition 2/12–13	Dog causing wounds or maiming		Half the maximum fine (not revenge)
Addition 3/1–2; 2–3	Small bones broken in the foot or hand; each rib		Two marks
Addition 3/3	Disability following the above		Two marks in silver
Addition 3/4–5	If so many bones are broken that the damage is obvious		½ mark per bone
Addition 4/1	If an ear is damaged but not totally cut off		One mark in silver (this was two marks in coin in the A-text)
Addition 4/1–2	If the long bones of the leg or arm are broken		Two marks in silver
Addition 4/3–5	If teeth are knocked out		One mark in silver for each of the two central upper or lower teeth, otherwise two marks in coin
Addition 5/2–4	If hair is pulled out leaving a bald patch larger in size than a palm; total hair loss		One mark in silver; two marks in silver[6]
Addition 5/4–5	If the scalp is cut		One mark in silver

[6] This series suggests that a mark in silver was worth four times a mark in coin at this period.

Addition 6/3–4	Providing too much ale for the wedding party	The general assembly	Twelve marks
Addition 8/1–3	Stealing by a slave or slaves of an *öre* or less		Three *öre*, payable by each master, the stolen goods being already recovered
Addition 8/3–5	Stealing by a slave of more than an *öre*		The stolen goods plus three times the value of the goods
Addition 8/5–7	Stealing by more than one slave of an *öre* or less		Three times the value of the missing goods (payable by each master)
Addition 8/15–20; 10–15	For taking a slave on suspicion without proof, even if he confesses		Six *öre*, unless there was no sign of a break-in (which constitutes proof)
Addition 8/23–28	Stealing by a slave of more than one *öre* [assumed], where there is material evidence		Three times the value (up to the value of the slave), plus the goods themselves (payable by the master unless he allows a search, in which case there is no triple fine)
Addition 8/23–28	For a theft greater than the slave's owner can afford		The slave to be handed over to the owner of the stolen goods
Addition 8/35–38	If a thief goes on the run		No triple compensation for food stolen, but return of what remains
Addition 8/39–43	Redeeming a slave: on land; in a boat; out of sight of land		Two *öre*; three *öre*; ½ mark
Addition 8/43–44; 48–50	If a slave escapes in an unlocked boat, or drowns at sea		Compensation is paid by the owner of the boat (to the owner of the slave) Three marks maximum
Addition 8/44–48	If a slave, in escaping, has stolen goods		from the slave's owner for the goods stolen

The maximum case a *siettungr* (sixth, district) assembly could hear was for three marks, the *þriþiungr* (riding) assembly six marks and the general assembly twelve marks. No fine limit is given for the local or hundred assemblies.

(iii) *Fees and rewards for stray animals*

Chapter and line	Type of animal	Number and type of assembly	Fine from owner if claimed	Fee per assembly if unclaimed	Paid for beast by finder	Paid to whom
40/2–5	Small livestock	Two, church plus (presumably) local assembly		Assembly fee	Value less the assembly fee	Parishioners
41/3–4; 6–7	Swine	Two local plus riding	*Örtug* per assembly	Assembly fee	Value less the assembly fee	Parishioners
42/2–5; 5–6	Tame sheep	Two local plus riding	The offspring	Riding assembly fee	No amount specified	Not applicable
43/2–3; 3–4	Unshorn rams	Unspecified	*Örtug*	'As for other sheep'	No amount specified	Not applicable
44/5–7; 7–8	Shorn rams in winter	Unspecified, possibly none held in winter	Unspecified	The ram itself	No amount specified	Not applicable
45/2–4	Goats	Two over two years; presumably riding assemblies	*Örtug* for a billy-goat and six pence for a nanny per assembly	Not specified	No amount specified	Not applicable
45a/2–5	Horses	Two local plus riding	Two *örtugar* per assembly	Not specified	No amount specified	Not applicable

APPENDIX E: OATHS AND WITNESSES REQUIRED

(i) *Oaths*

Page and line	Circumstances of 'character' oaths	Number of oath-takers
2/15	rehabilitation oath (*symdaraiþr*) in respect of innocence of infanticide	Six
2/28–30	as above, in the case where prosecution witnesses fail to put up their deposit	not specified
4/11–12	in respect of a man defending himself if accused of pagan practices	Six
4/12–14	as above at the local assembly	Six
4/15–17	as above at the general assembly	Twelve
13/57–58	in respect of a man claiming that he has offered compensation three times, with a year between each offer in respect of a manslaughter case; this was an oath in addition to actual witness as to fact (see below)	Twelve
16/17–18	in respect of the master of a slave claiming that he had nothing to do with the killing perpetrated by the slave, if the latter is not present to carry the case	Six
19/8–10	in respect of a wound compensated at more than three marks	Six, including the injured party
19/10–11	in respect of a wound compensated at three marks or less	Three, including the injured party
19/73; 76–77	in respect of a man injured so that he loses his hearing	Six, plus the same factual witness as for a wound (see below)
22/21–23	in respect of the defence of a man accused of rape, where the woman initially claims not to have recognised the assailant, but changes her mind	Twelve
22/23–27	in respect of a woman, who claims rape, being pregnant and giving birth at the appropriate time for it to have been the result of the rape	Twelve, plus her witnesses (see below)
32/2–4	in respect of a demand for payment in money, where there is disagreement over the sum involved	Six (at the most)

32/4–7	in respect of a demand for payment in land, where the value involved is a gold mark or greater	Eighteen
39/9–10	in respect of the defence of a man charged with slander	Three, with the witness of the parishioners
39/12	in respect of the remedy by a man found guilty of slander at parish level	Three, in church
39/16	as above, but when the insult is more public and is brought to the local assembly	Six, with the witness of the assembly

(ii) *Witnesses as to fact and juries*

Page and line	Circumstances for the witness as to fact; those marked * also swore oaths as to the facts	Number of witnesses
2/4–7	in respect of a woman claiming that her child was stillborn	Two (i.e. three with herself)
2/10–11	in respect of a woman guilty of infanticide having confessed and done penance	One (the shriving priest)
3/32–34*	in respect of proof that a man has lawfully taken part in the building and consecration of a new church	Three parishioners (including himself)
3/35–39	as above, when three or more years have passed	Two parishioners and the priest
4/5–7	confirmation that someone had held a sacrificial meal	Unspecified number of witnesses
13/53–56	in respect of a man claiming that he has offered compensation three times, with a year between each offer in respect of a manslaughter case	Three (who were present when the offers were made)
14/26–28*	in respect of a woman killed while pregnant	Husband or, if he is not alive, closest relative with two more landowners and a further nine of equal birth
18/4–7; 7–9	in respect of a woman who has a miscarriage as a result of being struck	Two landowners to witness the blow and her complaint and two female witnesses to witness the miscarriage
18/9–10*	as above, swearing that the child was alive when she was struck	Herself and five others; note that this says 'person-oath' rather than 'man-oath', indicating, perhaps, that some of the witnesses in this case might be women
19/6–8	witness (as to the fact of the wound) but not swear the oath	Three (two local magistrates and one district, i.e. sixth, judge)

19/71–72	in respect of a hand damaged so that it cannot tolerate hot and cold	Self-witness
19/117–121	in respect of a non-open wound causing the injured person to be bedridden for a year or more	Four landowners and three judges from the same sixth and then others to make up twelve in all
20/92–96	in respect of an illegitimate child's claim to inheritance, that his father and three successive female ancestors were trueborn Gotlanders	A genealogical table
20a/9–14*	in respect of a man denying a paternity suit, claiming that he had not been named before the child was born	Six (including two landowners from the woman's parish)
20a/15–18*	as above, in support of the woman, when the case is not found in favour of the man	Six (all of equal birth with her)
22/5–7	in respect of a woman being raped, whose shout immediately after the attack is heard	One, the witness to the 'shout'
22/7–10	in respect of a woman being raped, whose shout after the attack is not heard	An unspecified number of witnesses to her complaint, made within a day, who may also act as witness to her attack
22/23–26	in respect of a woman, pregnant as a result of being raped, to confirm the date of her rape	An unspecified number of witnesses to the fact, as in the previous entry
23/6–8	in respect of attacks upon a woman resulting in whole or partial removal of her headdress, according to witness	Unspecified number of eye-witnesses, including herself
23/14–15	in respect of laces being removed as to whether compensation and restitution have been made	The woman herself
25/2–3; 8–11*	in respect of disputes about woodland; the witness had to swear on oath, or it was invalid	Two: a neighbour and a work witness
25/11–17	in respect of disputes about cultivated land	Two: a (distant) kin witness and a work witness owning neighbouring land
25/32–33	in respect of the taking of timber from another's wood, to deny the justification to confiscate the one's property	The disputing parties and an eyewitness
26/60–61*	in respect of the taking of timber from his wood, that he has received restitution	Self, on oath
32/7–9	in respect of a dispute about the value of property owed, if of a mark in gold or more	Unspecified number of magistrates in the hundred to decide

32/14–16	in respect of a dispute about the value of property owed, if less than a mark in gold	Six–man jury to decide
37/11–15	in respect of the possession of disputed goods where their origin is agreed	The assignor
37/19–22	in respect of the possession of stolen goods, when the knowledge of their having been stolen is denied, and responsibility laid on the supplier	An unspecified number of those who were present when the goods were handed over, if the assignor denies responsibility
Addition 8/7–9	in respect of a theft in which the stolen goods are not to hand, how much has been taken	Self-witness
Addition 8/51–56	in respect of a man caught without the relevant stolen goods in his possession, to witness to what is said	Three magistrates from the same hundred or sixth to decide or witness

(iii) *Official witness for reference in the future in case of dispute*

Page and line	Circumstances for the official witness	Number of witnesses
16/23–25	in respect of a slave who has worked out his bondage time	Unspecified number of parishioners, perhaps all of them
20/114–116	in respect of the rights of illegitimate children	Unspecified number of parishioners, who will administer their rights
26/2–3; 4–5	in respect of declarations being made in a claim for a party fence; erection of a party fence	One neighbour or parishioner; an unspecified number of neighbours
26/17–19, 22–25	in respect of animals straying or breaking through a lawful fence being offered back to the owner	Unspecified number of neighbours
28/8–10	in respect of the sale or mortgage of property and the offering of the kinsman's portion	Unspecified number of (assembly members as) witnesses
28/25–28	in respect of property sold to a more distant relative and informing the receiver of the kinsman's portion	Unspecified number of parishioners
44/5–6, 7–9	in respect of a stray ram found before covering time and its being offered for redemption, and re-branded if unclaimed	Unspecified number of parishioners
45a/5–7	in respect of a stray bullock or draught pony being found and its being offered for redemption, and being available for use if unclaimed	Unspecified number of parishioners
61/8–9	that any new laws are true Gotlandic laws	The majority of the judges

BIBLIOGRAPHY AND ABBREVIATIONS
Abbreviations

The following abbreviations are used throughout for Swedish provincial laws and for the sections (*balkar*) within them. They are to a great extent those used in the series *Svenska landskapslagar* (*SL*), since these are widely current in the literature referenced. Where page numbers are given, they refer to the indicated volumes in the series *Corpus iuris sueo-gotorum* (*CIS*). Schlyter's editions of the laws of Magnus Eriksson (*CIS* X and *CIS* XI) are abbreviated to *MELL* and *MEStL*. The Swedish translations of these laws are referred to as *MELLNT* and *MEStLNT*. These two abbreviations are listed in the Bibliography, as are abbreviations of law texts in volumes in the series *Norges gamle love indtil 1387* (*NGL*) and *Danmarks gamle Landskabslove* (*DGL*).

BjR	The town law for Bjärkö (*CIS* VI, 111–34)
DL (*ÄVmL*)	The law of Dalarna (older law of Västmanland) (*CIS* V, 1–66)
daGL	Danish translation of the law of the Gotlanders (*CIS* VII, 169–218)
GL	The law of the Gotlanders (*CIS* VII, 1–112)
HL	The law of Hälsingland (*CIS* VI, 1–93)
KrLL	Kristoffer's national law (*CIS* XII)
MELL	Magnus Eriksson's national law (*CIS* X)
MEStL	Magnus Eriksson's town law (*CIS* XI)
SdmL	The law of Södermanland (*CIS* IV)
SkL	The law of Skåne (in general, regardless of edition)
CISk I	The law of Skåne (*CIS* IX, 1–238)
CISk II	Andreas Suneson's Latin text of the law of Skåne (*CIS* IX, 239–354)
CISk IV	The town law of Skåne (*CIS* IX, 397–434)
CISk V	Miscellaneous additions to the law of Skåne (*CIS* IX, 435–500)
tyGL	German translation of the law of the Gotlanders (*CIS* VII, 113–168)
UL	The law of Uppland (*CIS* III)
VgL III	Lydekinus' excerpts and notes on the laws of Västergötland (*CIS* I, 255-281)
VgL IV	Notes by the priest of Vidhem and the monk of St John on the laws of Västergötland (*CIS* I, 283–344)
VgLL	The laws of Västergötland as a group

VmL	The (younger) law of Västmanland (*CIS* V, 67–239)
VStL	The town law of Visby (*CIS* VIII, 1–182)
YVgL	The younger law of Västergötland (*CIS* I, 77–253, *VgL* II)
ÄVgL	The older law of Västergötland (*CIS* I, 2–74, *VgL* I)
ÖgL	The law of Östergötland (*CIS* II)

Add	Additions (to *YVgL*, etc.)
Bb	The section concerning building (*SdmL*, *MELL*, etc.)
	The section concerning community (village) law (*HL*, *UL*)
Db	The section concerning manslaughter (*YVgL*, *ÖgL*, *MELL*, *MEStL*)
Eb	The section concerning the King's oath
fl.	*flock*, chapter of the law
Fns	The first section concerning honour (*ÄVgL*)
Fnb	The second section concerning honour (*ÄVgL*)
	The section concerning personal injury (*YVgL*)
Gb	The section concerning matrimony
Jb	The section concerning land
Kgb	The section concerning the monarchy
Kkb	The section concerning church or Christian law
Kmb	The section concerning trade
Mb	The section concerning personal and property rights (*UL*, etc.)
Md	The section concerning killing (*ÄVgL*)
pr	principium (first or principal paragraph in each chapter)
Rb	The section concerning slaves and outlaws (*ÄVgL*, *YVgL*)
	The section concerning the legal process (*UL*, *VmL*, *MELL*, etc.)
Sb	The section concerning wounding (*ÄVgL*, *MELL*, *MEStL*)
Tjb	The section concerning theft
Urb	The section concerning outlawry cases (*ÄVgL*, *YVgL*)
Utb	The section concerning off-farm activities (*YVgL*)
Vb	Concerning accidental injury (*ÄVgL*, *YVgL*)
	The section concerning accidental injury, wounding, adultery, robbery and theft (*ÖgL*)
Äb	The section concerning inheritance

Manuscripts and unpublished works

Biblioteca Medicea Laurenziana, Florence. Codex Laur. Ashburnham, 1554. *c*.1120. The so-called 'Florensdokumentet'; list of bishoprics, church provinces, etc.

Det kongelige Bibliotek, Copenhagen. Den gamle kongelige samling (GKS) 3363 4to. Late 17th or early 18th century. *Lex Gothlandica 1470 scripta*.

Det kongelige Bibliotek, Copenhagen. Kalls samling 650 4to. Late 17th or early 18th century. Copy of *Lex Gothlandica 1470 scripta*.

Kungliga Biblioteket, Stockholm B 64. 14th century. *[Gottlandz landzlagh.]*

Kungliga Biblioteket, Stockholm B 65. 1401. *[Gottlands landslag på Plattyska.]*

Kungliga Biblioteket, Stockholm B 68 4to. Early 17th century. *[Van gamla gullands love 4to.]*

Kungliga Biblioteket, Stockholm C 81 4to. Late 16th century. *[K Hanses recess paa Gullands lov 1492 4to.]*

Neogard, Lars Nilsson 1732. *Gautau-Minning, Thet är, Något om then ofgamla Gautaun ell Gjötiska Ön Guthiland, nu kallad Gothland, Med någon dryg tidspillan sammanhemtat af Lars Neogard 1732*. Copies held in the libraries of Visby Läroverk and Uppsala University.

University Library, Copenhagen. Den arnamagnaeanske håndskriftsamling AM 54 4to. 1587. *Guta lag*. Copy by David Bilefeld of a lost manuscript from 1470.

University Library, Copenhagen. Den arnamagnaeanske håndskriftsamling AM 55 4to. Mid 16th century. *Den gamle Gullands Low*. Danish translation from *c*.1492.

Printed works

Aakjær, Svend 1936. 'Maal, Vægt og Taxter i Danmark'. In *NK XXX*, 175–282.

Aasen, Ivar Andreas 2003. *Norsk ordbog med dansk forklaring*. Ed. Kristoffer Kruken and Terje Aarset.

AEW = Jan de Vries 1961. *Altnordisches etymologisches Wörterbuch*.

AL = Adolf Noreen 1904. *Altschwedisches Lesebuch. Mit Anmerkungen und Glossar. Zweite Auflage*.

Almquist, Jan Eric 1923. *Det processuella förfarandet vid ägotvist: studier över jordabalkens 14 och 15 kapitel*.

Almquist, Jan Eric 1942. 'Om formerna för tingsfridens lysning i Sverige under äldre tid'. In *Historiska studier tillägnade Sven Tunberg, den 1 februari 1942*. Ed. Adolf Schück and Åke Stille, 61–81.

Ambrosiani, Sune 1939. 'Mark och markland. "Marca" and "marca terræ"'. *Rig. Tidskrift utgiven av Föreningen för svensk kulturhistoria* 22, 153–65.

Amira, K. von 1882–95 (reprint 1973). *Nordgermanisches Obligationenrecht*. 2 vols.

Amira, Karl von 1913 (3rd revised and enlarged edn). *Grundriss des germanischen Rechts*.

Amira, Karl von 1922. *Die germanischen Todesstrafen: Untersuchungen zur Rechts- und Religionsgeschichte*.

Beckman, Natanael 1920. 'Gutalagens inledningsord och Gotlands kristnande'. *Minnesskrift utgiven af Filologiska samfundet i Göteborg på tjugoårsdagen av dess stiftande den 22 oktober 1920* in *Göteborgs högskolas årsskrift* 26:2, 9–14.

BjarkR = *Den ældre By-lov eller Bjarkö-Ret* 1846. Ed. R. Keyser and P. A. Munch. (*NGL* 1, 301–36).

Björkander, Adolf 1898. *Till Visby stads äldsta historia. Ett kritiskt bidrag*.

Björling, Carl Georg Emanuel 1893. *Om bötesstraffet i den svenska medeltidsrätten*.

BoG = *Boken om Gotland* 1945. Ed. (Vol. I) Mårten Stenberger, (Vol. II) Richard Steffen. 2 vols.

Bohman, Lennart 1951. 'Gotlands förbindelser med Stockholm före Kalmarunionen'. *GArk* 23, 30–56.

BorgL = *Den ældre Borgathings- eller Vikens-Christenret* 1846. Ed. R. Keyser and P. A. Munch. (*NGL* 1, 337–72).

Brunner, Heinrich 1906–28 (2nd edn). *Deutsche Rechtsgeschichte (2. Aufl. / neu bearbeitet von Claudius von Schwerin)*. 2 vols.

Brøgger, A. W. and Shetelig, Haakon 1950. *Vikingeskipene: deres forgjengere og etterfølgere*.

Bugge, Alexander 1899. 'Gotlændingernes handel paa England og Norge omkring 1300'. *Historisk tidsskrift utgitt av Den norske historiske forening* Række 3, Band 5, 145–80.

Bugge, Sophus 1877–78. 'Sproglige Oplysninger om Ord i gamle nordiske Love. I. Svenske Ord'. *Nordisk Tidskrift for Filologi* 3 (Ny række), 258–75.

Carlsson, Lizzie 1934. 'Bödelsämbetet i det medeltida Stockholm'. *Samfundet S:t Eriks årsbok* 32, 95–118.

CCS = Corpus codicum suecicorum medii aevi. . . 1943–67. Ed. Elias Wessén. 20 vols.

Christiansen, Eric 1997. *The northern crusades.*

CIG = GL, tygL and *daGL.* In *Codex iuris Gotlandici, cum notis criticis, variis lectionibus, nova versione suecana, glossariis et indicibus nominum propriorum. Gotlands-lagen* 1852. Ed. C. J. Schlyter. (*CIS* VII).

CIS = Corpus iuris sueo-gotorum antiqui . . . Samling af Sweriges gamla lagar 1827–77. Ed. (Vols I–II) H. S. Collin and C. J. Schlyter; (Vols III–XIII) C. J. Schlyter. 13 vols.

CIS I = *Codex iuris Vestrogotici, . . . Westgöta-lagen utgifven av H. S. Collin och C. J. Schlyter [Facsimile edition with an addendum by Otto von Friesen, Our oldest manuscript in Old Swedish]* 1976. Ed. Gösta Holm.

CIS II = *Codex iuris Ostrogotici, . . . Östgöta-lagen utgifven av H. S. Collin och C. J. Schlyter [Facsimile edition with addendum by the main part of Emil Olson, Östgötalagens 1300-talsfragment (reprint) and Carl Ivar Ståhle, De Liedgrenska fragmenten av Östgötalagens C-text (first print)]* 1980. Ed. Gösta Holm and Carl Ivar Ståhle.

CIS III = *Codex iuris Uplandici, . . . Upplands-lagen* 1834. Ed. C. J. Schlyter.

CIS IV = *Codex iuris Sudermannici, . . . Södermanna-lagen* 1838. Ed. C. J. Schlyter.

CIS V = *Codex iuris Vestmannici, . . . Westmanna-lagen* 1841. Ed. C. J. Schlyter.

CIS VI = *Codex iuris Helsingici; Codicis iuris Smalandici pars de re ecclesiastica; et, Juris urbici codex antiquior. Helsinge-lagen; Kristnu-balken af Smålands-lagen; Bjärköa-rätten* 1844. Ed. C. J. Schlyter.

CIS VIII = *Codices iuris Visbyensis urbici et maritimi. Wisby stadslag och sjörätt* 1853. Ed. C. J. Schlyter.

CIS IX = *Codex iuris Scanici, . . . Skåne-lagen* 1859. Ed. C. J. Schlyter.

CIS X = *Codex iuris communis Sueciae Magnaeanus. Konung Magnus Erikssons landslag* 1862. Ed. C. J. Schlyter.

CIS XI = *Codex iuris urbici Magnaeanus. Konung Magnus Erikssons stadslag* 1865. Ed. C. J. Schlyter.

CIS XII = *Codex iuris communis Sueciae Christophorianus. Konung Christoffers landslag* 1869. Ed. C. J. Schlyter.

CISG = Glossarium ad corpus iuris sueo-gotorum antiqui. . . Ordbok till samlingen af Sweriges gamla lagar 1877. Ed. C. J. Schlyter. (*CIS* XIII).

CODEE = The Concise Oxford Dictionary of English Etymology 1986. Ed. T. F. Hoad.

C-V = Richard Cleasby and Gudbrand Vigfusson 1957 (2nd edn William A. Craigie). *An Icelandic-English dictionary.*

DD III = *Diplomatarium Danicum (1340–1412)* 1958–82. Ed. C. A. Christensen (and Herluf Nielsen for later volumes). Række III, 9 vols.

Delin, Carl 1909. *Om oäkta börd samt om oäkta barns rättställning enligt äldre svensk rätt.*

Delin, Carl 1926. 'Om blodshämnden och götalagarnas straffbestämmelser för enkelt viljadråp'. In *Skrifter tillägnade Johan C. W. Thyrén vid hans avgång från professorsämbetet den 31 maj 1926*, 238–305.

Delisle, M. Léopold 1886. *Notice sur des manuscrits du fonds libri conservés . . . la Laurentienne, . . . Florence.*

DGL = Danmarks gamle Landskabslove med Kirkelovene 1933–61. Ed. Johs. Brøndum-Nielsen and Poul Johs. Jørgensen. 8 vols and a supplement to vol. 4 edited by Eric Buus.

Dovring, Folke 1947. *Attungen och marklandet: studier över agrara förhållanden i medeltidens Sverige.*

DS = Diplomatarium Suecanum 1829–1995. Ed. John Gustaf Liljegren et al. 8 vols and 2 appendices.

DS I = *Diplomatarium Suecanum* 1829. Vol. I. Ed. John Gustaf Liljegren et al.

DS II = *Diplomatarium Suecanum* 1834, 1837. Vol. II. Ed. John Gustaf Liljegren.

DS Appendix 1 = *Diplomatarium Svecanum appendix. Acta pontificum Svecica. Acta cameralia. Auspiciis archivi regni Sveciae* 1936–42. Vol. I. Ed. L. M. Bååth.

Edda = Edda: Die Lieder des Codex Regius nebst verwandten Denkmälern I: Text 1962 (3rd edn, revised Hans Kuhn). Ed. Gustav Neckel.

EidsL = Den ældre Eidsivathings-Christenret 1846. Ed. R. Keyser and P. A. Munch. (*NGL* 1, 373–406).

Ekelund, Samuel 1906. *Studien über eine mitteldeutsche Übersetzung des altgutnischen Rechtes. Akademische Abhandlung.*

Eriks SjL1 = Eriks sjællandske Lov Text 1–2 1932. Ed. Peter Skautrup. (*DGL* 5).

Erikskrönikan = Erikskrönikan enligt Cod. Holm. D2 1921 and 1963. Ed. Rolf Pipping.

Erixon, Sigurd 1955. 'Den till fångstnäringarna knutna rörliga bebyggelsen'. In *NK* XI–XIIA, 124–35.

Fabre and Duchesne 1910 = Honorius III, Pope [Cencio Savelli] 1910. *Le Liber Censuum de l'Église Romaine. Publié avec une préface et un commentaire par . . . P. Fabre . . . et L. Duchesne. (G. Mollat).* Ed. Paul Fabre and Louis Duchesne. (Guillaume Mollat). 3 vols.

Falk, Hjalmar 1919. *Altwestnordische Kleiderkunde: mit besonderer Berücksichtigung der Terminologie.*

FL = *Ett forn-svenskt legendarium: innehållande medeltids klostersagor om helgon, påfvar och kejsare ifrån det I:sta till det XIII:de århundradet efter gamla handskrifter* 1847–58, 1874. Ed. George Stephens. 3 vols.

Friesen, Otto von 1933. 'II De nordiska (yngre) runorna: 3 De svenska runinskrifterna'. In *NK* VI, 145–248.

Fritzner = Johan Fritzner 1883, 1891, 1896 (reprint 1954). *Ordbog over det gamle norske sprog.* Vols I–III [Third volume includes 'Bemærkninger af Sophus Bugge', 1101–1110]. Vol. IV: Finn Hødnebø 1972. *Ordbog over det gamle norske sprog af Dr. Johan Fritzner. Rettelser og tillegg.*

FrostL = *Den ældre Frostathings-Lov* 1846. Ed. R. Keyser and P. A. Munch. (*NGL* 1, 119–300).

G 351 = Inscription 351 in Snædal 2002, 87–88.

Gannholm, Tore 1994. *Guta lagh med Gutasagan.*

GArk = *Gotländskt arkiv. Meddelanden från föreningen Gotlands fornvänner* 1929–.

GGD = *Guterlov og Gutersaga paa dansk* 1910. Ed. Lis Jacobsen.

Gigas, E. 1903, 1906, 1911–15. *Katalog over Det store kongelige Bibliotheks Haandskrifter vedrørende Norden, særlig Danmark.* 3 vols.

G-L = *Guta-Lagh das ist: Der Insel Gothland altes Rechtsbuch* 1818. Ed. Karl Schildener.

GLGS = *Guta lag och Guta saga jämte ordbok* 1905-07. Ed. Hugo Pipping.

GO = *Gotländsk ordbok på grundval av C. och P. A. Säves samlingar* 1918–40, 1941–45 (facsimile reprint in 1991). Ed. G. Danell (a–ba), A. Schagerström (be–ben) and Herbert Gustavson. 2 vols.

Gothlandz-Laghen = *Gothlandz-Laghen på gammal Göthiska* 1687. Ed. Johan Hadorph.

Grágás = *Grágás: Islændernes Lovbog i Fristatens Tid udgivet efter det Kongelige Bibliotheks Haandskrift* 1852–70. Tr. into Danish and ed. Vilhjálmur Finsen. 2 vols.

Grieg, Sigurd 1943a. 'Skjoldene i middelalderen'. In *NK* XIIB, 67–89.

Grieg, Sigurd 1943b. 'Hugg- og støtvåpen fra middelalderen'. In *NK* XIIB, 90–133.

Grønbech, Vilhelm Peter 1955. *Vor folkeæt i oldtiden.* 2 vols (new edition).

GS = *Guta saga. The History of the Gotlanders* 1999. Ed. and trans. Christine Peel.

GU = Säve, Carl 1859. *Gutniska urkunder: Guta lag, Guta saga och Gotlands runinskrifter språkligt behandlade. Academisk afhandling.*

GulKrR = *Den nyere Gulathings Christenret* 1848. Ed. R. Keyser and P. A. Munch. (*NGL* 2, 306–38.)

GulL = *Den ældre Gulathings-Lov* 1846. Ed. R. Keyser and P. A. Munch. (*NGL* 1, 1–118.)

GulL supp. = *Supplement to Gulathings-Lov* 1848. Ed. R. Keyser and P. A. Munch. (*NGL* 2, 493–523.)

Gustavson, Herbert 1940–42, 1948. *Gutamålet: en historisk-deskriptiv översikt.* 2 vols.

Gædeken, Poul 1934. *Retsbrudet og Reaktionen derimod i gammeldansk og germansk Ret.*

Hafström, Gerhard 1949. *Ledung och marklandsindelning.*

Hafström, Gerhard 1970 (4th revised edn). *Land och lag.*

Hald, Kristian 1975. 'Tre ord fra *Gutalagen*'. In *Nordiske studier. Festskrift til Chr. Westergård-Nielsen på 65-årsdagen den 24. november 1975*, 53–58.

Hammerich, Louis Leonor 1941. *Clamor: eine rechtsgeschichtliche Studie.*

Hammerich, Louis Leonor 1959. 'Was ist germanische Rechtsgeschichte?' *Saga och sed. Kungl. Gustav Adolfs Akademiens årsbok*, 177–99.

HansUB I = *Hansisches Urkundenbuch* 1876–1916. Vol. 1 of 11. Ed. Konstantin Höhlbaum et al.

Harrison, Dick 2002. *Jarlens sekel. En berättelse om 1200-talets Sverige.*

Hasselberg, Gösta 1953. *Studier rörande Visby stadslag och dess källor.*

Hauberg, P. 1891. 'Gullands myntvæsen'. *Aarbøger for nordisk Oldkyndighed og Historie* 26 (II række, 6 bind), 1–72.

Hayes, M. Horace 1968 (16th revised edn). *Veterinary Notes for Horse Owners. A manual of horse medicine and surgery.* Revised by J. F. Donald Tutt.

HBU = *Heliga Birgittas Uppenbarelser efter gamla handskrifter* 1857–98, 1860, 1861, 1862, 1883–84. Ed. G. E. Klemming. 5 vols.

Hegel, Karl 1891. *Städte und Gilden der germanischen Völker im Mittelalter.* 2 vols.

Heiðreks saga = *The saga of King Heidrek the Wise: Saga Heiðreks konungs ins vitra* 1960. Ed. and trans. Christopher Tolkien.

Hellquist, Elof 1980 (3rd edn). *Svensk etymologisk ordbok.*

Hellsten, Nils E. 1943. 'Fäktning i norden under forntid och medeltid'. In *NK* XIIB, 173–92.

Hemmer, Ragnar 1928. *Studier rörande straffutmätningen i medeltida svensk rätt.*

Hemmer, Ragnar 1945. 'Hemfridens lokala utsträckning enligt svensk landskapsrätt'. *Svensk juristtidning* 30, 232–58.

Hemmer, Ragnar 1960. 'Recension av Per-Edwin Wallén: *Die Klage gegen den Toten im nordgermanischen Recht*'. *Tidskrift utgiven av Juridiska föreningen i Finland (FJFT)* 96:4, 186–94.

Heurgren, Paul 1925. *Husdjuren i nordisk folktro.*

Hildebrand, Hans 1879–94, 1884–98, 1898–1903, 1953. *Sveriges medeltid: kulturhistorisk skildring.* 4 vols (Vol. 4 is an index edited by Sven Tunberg).

Hjärne, Erland 1929. 'Vederlag och sjöväsen. Ett bidrag till det danska statsskickets äldsta historia'. *NoB* 17, 83–116.

Hjärne, Erland 1947. 'Roden. Upphovet och namnet. Om rådet och jarlen'. *NoB* 35, 1–96.

Hkr = Snorri Sturluson 1941, 1945, 1951. *Heimskringla.* Ed. Bjarni Aðalbjarnarson. 3 vols. *ÍF* XXVI–XXVIII.

Holmbäck, Åke 1919. *Ätten och arvet enligt Sveriges medeltidslagar.*

Holmbäck, Åke 1920. 'Studier över de svenska allmänningarnas historia. 1. Rättsreglerna för intaga av jord vid den fasta bosättningen. Uppkomsten av särskilda slag av allmänningar'. *Uppsala universitets årsskrift. Juridik* 1, 1–34.

HRSH = *Handlingar rörande Skandinaviens historia* (From vol. 11 *Nya handlingar rörande Skandinaviens historia* and renumbered from 1) 1816–60, 1865. 40 vols plus an index.

HRSH29 = *Nya handlingar rörande Skandinaviens historia* 1848. Vol. 29 (19).

ÍF = *Íslenzk fornrit* 1933–.

Ihre, Johannes 1769. *Glossarium Suiogothicum.* 2 vols.

ÍO = Ásgeir Blöndal Magnússon 1989. *Íslensk orðsifjabók.*

Iuul, Stig 1940. *Fællig og Hovedlod.*

Jansson, Sam Owen 1936. 'Mått, mål och vikt i Sverige till 1500-talets mitt'. In *NK* XXX, 1–57.

Jansson, Valter 1935. 'Runsten från Bro socken, Gotland'. *Acta Philologica Scandinavica* 10, 1–13.

JL1 = *Jyske Lov Text 1: NkS 295 8vo* 1933. Ed. Peter Skautrup. (*DGL* 2).

KL = *Kulturhistoriskt lexikon för nordisk medeltid* 1956–78. 22 vols.

Kock, Axel 1895. 'Studier i fornnordisk grammatik'. *Arkiv för nordisk filologi* 11 (ny följd 7), 117–53.

Kock, Axel 1904. 'Bidrag till nordisk ordforskning'. *Arkiv för nordisk filologi* 20 (ny följd 16), 44–75.

Kock, Axel 1912. 'Etymologisk belysning av några nordiska ord och uttryck'. *Arkiv för nordisk filologi* 28 (ny följd 24), 167–218.

Kock, Axel 1918. 'Belysning av forndanska och forngutniska ord'. In *Studier tillegnade Esaias Tegnér den 13. januari 1918*, 355–68.

Kock, Ebbe 1926. *Om hemföljd (förtida arv) i svensk rätt t.o.m. 1734 års lag.*

Kristnisaga = *Kristnisaga*. In *Kristnisaga*. *Þáttr Þorvalds ens víðfǫrla. Þáttr Isleifs biskups Gizurarsonar. Hungrvaka* 1905. Ed. B. Kahle.

Larson, Laurence M. 1935. *The Earliest Norwegian Laws.*

Laxdæla saga 1944. *ÍF* V. Ed. Einar Ól. Sveinsson.

LEI = *Laws of early Iceland, Grágás: the Codex Regius of Grágás with material from other manuscripts* 1980, 2000. Tr. and ed. Andrew Dennis, Peter Foote, Richard Perkins. 2 vols.

Lemke, Otto Wilhelm 1868. *Visby stifts herdaminne, efter mestadels otryckta källor utarbetadt.*

LG = *Lex Gotlandiae svecice et germanice e codicibus B 64 et B 65 Bibl. Reg. Holm. Suecice et Britannice praefatus* 1945. Ed. Elias Wessén. (*CCS* V).

Lidén, Evald 1892. 'Smärre språkhistoriska bidrag'. In *Uppsalastudier*, 79–96.

Lidén, Evald 1911. 'Om några fornsvenska lagord'. *Arkiv för nordisk filologi* 27 (ny följd 23), 259–85.

Lilienberg, V. E. 1908. *Om svenska mynt och myntvärden*. (Offprint of *Föredrag i Numismatiska klubben den 4. dec. 1907*.)

Lindkvist, Thomas 1989. 'Medeltidens lagar. [Review of *Sveriges medeltidslagar. Europeisk rättstradition i politisk omvandling* by Elsa Sjöholm]'. *Svensk historisk tidskrift* 109; 51 (2: e följd), 413–20.

Lindström, G. 1892, 1895. *Anteckningar om Gotlands medeltid.* 2 vols.

Lithberg, Nils and Wessén, Elias 1939. *Den gotländska runkalendern.*

Låle = 1889–94; 1891–92. *Östnordiska och latinska medeltidsordspråk. Peder Låles ordspråk och en motsvarande svensk samling.*

Ed. (Vol. I) Axel Kock and Carl af Petersens, (Vol. II) Axel Kock. 2 vols.

Läffler, Leopold Fredrik Alexander 1878. 'Bidrag till svensk språkhistoria'. *Antiqvarisk tidskrift för Sverige* 5, 216–94 (1–79 in the särtryck).

Lönnroth, Eric 1940. 'Statsmakt och statsfinans i det medeltida Sverige: studier över skatteväsen och länsförvaltning'. *Göteborgs högskolas årsskrift* 46:3.

Mau, Jens Christian Eduard Theodor 1879. *Dansk Ordsprogs-Skat, eller Ordsprog, Skjæmtesprog, Rimsprog, Mundheld, Talemaader, Tankesprog.* 2 vols.

Maurer, Konrad 1878. *Udsigt over de nordgermaniske Retskilders Historie.*

MD = Svenska medeltids dikter och rim 1881–82. Ed. G. E. Klemming.

MELLNT = Magnus Erikssons landslag i nusvensk tolkning 1962. Ed. Åke Holmbäck and Elias Wessén.

MEStLNT = Magnus Erikssons stadslag i nusvensk tolkning 1966. Ed. Åke Holmbäck and Elias Wessén.

Mitchell, Stephen A. 1984. 'On the composition and function of *Guta Saga*'. *Arkiv för nordisk filologi* 99, 151–74.

MLBL = Den nyere Bylov (Magnus lagabøters bylag) 1848. Ed. R. Keyser and P. A. Munch. (*NGL* 2, 179–290).

MLLL = Den nyere Landslov (Magnus lagabøters landslag) 1848. Ed. R. Keyser and P. A. Munch. (*NGL* 2, 1–178).

Mogk, E. 1909. 'Die Menschenopfer bei den Germanen'. *Abhandlungen der philologisch-historischen Klasse der königlich sächsischen Gesellschaft der Wissenschaften* 57, Part 17, 601–44.

MRL = Medieval Russian laws 1979. Tr. George Vernadsky.

Munktell, Henrik 1939. 'Tortyren i svensk rättshistoria'. *Lychnos. Lärdomshistoriska samfundets årsbok*, 102–35.

Nevéus, Clara 1974. *Trälarna i landskapslagarnas samhälle. Danmark och Sverige.*

NGL = Norges gamle love indtil 1387 1846–95. Ed. Rudolph Keyser and Peter Andreas Munch. 5 vols.

NK = Nordisk kultur 1931–56. 32 vols.

NK VI = Runorna 1933. Ed. Otto von Friesen.

NK VIII: A = Litteraturhistoria: Danmark, Finland och Sverige 1943. Ed. Sigurður Nordal.

NK XI/XII: A = Fångst, jakt och fiske 1955. Ed. Sigurd Erixon.

NK XII: B = Vapen / Vaaben 1943. Ed. Bengt Thordeman.

NK XXIX = *Mønt* 1936. Ed. Svend Aakjær.

NK XXX = *Maal og vægt* 1936. Ed. Svend Aakjær.

Nordén, Arthur 1931. 'Ett rättsdokument från en fornsvensk offer-lund'. *Fornvännen* 26, 330–51.

Nordström, Johan Jacob 1839–40. *Bidrag till den svenska samhälls-författningens historia*. 2 vols.

Noreen, Adolf 1894. *Abriss der urgermanischen Lautlehre mit beson-derer Rücksicht auf die nordischen Sprachen zum Gebrauch bei akademischen Vorlesungen*.

Noreen, Adolf 1897. *Svenska etymologier*.

Ohlmarks, Åke 1976. *De svenska landskapslagarna i komplett över-sättning, med anmärkningar och förklaringar*.

Óláfs saga helga 1945. *ÍF* XXVII. Ed. Bjarni Aðalbjarnarson.

Ólafur Halldórsson 1990. 'Því flýgur krákan víða'. In *Grettisfærsla. Safn ritgerða eftir Ólaf Halldórsson gefið út á sjötugsafmæli hans 18. apríl 1990*, 111–34.

Olsen, Olaf 1965. 'Hørg, hov og kirke: historiske og arkæologiske vikingetidsstudier'. *Aarbøger for nordisk oldkyndighed og historie*.

Olsson. Ingemar 1976. *Gotlands stavgardar—en ortnamnsstudie*.

Olsson, Ingemar 1992. 'Stavgardsproblemet—ännu en gång'. *Forn-vännen* 87, 91–97.

Orosius = *The Old English Orosius* 1980. Ed. Janet Bately.

OSMS = Söderwall, K. F. 1884–90, 1891–1918, 1953, 1953–73. *Ordbok öfver svenska medeltids-språket*. 4 vols (vols 3 and 4 supplements edited by K. F. Söderwall, W. Åkerlund, K. G. Ljunggren and E. Wessén).

Pernler, Sven-Erik 1977. *Gotlands medeltida kyrkoliv—biskop och prostar. En kyrkorättslig studie. Mit einer deutschen Zusammen-fassung*.

Pipping, Hugo 1901. *Gotländska studier*.

Pipping, Hugo 1904. 'Nya gotländska studier'. *Göteborgs högskolas årsskrift* 10, 3–24.

Pipping, Rolf 1926. *Kommentar till Erikskrönikan. (Skrifter utgivna av svenska litteratursällskapet i Finland* 187).

Pipping, Rolf 1938; 1954; 1960; 1962; 1963. 'Ordspråksstudier I–II'. *Studier i nordisk filologi* 28; 43; 50; 52; 53.

PRF = *Privilegier, resolutioner och förordningar för Sveriges städer* 1927–85. Ed. (Vol. I) Nils Herlitz. 6 vols.

Rehfeldt, Bernhard 1942. *Todesstrafen und Bekehrungsgeschichte. Zur Rechts- und Religionsgeschichte der germanischen Hinrichtungs-bräuche*.

Rietz, Johan Ernst 1862–67, 1955. *Svenskt dialekt-lexikon. Ordbok öfver svenska allmogespråket.*

RS3 = Rättshistoriska studier 1969. Ed. Kjell Ä. Modéer. *(Skrifter utgivna av Institutet för Rättshistorisk Forskning grundat av Gustav och Carin Olin. Serien II* 3).

Ruthström, Bo 2002. Land *och* fæ. *Strukturellt-rättsfilologiska studier i fornnordiskt lagspråk över beteckningar för egendom i allmänhet med underkategorier.*

Rydqvist, Johan Erik 1850–83. *Svenska språkets lagar.* 6 vols.

Sandström, J. 1927. 'Markland och bördsrätt: till frågan om marklandsuppskattningens uppkomst i svea-landskapen'. *Upplands fornminnesförenings tidskrift* 10, Bilaga 3.

Schück, Adolf 1945. 'Gotlands politiska historia intill Brömsebrofreden'. In *BoG* I, 178–225.

Schwerin, C. von 1941. '[Review of] T. Wennström's *Brott och böter'. Zeitschrift der Savigny-Stiftung für Rechtsgeschichte Germanistische (Romanistische, Kanonistische) Abteilung* 61, 480–85.

SD = Svenskt diplomatarium från och med år 1401 1875–1904. Ed. Carl Silfverstolpe and K. H. Karlsson. 4 vols.

Siltberg, Tryggve 2005. 'Gotlands landskapssigill och äldre judiciella sigill'. In *Landsarkivet i Visby 1905–2005.* Ed. Tommy Sundberg, 277–370.

Sjöberg, Sigfrid 1969. 'Om tingstider under landskapslagarnas och landslagarnas tid före 1614'. In *RS3*, 49–103.

Sjöholm, Elsa 1976. *Gesetze als Quellen mittelalterlicher Geschichte des Nordens.*

SkL = Skånske Lov 1933. Ed. Svend Aakjær and Erik Kroman. (*DGL* 1:1, 1–199).

SkL Add = Skånske Lov: Tillæg til Skånske Lov 1933. Ed. Svend Aakjær and Erik Kroman. (*DGL* 1:2, 719–818).

SkLAS = Skånske Lov: Andreas Sunesøns parafrase, Skånske Kirkelov m.m. 1933. Ed. Svend Aakjær and Erik Kroman. (*DGL* 1:2, 467–667).

Skov, Sigvard 1946. 'Anders Suneson og Guterloven'. In *Festskrift til Erik Arup: den 22. november 1946.* Ed. Astrid Friis and Albert Olsen, 107–17.

SL = Svenska landskapslagar tolkade och förklarade för nutidens svenskar 1933–46; reprint 1979. Ed. Åke Holmbäck and Elias Wessén. 5 vols.

SL I = *Östgötalagen och Upplandslagen* 1933; reprint 1979. Ed. Åke Holmbäck and Elias Wessén.

SL II = *Dalalagen och Västmannalagen* 1936; reprint 1979. Ed. Åke Holmbäck and Elias Wessén.

SL III = *Södermannalagen och Hälsingelagen* 1940; reprint 1979. Ed. Åke Holmbäck and Elias Wessén.

SL IV = *Skånelagen och Gutalagen* 1943; reprint 1979. Ed. Åke Holmbäck and Elias Wessén.

SL V = *Äldre västgötalagen, Yngre västgötalagen* 1946; reprint 1979. Ed. Åke Holmbäck and Elias Wessén.

SND = *Scottish national dictionary* 1929–76. 10 vols.

Snædal, Thorgunn 2002. *Medan världen vakar: studier i de gotländska runinskrifternas språk och kronologi = While the world wakes: studies in the language and chronology of the runic inscriptions of Gotland.*

Spegel = Haquin Spegel 1901. *Rudera gothlandica. Kort beskrivning om then øøn Gothland. Anno 1683.* Ed. O. v. Wennersten.

SRS = *Scriptores rerum svecicarum medii ævi* 1818, 1871, 1876. Ed. E. M. Fant, E. G. Geijer, J. H. Schröder and Claudius Annerstedt. 3 vols.

Stadga = *Stadga för S. Karins Gille i Björke socken på Gotland 1443.* In *Småstycken på fornsvenska* 1868–81. Ed. G. E. Klemming.

Steffen, Richard 1943. *Gotlands administrativa, rättsliga och kyrkliga organisation från äldsta tider till år 1645.*

Steffen, Richard 1945. 'Gotlands indelning och organisation'. In *BoG* I, 226–53.

Steinnes, Asgaur 1936. 'Mål, vekt og verderekning i Noreg'. In *NK* XXX, 84–154.

STFM = *Sveriges traktater med främmande magter jemte andra dit hörande handlingar* 1877–1934. Ed. Olof Simon Rydberg. 15 vols.

Ström, Folke 1942. *On the sacral origin of the Germanic death penalties.* Tr. Donald Burton.

Strömbäck, Dag 1942. 'Hade de germanska dödsstraffen sakralt ursprung?' *Saga och sed. Kungl. Gustav Adolfs Akademiens årsbok*, 51–69.

STUAGNL = *Samfund til udgivelse af gammel nordisk litteratur* 1880–1976. Vols 1–67.

Styffe, Carl Gustaf 1864. *Framställning af de så kallade grundregalernas uppkomst och tillämpning i Sverige intill slutet af sextonde århundradet med anledning af den uppdiktade berättelsen om ett riksdagsbeslut på Helgeandsholmen år 1282.*

Söderberg, Bengt G. 1956. 'Den gutniska bonderepubliken'. In *Från farmannabonde till föreningsbonde.* Ed. Valton Johansson, 1–16.

Söderwall, K. F. 1870. *Hufvudepokerna af svenska språkets utbildning.*

234 THE LAW OF THE GOTLANDERS

Tacitus, Cornelius 1914. *De vita Iulii Agricolae, De origine et moribus Germanorum.* Ed. J. H. Sleeman.

Tamm, Fredrik August 1883–84. 'Germanska språk. [Review of J. E. Rydqvist. 1883. *Svenska språkets lagar. Kritisk afhandling.* Volume 6. Ed. K. F. Söderwall]'. *Nordisk revy. Tidning för vetenskaplig kritik och universitetsangelägenheter* 1, No 10, 310–11.

Thomsen, Wilh. 1870. *Über den Einfluss der germanischen Sprachen auf die finnisch-lappischen: eine sprachgeschichtliche Untersuchung.*

Thomson, Arthur 1972. *I stocken. Studier i stockstraffets historia.*

Thordeman, Bengt Johan Nerén 1936. 'Sveriges medeltidsmynt'. In *NK* XXIX, 1–92.

Thulin, Gabriel 1911. *Historisk utveckling af den svenska skifteslagstiftningen med särskildt afseende å frågan om delningsgrund vid skifte.*

Tunberg, Sven August Daniel 1911. *Studier rörande Skandinaviens äldsta politiska indelning.*

Tunberg, Sven August Daniel 1913. 'En romersk källa om Norden vid 1100-talets början'. *Språkvetenskapliga sällskapets i Uppsala förhandlingar. Bil. B; F.* in *Uppsala Universitets årsskrift. Filosofi språkvetenskap och historiska vetenskaper* 1, 14–34; 96–98.

U 614 = Inscription 614 in *UR3.* (*Sveriges runinskrifter* 8).

Uppsalastudier = *Uppsalastudier tillegnade Sophus Bugge* 1892.

UR = *Upplands runinskrifter* 1940–43; 1943–46; 1949–51; 1953–58. Ed. Elias Wessén and Sven B. F. Jansson. (*Sveriges runinskrifter* 6–9.)

UR3 = *Upplands runinskrifter* 1949–51. Ed. Elias Wessén and Sven B. F. Jansson. (*Sveriges runinskrifter* 8).

Vries, Jan de 1956–57. *Altgermanische Religionsgeschichte.* 2 vols.

Wadstein, Elis 1890–92. 'Recension: *Ordböjning i Västmannalagen* I. *Substantivets böjning. Akademisk afhandling för vinnande af filosofisk doktorsgrad af Karl K:son Siljestrand.* Linköping 1890'. *Nordisk Tidskrift for Filologi* 10 (Ny Række), 226–33.

Wadstein, Elis 1894–95. 'Förklaringar och anmärkningar till fornnordiska lagar'. *Nordisk Tidsskrift for Filologi* 3 (Tredie Række), 1–16.

Wallén, Per-Edwin 1958. *Die Klage gegen den Toten im nordgermanischen Recht.*

Wennström, Torsten 1931. *Studier över böter och myntvärden i Västgötalagarna.*

Wennström, Torsten 1936. *Tjuvnad och fornæmi: rättsfilologiska studier i svenska landskapslagar.*

Wennström, Torsten 1940. *Brott och böter: rättsfilologiska studier i svenska landskapslagar.*

Wennström, Torsten 1946. *Lagspråk och lagtexter: rättsfilologiska studier över medeltida svenska lagar.*

Wessén, Elias 1924. 'Studier till Sveriges hedna mytologi och fornhistoria'. *Uppsala universitets årsskrift. Filosofi, språkvetenskap och historiska vetenskaper* 6, 1–198.

Wessén, Elias 1932. 'Om nordiska inbyggarnamn'. In *Germanska namnstudier tillägnade Evald Lidén den 3 oktober 1932*, 71–89.

Wessén, Elias 1945. 'Gutasagan och Gotlands kristnande'. In *BoG* I, 153–64.

Westholm, Gun 2007. *Visby 1361 invasionen.*

Westman, Karl Gustaf 1902/1905. 'Om delaktighet i dråp enligt de svenska landskapslagarna'. *Antiqvarisk tidskrift för Sverige* 17: 2, 1–53.

Westman, Karl Gustaf 1912a. *Den svenska nämnden. Dess uppkomst och utveckling.* Vol. 1.

Westman, Karl Gustaf 1912b. *De svenska rättskällornas historia: föreläsningar.*

Westman, Karl Gustaf 1944. 'Magiskt rop i svensk folktro och i forntidsrätten'. *Saga och sed. Kungl. Gustav Adolfs Akademiens årsbok*, 52–56.

Wilda, Wilhelm Eduard 1960 (facsimile of 1842 edn). *Geschichte des deutschen Strafrechts I. Das Strafrecht der Germanen.*

Wildte, Fridolf 1926. 'Tingsplatserna i Sverige under förhistorisk tid och medeltid'. *Fornvännen* 21, 211–30.

Wildte, Fridolf 1931. 'Västergötlands medeltida tingställen'. *Rig. Tidskrift utgiven av Föreningen för svensk kulturhistoria* 14, 174–84.

Wildte, Fridolf 1933–34. 'Östergötlands tingställen före år 1600'. *Meddelande från Östergötlands Fornminnes- och Museiförening*, 171–88.

Wimmer, Ludvig Frans Adalbert 1887. *Døbefonten i Åkirkeby kirke.*

Yrwing, Hugo Nilsson 1940. *Gotland under äldre medeltiden: Studier i baltisk-hanseatisk historia.*

Yrwing, Hugo Nilsson 1963. 'Biskop Bengts brev för Mariakyrkan i Visby'. In *Historia kring Gotland*. Ed. Å. G. Sjöberg, 71–99.

Yrwing, Hugo Nilsson 1978. *Gotlands medeltid.*